D1093292

THE LIVES OF LGBT
OLDER ADULTS

THE LIVES OF LGBT OLDER ADULTS

UNDERSTANDING CHALLENGES AND RESILIENCE

EDITED BY
NANCY A. OREL AND CHRISTINE A. FRUHAUF

American Psychological Association • Washington, DC

NOV 12 2014

PROPERTY OF
SENECA COLLEGE
LIBRARIES
KING CAMPUS

Copyright © 2015 by the American Psychological Association. All rights reserved. Except as permitted under the United States Copyright Act of 1976, no part of this publication may be reproduced or distributed in any form or by any means, including, but not limited to, the process of scanning and digitization, or stored in a database or retrieval system, without the prior written permission of the publisher.

Published by
American Psychological Association
750 First Street, NE
Washington, DC 20002
www.apa.org

To order
APA Order Department
P.O. Box 92984
Washington, DC 20090-2984
Tel: (800) 374-2721; Direct: (202) 336-5510
Fax: (202) 336-5502; TDD/TTY: (202) 336-6123
Online: www.apa.org/pubs/books
E-mail: order@apa.org

In the U.K., Europe, Africa, and the Middle East, copies may be ordered from
American Psychological Association
3 Henrietta Street
Covent Garden, London
WC2E 8LU England

Typeset in Goudy by Circle Graphics, Inc., Columbia, MD

Printer: Maple Press, York, PA
Cover Designer: Mercury Publishing Services, Rockville, MD

The opinions and statements published are the responsibility of the authors, and such opinions and statements do not necessarily represent the policies of the American Psychological Association.

Library of Congress Cataloging-in-Publication Data
The lives of LGBT older adults : understanding challenges and resilience / edited by Nancy A. Orel and Christine A. Fruhauf. — First edition.
    pages cm
  Includes bibliographical references and index.
  ISBN-13: 978-1-4338-1763-2
  ISBN-10: 1-4338-1763-2
  1. Older sexual minorities—United States—Social conditions. 2. Older sexual minorities—Services for—United States. 3. Older sexual minorities—Family relationships—United States. I. Orel, Nancy A. II. Fruhauf, Christine A.
  HQ76.27.O44L58 2015
  306.76084'60973—dc23

                                    2014006152

British Library Cataloguing-in-Publication Data
A CIP record is available from the British Library.

Printed in the United States of America
First Edition

http://dx.doi.org/10.1037/14436-000

CONTENTS

CONTRIBUTORS

Michael Adams, Executive Director, Services & Advocacy for GLBT Elders, New York, NY

Shari Brotman, PhD, School of Social Work, McGill University, Montreal, Quebec, Canada

Morgan Bunting, BS, Gerontology Program, Bowling Green State University, Bowling Green, OH

Sean Cahill, PhD, Fenway Institute, Boston, MA

Loree Cook-Daniels, MS, FORGE, Inc., Milwaukee, WI

Brian de Vries, PhD, Gerontology Program, San Francisco State University, San Francisco, CA

James P. Fedor, LCSW, School of Social Work, Rutgers, The State University of New Jersey, New Brunswick

Ilyan Ferrer, PhD Candidate, School of Social Work, McGill University, Montreal, Quebec, Canada

Karen I. Fredriksen-Goldsen, PhD, School of Social Work, University of Washington, Seattle

Christine A. Fruhauf, PhD, Department of Human Development & Family Studies, Colorado State University, Fort Collins

Jayn Goldsen, BS, School of Social Work, University of Washington, Seattle

Charles P. Hoy-Ellis, PhD, MSW, LICSW, School of Social Work, University of Washington, Seattle

Hyun-Jun Kim, PhD, School of Social Work, University of Washington, Seattle

Douglas C. Kimmel, PhD, Department of Psychology, Emeritus, City College of the City University of New York; Hancock, ME

Anna Muraco, PhD, Department of Sociology, Loyola Marymount University, Los Angeles, CA

Nancy A. Orel, PhD, LPC, College of Health and Human Services, Bowling Green State University, Bowling Green, OH

Brenda Richard, PhD, School of Social Work, Dalhousie University, Halifax, Nova Scotia, Canada

Bill Ryan, MSW, School of Social Work, McGill University, Montreal, Quebec, Canada

Kristin S. Scherrer, PhD, LCSW, School of Social Work, Rutgers, The State University of New Jersey, New Brunswick

Tamara Sussman, PhD, School of Social Work, McGill University, Montreal, Quebec, Canada

Cody Swartz, BS, LNHA, Gerontology Program, Bowling Green State University, Bowling Green, OH

FOREWORD

MICHAEL ADAMS

The publication of this volume could not be more timely given the notable recent progress toward a lesbian, gay, bisexual, and transgender (LGBT)-inclusive approach to aging in the United States and the critical need to continue and accelerate that progress in the years ahead. It is easy to forget that it was less than a decade ago that Services and Advocacy for GLBT Elders (SAGE) joined other activists to advocate aggressively at the last White House Conference on Aging for attention to the needs of LGBT older adults and other diverse elders, only to see the exclusive acknowledgment of our mere existence relegated to a footnote in the conference report. Yet just 4 years later, in 2009, the Department of Health and Human Services explicitly recognized the unique needs of LGBT older adults, and the federal government's responsibility to help address those needs, in announcing the creation of the country's first National Resource Center on LGBT Aging. In 2012, the White House convened its first-ever Conference on LGBT Aging, bringing together leading governmental figures and advocates to explore how to work together to better address the needs of LGBT older adults. To add a dramatic touch to the growing visibility of older members of the LGBT community, it was an 84-year-old lesbian named Edie Windsor who decided to fight the federal government's refusal to recognize her marriage to her life partner Thea Spyer, took her case all the way to the U.S. Supreme Court, and convinced the Court to overturn the Defense of Marriage Act.

Developments such as these have grabbed headlines for LGBT aging issues; at least as important, they are emblematic of significant systemic advances that are starting to improve the quality of life for LGBT older adults across the country. Community-based providers are introducing and expanding services for LGBT older adults in a growing number of cities across the country; in 2012, SAGE introduced the country's first full-fledged LGBT senior city in New York City. Meanwhile, incipient progress is being made on LGBT elder housing, with projects up and running or under construction in a small but growing number of communities. The National Resource Center on LGBT Aging is spearheading an expanded and more intentional approach to training designed to create cultural competence among providers of services and health care for the aged. And as evidenced by this volume, researchers are starting to pay attention to the health needs and well-being of LGBT older adults.

Efforts like these must be buttressed by policy change in order to be successful and replicated; fortunately, there have been unmistakable signs in recent years of an emerging LGBT aging policy agenda, along with early signs of policy progress. For example, over the past year, the federal government has removed obstacles to protection of same-sex couples from spousal impoverishment in the Medicaid program; couples-based protection in Medicaid and Social Security will expand with the overturn of the Defense of Marriage Act. Moreover, the Department of Health and Human Services has advised states that LGBT older adults can be treated as an older population of great socioeconomic need under the Older Americans Act (OAA). Efforts to amend the OAA, which directs billions of federal dollars for local aging services, to be LGBT-inclusive are starting to build steam with the introduction in Congress of the LGBT Elder Americans Act. Furthermore, states are emerging as important laboratories for LGBT aging policy progress; for example, California has shown leadership on ameliorative LGBT aging legislation, Washington has provided early innovation in Medicaid, and New York is a pioneer on LGBT-inclusive data collection in long-term care.

More broadly, LGBT aging and older people are starting to capture more "mind share" on important fronts. For example, the American Association of Retired Persons, widely recognized as a "best of breed" organization for the effectiveness of its advocacy and marketing efforts in the 50-and-older space, has visibly increased its attention to LGBT aging issues in recent years. Less known but nonetheless important aging field leaders like the American Society on Aging and National Senior Citizens Law Center have also increased their efforts. Media attention to LGBT aging issues has grown dramatically as well.

Although progress has been made in recent years, it is only a start in the right direction. Services for LGBT older adults are still confined for the most part to a limited number of urban areas, and even these are thin in terms of their offerings. The current service infrastructure does not begin to reflect the breadth and depth of need among LGBT older people across the country. Apart from severe geographic limitations, the needs and voices of especially vulnerable LGBT older adults—including those who are people of color or transgender (or both)—have received precious little attention from providers, policymakers, researchers, or funders. Policy progress is still in its earliest stages and will require years of concentrated and strategic effort to achieve LGBT-inclusive aging policies at the federal, state, and local levels. Cultural competency training for service and health providers is expanding quickly but is still only scratching the surface in terms of reaching a critical mass of providers and achieving sustainable culture change within service delivery systems. Ageism—the still dominant discourse that privileges and glorifies youth while devaluing those who are old and older—remains prevalent both within the LGBT community and in society at large. Furthermore, although the work of practitioners is strengthened by the extensive "on-the-ground" expertise of organizations such as SAGE and the life experiences and voices of LGBT older adults themselves, formal research on a wide array of LGBT aging issues is still lacking. Here again, this is especially true with regard to research and data on the most marginalized of LGBT older adults; as this volume's authors repeatedly point out, research on the lives, experiences, and needs of LGBT elders of color, transgender and bisexual elders, and other at-risk subpopulations is in critically short supply.

Against this backdrop, the importance of this volume becomes readily apparent. The various authors shed important new light on critical issues by distilling the best available evidence and providing the reader with powerful themes, trends, and insights from the small but growing body of research on key LGBT aging topics. The volume's interconnected focus on health and stigma among LGBT older adults is both instructive and reflective of the practice-based experience of LGBT aging organizations. Although no longer news, it is sobering to be reminded of the disproportionate levels of physical and mental health challenges and disability among LGBT older people. The volume's powerful connection of these documented health outcomes to experiences with stigma throughout the life course is an important observation for practitioners seeking to craft effective health-related interventions. Similarly, service providers and policymakers must grapple with the fact that HIV should be front and center in any LGBT aging agenda, as we are reminded that by 2015, 50% of the 1.2 million Americans living with HIV will be 50 and over.

Another of the book's essential contributions is the in-depth examination of how LGBT older adults both construct and value "families of choice" and relate to their families of origin. This is important for many reasons, including its implications for caregiving. The fact that only 11% of LGBT older adults receiving care get that support from a biological family member is a powerful indicator of the preeminent significance of caregiving and caregivers for LGBT people and their friends and loved ones (who provide the care that heterosexual older adults are much more likely to receive from their families of origin).

The volume's close examination of transgender aging issues is especially welcome, given that so little attention has been paid to this important topic to date. Last year, SAGE and the National Center for Transgender Equality together issued a report that reviewed available literature, profiled the experiences of transgender elders around the country, and made concrete recommendations for policymakers and practitioners. It is heartening that this volume deepens that discussion, contextualizes it within a comprehensive discussion of cross-cutting LGBT aging issues and aging theory, and makes this knowledge available to new audiences.

It is also noteworthy, and highly welcomed, to see the volume's repeated recognition of resilience among LGBT older adults and the linking of this resilience with notions of positive aging. LGBT elders have pioneered progress for younger members of the LGBT community precisely because of their fortitude and ingenuity. There is no doubt that LGBT older adults face substantial challenges as they age; many are in need of services and support as a result of typical aging experiences as well as discrimination, marginalization, intracommunity ageism, and internalized stigma. At the same time, there should also be no doubt that many LGBT older adults remain deeply resilient and resourceful in their later years. This is made clear not only by the research cited in this book but also by the repeated examples of leadership and agency offered by LGBT older adults themselves on a daily basis.

Apart from the knowledge to be gleaned from the thoughtful offerings of its authors, this volume makes an invaluable contribution by coupling a focus on current research with attention to clinical applications. Fortunately, the concept here is praxis in the broadest sense of the term, inclusive of a wide array of service modalities and community supports rather than a narrower focus on clinical work per se. This generous approach to practice—including references throughout the volume to social services, congregate programs, nutrition, supportive housing, patient-centered health care, and older adult empowerment—makes this book especially relevant to those who work on services, advocacy, policy, or training in the field of LGBT aging. The consistent theory–praxis orientation of the volume is a powerful reminder of one of the key justifications for investing more research resources on LGBT aging—to make a difference in the quality of life of LGBT older adults. For practice-oriented organizations like SAGE and our partners, this book contains an evident invitation for future collaboration and bridging of gaps between researchers and practitioners. We warmly welcome and embrace that invitation.

As one who tends toward a proactive agenda, my inevitable question in completing a foreword like this is: What now? I would suggest that *The Lives of LGBT Older Adults: Understanding Challenges and Resilience* lays before us an agenda that is as concise as it is ambitious. First, we must dramatically deepen the research available to elucidate the full breadth of issues central to the lives of LGBT older adults, in the face of precious little formal research to date. Second, we must expand and adapt our nation's aging services and policies to effectively and expansively embrace those living at the intersections of the aging process and LGBT identities. And third, we must craft our research, services, and policies with an explicit emphasis toward those LGBT older adults who are most at risk.

I congratulate the American Psychological Association and the authors of this volume for this outstanding effort to deepen our collective understanding of LGBT aging, and I welcome their continued contributions to theory and practice as we work together to realize this shared agenda of transforming the landscape for LGBT older adults and their families.

THE LIVES OF LGBT OLDER ADULTS

1

THE INTERSECTION OF CULTURE, FAMILY, AND INDIVIDUAL ASPECTS: A GUIDING MODEL FOR LGBT OLDER ADULTS

NANCY A. OREL AND CHRISTINE A. FRUHAUF

The U.S. population is aging. Whereas the overall U.S. population has tripled over the past century, the number of people aged 65 and older has increased 11-fold (Administration on Aging, 2010; U.S. Census Bureau, 2000). Currently, more than 41 million Americans are 65 years or older, representing 13.3% of the population, or one in eight individuals in the United States (Administration on Aging, 2012). The U.S. population will continue to age. During the next 25 years, as baby boomers (i.e., those born between 1946 and 1964) reach later life, the number of American elders will almost double to 69.4 million (Administration on Aging, 2012). As of January 1, 2011, approximately 10,000 baby boomers are turning age 65 each day (Cohn & Taylor, 2010). It is estimated that in 2030, one in five Americans will be age 65 years or older.

DOI: 10.1037/14436-001
The Lives of LGBT Older Adults: Understanding Challenges and Resilience, N. A. Orel and C. A. Fruhauf (Editors)
Copyright © 2015 by the American Psychological Association. All rights reserved.

The primary reason for the tremendous growth in the older adult population is the dramatic increase in life expectancy, which has risen from 49.2 years in 1900 to 77.8 years in 2006 (Tootelian & Varshney, 2010). Specifically, life expectancy for males has increased from 48 years to 75 years since 1900, and life expectancy for females has increased from 51 years to 80 years. This demographic trend not only demands societal attention (e.g., through research, practice, and policy) to the challenges and opportunities of an aging population but also changes the very landscape of the United States with strong, positive images of older adults and their families.

Paralleling the general older population in the United States, the number and proportion of lesbian, gay, bisexual, and transgender (LGBT) older adults are also significantly increasing (Gates, 2011). It is anticipated that by 2050, there will be accurate statistics on the number of LGBT older adults in the United States (and globally) because the pervasive homophobic attitudes of society that discouraged LGBT older adults from "coming out" and being counted (Hunter, 2007) will no longer be prevalent. Ideally, this once "invisible" minority will be visible, and the specific needs and concerns of LGBT older adults will be addressed.

Researchers and practitioners have become increasingly aware that LGBT persons have unique and varying needs. However, there is a dearth of empirical research on the specific needs and concerns of LGBT older adults and their families because sexual orientation as a research variable is basically absent in all major gerontological research studies. As a result, it is apparent that the available research on the specific needs and concerns of this "invisible" minority group must be made visible and accessible to all professionals who work with the older adult population. Thus, this book represents a comprehensive overview of cutting-edge research on LGBT older adults and their families. The primary purpose of the book is to inform researchers, practitioners, and policymakers of key research findings and describe practical implications for policy and practice related to LGBT aging individuals and families. Another key aspect of this book is its focus on the strengths and resiliency of the LGBT older adult population and the innovative ways in which individuals have overcome heterosexism and homophobia throughout their lives. The focus on strengths and resiliency is an important advancement in the field given that much of the previous literature on LGBT older adults neglected to address such topics.

The content of the book has been written by experts in the field, and all contributors have focused on those aspects of LGBT older adults that have enabled them to successfully adapt to aging. This includes a focus on resiliency, coping, adaptation, and managing disclosure. This book is therefore a catalyst for a new and burgeoning area of research on LGBT elders and their families focusing on strengths and resiliency. Additionally, because older adults are a diverse and heterogeneous group of individuals, with age being the common denominator, the content of the book specifically highlights the cultural factors, personal attributes, and family dynamics that intersect and define the unique and varying subgroups of the older adult population. All contributors have paid particular attention to the diversity that exists within the LGBT older adult population.

The remainder of this chapter presents a framework that can be used to illustrate the heterogeneity of the older adult population in general and the LGBT older adult population specifically. We conclude with a brief overview of the chapters in this book.

ADDRESSING FRAMEWORK

Drawing on the work of Hays (1996, 2008), the acronym ADDRESSING can be a helpful guide that illustrates the cultural factors and personal attributes that influence aging and the importance of these constructs in physical health, mental health, familial relationship, social relationships, and overall wellness. This model can also be used to illustrate how cultural factors and personal attributes contribute to an individual's ability to access services; the model can also potentially shed light on the difficulty in designing services and programs that would meet the needs of any specific subgroup of older adults—especially LGBT older adults and their families.

ADDRESSING diversity in aging requires practitioners (e.g., psychologists, physicians, social workers, nurses, administrators) to consider 10 primary cultural influences: age and cohort effects, degree of physical ability, degree of cognitive ability, religion, ethnicity and race, socioeconomic status, sexual orientation, individualistic life experiences, national origin, and gender. It is important to note that we modified Hays's (2008) original model from *indigenous heritage* to *individualistic life experiences* because of the impact that the latter have on individuals in general, but as will be seen in this introductory chapter and throughout this book, individualistic life experiences have a tremendous impact on the collective memories of LGBT older adults (Orel & Watson, 2012) across the life course.

A key task for health care practitioners, researchers, and other professionals when attempting to understand the general older adult population, and specifically the LGBT older population, is to discover and determine the cultural factors and personal attributes that are distinctive to their lives and thus contribute to their health and well-being over time. The ADDRESSING framework is of particular importance when investigating the LGBT older adult population because it can increase awareness of "specific cultural influences and minority identities that might otherwise be overlooked" (Hays,

1996, p. 335) as well as decrease the likelihood that important aspects of LGBT older adults' lived experiences over the life course would be unnoticed, ignored, or disregarded. This requires all researchers to possess culture-specific knowledge and skills when investigating the lives of LGBT older adults. To appropriately and adequately serve LGBT older adults, we must seek to understand the LGBT elder's perspective and how each of these areas of diversity bears on one's attitudes, experiences, and needs.

Despite having both age and sexual orientation as common denominators, LGBT older adults also possess heterogeneous aspects of their selves and individualistic life experiences that have undoubtedly affected their views and lived experiences. For example, consider the following LGBT individuals visiting a special LGBT senior center.

Edna is a 75-year-old White lesbian who has been in a long-term relationship with her partner, Sue, for more than 45 years. Edna and Sue are first-generation Americans who emigrated from Poland when they were children. They have lived within the same Polish neighborhood for more than 30 years, and members within the community refer to them as the "Polish Spinsters." Edna has not minded this label because it was her desire to keep her sexual orientation and her relationship with Sue a secret. However, Sue is starting to show signs and symptoms of mild dementia, and Edna is worried that soon Sue will display her affection for Edna publically. Edna's goal is to discover what types of programs she and Sue would be eligible for and what types of services would be available for Sue as her condition worsens.

Jack is a White 67-year-old gay man. He is a veteran of the Vietnam War and lives alone. His longest relationship was with Mark, whom he loved dearly. Mark was diagnosed as HIV positive in 1983, and he died in 1984. Since Mark's death, Jack has felt guilty that he remained healthy and HIV negative. Jack is financially struggling, and his general health is not good. He is hoping that the staff at the LGBT senior center will provide financial resources as well as health screenings.

Cheryl is a 64-year-old African American lesbian who lives with Carol, her partner of 10 years. Cheryl has a grown daughter and son from a previous heterosexual relationship and four grandchildren (ages 3 months and 2, 4, and 7 years). Cheryl has not told her grown children and grandchildren about her sexual relationship with Carol, but she assumes that they might know. Carol wants Cheryl to be open and honest with her family and has indicated that she will "out" Cheryl if she doesn't disclose her sexual orientation. Carol wants to be treated like family and resents that she is not invited to family events and activities. Cheryl is coming to the LGBT senior center to see if there might be other lesbian grandmothers who she could talk with and ask for advice.

Tanna is a Hispanic woman with long dark hair, wearing a dress and shawl. She appears to be much younger than the 64 years indicated on her green card. Tanna's physical complaints are numerous. She has chronic back pain, and walking is becoming increasingly difficult. Tanna also recognizes that she is having more difficulty getting up in the morning and would prefer to stay in bed all day. She pulled herself out of bed today to come to the LGBT senior center hoping that perhaps someone there would understand her unique needs as a transgender person.

These four individuals are visiting the LGBT senior center to find services and programs that would meet their specific needs and concerns. The center seems like an appropriate venue for each of them. However, each one possesses unique physical and mental health needs and is experiencing unique social and familial concerns. Individuals like these have practical concerns that are at the heart of the research reviewed in this book. We return to them in the final chapter.

As previously indicated, a key task for professionals who are assessing the needs and concerns of LGBT older adults is to discover and determine what cultural factors and personal attributes are important to their lives and thus contribute to their well-being. The ADDRESSING framework and its potential application to the lived experiences and the life course of LGBT older adults are briefly discussed in the following sections. The next sections also draw connections between the framework and the materials covered in the chapters of this book.

Age and Cohort Effects (A)

The experience of aging is a multilevel process that is extremely diverse, with the actual self-identification of *aged* being individualistic. There are numerous theories of aging, and collectively they can illuminate our understanding of aging from a microlevel that focuses on individual aging processes to a macrolevel that focuses more on the relationship between age and social status (Hagestad & Dannefer, 2001). Throughout the chapters in this book are examples of how various theoretical approaches have been used with the LGBT older adult population, with special emphasis on a life course perspective, which emphasizes that an individual's life span is "historically embedded and reflects, to a significant degree, the conditions, constraints, and opportunities of the historical context" (George, 2013, p. 151). What is extremely important when working with LGBT older adults is to recognize the historical context and the experiences of LGBT older adults who came of age in different historical and social contexts (i.e., cohort effects). The oldest cohorts of LGBT persons came of age during a significantly different sociohistorical context in which heterosexism went unchallenged and negative views toward homosexuality were made explicit in culture and social institutions. Before the Stonewall Rebellion of 1969, LGBT persons were forced to live secreted lives in which their sexual orientation was "closeted" so that a public heterosexual identity could be managed. However, current cohorts of LGBT older adults (e.g., baby boomers) have experienced greater opportunities to openly disclose their sexual orientation without fear of imprisonment or institutionalization. Because of this, many LGBT older adults are also able to openly engage in family roles as parents and grandparents without intense fears of being estranged from their families of origin. Current research that has quantitatively and qualitatively investigated the lived experiences of LGBT older adults is highlighted throughout this book.

It is important to recognize that LGBT older adults' attitudes and experiences have been shaped by culture and the historical events related to sexual orientation. Exhibit 1.1 lists a few of the historical events that LGBT older adults have experienced related to sexual orientation and gender. From this brief listing, it is evident that the current cohort of LGBT older adults has witnessed tremendous historical conditions, constraints, and opportunities. There can be no doubt that LGBT cohorts who were children and adolescents before the 1969 Stonewall riots (and the start of the gay rights movement) differ in many ways—ranging from political and religious attitudes to familial stability—from cohorts who succeeded them. Current cohorts of LGBT older adults are probably less likely than younger cohorts to openly discuss their sexual orientation. All practitioners who work with LGBT older adults must recognize that these elders have been influenced by different political and historical forces, with distinctive sets of social attitudes and opportunities.

Degree of Physical Ability (D)

Research indicates that medical and health care needs are a primary source of concern for the majority of LGBT older adults. These concerns are primarily related to rising health care costs, financial constraints in seeking medical care, and failing health (Orel, 2014). Research has also repeatedly indicated that there continues to be health disparities among LGBT persons, and LGBT older adults specifically. Research has suggested that LGBT persons are disproportionately at risk for violent hate crimes, sexually transmitted infections including HIV/AIDS, a variety of mental health conditions (Cochran, 2001; Cochran & Mays, 2000, 2009; Ferguson, Horwood, & Beautrais, 1999; Herek, 2008; Institute of Medicine, 2011; Koh & Ross, 2006), body weight problems (Carlat, Camargo, & Herzog, 1997; Carpenter, 2003; Deputy & Boehmer, 2010), substance use and abuse (Cochran & Mays, 2006; Skinner & Otis, 1996; Stall & Wiley, 1988), smoking (DuRant, Krowchuk, & Sinal, 1998; Stall, Greenwood, Acree, Paul, & Coates, 1999; Tang et al., 2004), and certain cancers (Cochran et al., 2001; Daling et al., 1987; Dibble, Vanoni, & Miaskowski, 1997; Koblin et al., 1996; Zaritsky & Dibble, 2010).

EXHIBIT 1.1
Select Historical Events Lesbian, Gay, Bisexual,
and Transgender Older Adults Have Experienced Related
to Sexual Orientation and Gender Identity

Year	Event
1924	First known gay rights organization is founded by Henry Gerber in Chicago but is forced to disband within a few months
1925	Ma Rainey is arrested in her home in Harlem for having a lesbian party
1928	Margaret Mead concludes that attitudes toward sex are culturally prescribed
1934	Gay/bisexual men are forced to wear pink triangles and lesbian/bisexual women are forced to wear black triangles in Nazi Germany
1941	Gays are banned from the U.S. military
1948	Kinsey Report findings include the statistics that 50% of men had experienced erotic attractions for other men and 4% were exclusively homosexual
1950s	Senator Joseph McCarthy defines 650 employees at the U.S. State Department as "subversive" because they are gay/lesbian
1951	Mattachine Society (the first sustained U.S. homosexual organization) is founded by Harry Hay
1951	British author Radclyffe Hall's *The Well of Loneliness*, an account of the challenges faced by a gender nonconforming lesbian at the start of the 20th century, is published
1953	First American (Christine Jorgenson) undergoes gender reassignment surgery
1953	Evelyn Hooker publishes a study that shows homosexuals are not mentally disturbed
1955	Daughters of Bilitis, the first lesbian civil and political rights organization in the United States, is formed by Del Martin and Phyllis Lyon
1957	The Wolfenden Report, issued by the British Departmental Committee on Homosexual Offenses and Prostitution, states that homosexual behavior between consenting adults should no longer be considered a criminal offense
1960	First national lesbian convention is held in San Francisco
1961	Hollywood's production code is revised to allow films to portray homosexuality
1961	Illinois becomes the first U.S. state to decriminalize homosexual acts
1969	The Stonewall riots, a series of spontaneous, violent demonstrations by members of the gay community in New York in response to a police raid of the Stonewall Inn, mark the beginning of the gay liberation movement
1970	The National Organization for Women passes a resolution recognizing the "double oppression" of lesbians
1973	The American Psychiatric Association removes homosexuality as a disease category from the *Diagnostic and Statistical Manual of Mental Disorders*
1973	Rita Mae Brown publishes *Rubyfruit Jungle*, which has become a classic of lesbian fiction
1977	Anita Bryant founds "Save Our Children" and leads a campaign to repeal a gay civil rights ordinance in Dade County, Florida
1977	Formation of SAGE—Senior Action in a Gay Environment
1978	Harvey Milk, San Francisco's first openly gay elected city supervisor, is assassinated along with Mayor George Moscone
1979	First national march on Washington DC for gay rights
1981	First cases of "unexplained" deaths among gay men in San Francisco, later called GRID (gay-related infectious disease) and then AIDS (acquired immunodeficiency syndrome), are reported

(*continues*)

EXHIBIT 1.1
Select Historical Events Lesbian, Gay, Bisexual,
and Transgender Older Adults Have Experienced Related
to Sexual Orientation and Gender Identity *(Continued)*

Year	Event
1981	J. R. Roberts publishes *Black Lesbians—an Annotated Bibliography*, written to counteract the "overwhelming whiteness of lesbian and women's studies"
1982	Wisconsin is the first state to outlaw discrimination on the basis of sexual orientation
1986	The Supreme Court rules in *Bowers v. Hardwick* that homosexual relations between consenting adults in the privacy of their own homes is not protected under the U.S. Constitution
1987	The Gay March on Washington revitalizes the gay movement
1992	Measure 9 (an antigay initiative) in Oregon is narrowly defeated[a]
1993	k. d. lang, a well-known lesbian country singer, appears on the cover of *Vanity Fair* with Cindy Crawford, a heterosexual supermodel
1993	"Don't Ask, Don't Tell" policy is established in the U.S. Armed Forces
1996	A Hawaii court rules that the state has not proved it has a "compelling interest" to ban gay marriage
1996	The U.S. Supreme Court strikes down Colorado's Amendment 2, which denied gays and lesbians protection from discrimination in that state
1996	The federal Defense of Marriage Act (DOMA) restricts LGEX partnership rights, permitting states to refuse to recognize same-sex marriages granted under other states' laws
1997	Forty-two million viewers watch Ellen DeGeneres in the "Coming Out" episode of *The Ellen Show*
1998	Matthew Shepard, a 21-year-old college student, is murdered in Laramie, Wyoming, for being gay
1998	Voters in Alaska and Hawaii approve measures to block same-sex marriage
1999	The Vermont Supreme Court rules that the state must grant gay and lesbian couples the same rights as married heterosexual couples receive
1999	A jury awards $25 million to the Amedure family when their gay son was slain after revealing during the taping of the *Jenny Jones* show that he had a crush on a male guest.
2000	Civil unions are permitted in Vermont
2000	California voters approve a ballot measure to block recognition of same-sex marriage
2000	The U.S. Census includes data for same-sex households with partners ages 55 and older
2001	Reverend Jerry Falwell suggests that homosexuals were partly responsible for the September 11 terrorist attack on the World Trade Center; on September 14, he apologizes for his comments
2002	Alabama Supreme Court Justice Roy Moore says that homosexuality is "an inherent evil"
2002	Clinton Risetter is set on fire because he was gay and subsequently dies in Santa Barbara, California
2003	The U.S. Supreme Court overturns *Bowers v. Hardwick* and discriminatory sodomy laws
2004	Voters in 11 states pass constitutional amendments to define *marriage* as between a man and a woman
2004	Legal same-sex weddings begin in Massachusetts
2005	Pope Benedict XVI proposes guidelines barring gay men from the priesthood

EXHIBIT 1.1
Select Historical Events Lesbian, Gay, Bisexual,
and Transgender Older Adults Have Experienced Related
to Sexual Orientation and Gender Identity   *(Continued)*

Year	Event
2007	The Chelsea Jewish Nursing Home Foundation engages in a $26 million capital campaign to construct a nursing home to cater to LGBT elders
2007	New Jersey becomes the third state (after Vermont and Connecticut) to recognize civil unions; 45 states have legal or constitutional bans on same-sex marriages
2007	Senator Larry Craig (Idaho) resigns from the Senate after pleading guilty to "inappropriate" behavior with a male police officer in a restroom at a Minnesota Airport
2008	Marriage for same-sex couples is legal in California for several months until voters pass Proposition 8
2009	Laws permitting same-sex marriage come into effect in Iowa and Vermont, while Maine bans same-sex marriage
2009	Barbra "Babs" Siperstein is nominated and confirmed as an at-large member of the Democratic National Committee, becoming its first openly transgender member
2010	Laws permitting same-sex marriage come into effect in New Hampshire and Washington, DC
2010	Australia becomes the first country in the world to recognize a "nonspecific" gender
2010	The U.S. Census reports counts of both same-sex partners and same-sex spouses for the first time
2010	Creation of the National LGBT elder resource center
2011	The first baby boomers turn 65 years of age
2011	Same-sex marriage becomes legally recognized in New York State
2011	End to "Don't Ask, Don't Tell"—the ban on openly gay and lesbian individuals in the military
2011	Chaz Bono appears on the 13th season of *Dancing With the Stars*, marking the first time an openly transgender man has starred on a major network television show for something unrelated to being transgender
2012	Maine, Maryland, and Washington are the first states to legalize same-sex marriage by popular vote
2012	The U.S. Department of Housing and Urban Development issues a regulation to prohibit LGEX discrimination in federally assisted housing programs
2012	Barack Obama becomes the first U.S. president to publicly announce support for same-sex marriage on May 9
2012	Berkeley, California, becomes the first city in the United States to officially proclaim a day recognizing bisexuals
2012	Minnesota votes down Amendment 1, a constitutional amendment that would have defined marriage as being a union solely between a man and a woman, becoming the first state in the country to vote against such an amendment
2013	Colorado Senate Bill 11 legalizing civil unions is signed by the governor
2013	The U.S. Supreme court declares the Defense of Marriage Act unconstitutional; this advances the legalization of same-sex marriage nationwide
2013	France becomes the 14th country to legalize same-sex marriage

aMeasure 9 would have prohibited all governments in Oregon from allocating money or property "to promote, encourage or facilitate homosexuality, pedophilia, sadism, or masochism." Additionally, Measure 9 would have required all levels of government, including public education systems, to assist in setting a standard recognizing that these behaviors are "abnormal, wrong, unnatural and perverse and . . . to be discouraged and avoided."

Lesbians are significantly less likely than nonlesbian women to receive routine preventive health care (e.g., pap smears, breast cancer screening; Denenberg, 1995; Institute of Medicine, 1999; Koh, 2000; Robertson & Schachter, 1981), and gay adults are significantly more likely than nongay adults to report unmet medical needs and difficulty obtaining care (Diamant, Schuster, & Lever, 2000; Diamant, Wold, Spritzer, & Gelberg, 2000; Ponce, Cochran, Pizer, & Mays, 2010). The exact causes of these health disparities are still understudied and therefore not well understood, but Meyer and Northridge (2007) suggested that the social stigma and systematic discrimination based on sexual orientation and gender identity create a stressful social environment that has a significant negative impact on the overall health of LGBT individuals.

Degree of Cognitive Ability (D)

"The topic of individual differences in cognition is somewhat controversial in contemporary society because cognitive ability is one of the most valued human characteristics, and consequently there is considerable reluctance to discuss individual or group differences in this characteristic" (Salthouse, 2012, p. 3). A great deal of research has examined the cognitive abilities of older adults. This research has focused primarily on domains related to instrumental activities of daily living (e.g., shopping, arranging transportation, handling finances, comprehending instructions) and the consequences of declines that may occur with increasing age. The majority of research on the negative consequences of age-related declines in cognitive ability is concentrated on the development of organic deterioration of the brain, or dementias. Numerous modifiable lifestyle interventions have been proposed to prevent dementia. Although there is no clear cause-and-effect conclusion as to their ability to improve brain functioning, physical exercise, real-life skills training, mental stimulation, and stress reduction have been suggested as interventions to reduce the risk of dementia or prevent cognitive decline. The minority stress model (Meyer, 2003) clearly illustrates the unique stressors experienced by sexual minority individuals. Therefore, when discussing the LGBT older adult population, it is extremely important to realize that discrimination, victimization, and internalized stigma are significant predictors of adverse cognitive and mental health among LGBT older adults (D'Augelli, Grossman, Hershberger, & O'Connell, 2001; Fredriksen-Goldsen et al., 2011; Jacobs & Kane, 2012; Meyer, 2003). However, other researchers have found that the ability of and necessity for LGBT individuals to cope with discrimination and overcome adversity across the life course has prepared LGBT older adults for the demands of aging within an ageist culture (Cahill, South, & Spade, 2000; Orel, 2014; Shippy, Cantor, & Brennan, 2004).

Religion (R)

Although the gerontological literature has suggested that religious involvement and spirituality appear to improve health, reduce disability, increase self-esteem, reduce symptoms of depression, enhance life satisfaction, and provide potent resources for coping with loss (Koenig, 2002; Krause, 2003; Wink & Dillon, 2001) for the general older adult population, there have been few systematic studies on the impact of religious involvement and spirituality for LGBT older adults (Brennan-Ing, Seidel, Larson, & Karpiak, 2013; Porter, Ronneberg, & Witten, 2013). When working with LGBT older adults, it is imperative that religious and spiritual beliefs are recognized and honored. Limited research indicates that religious and spiritual beliefs can play a significant role in the lives of LGBT older adults (Brennan-Ing et al., 2013).

There are theological guidelines regarding sex, sexual activities, and sexual orientation and there are considerable differences in sexual morality among followers of different religious traditions. For example, Christianity, the dominant religion in the United States, sanctions sexual activity mainly between a husband and wife, and sex is seen as serving the purpose of procreation. Therefore, older adults who are engaging in sexual activity with individuals of the same sex without the purpose of procreation "may experience higher levels of stress when attempting to integrate their sexual identify with their religious and/or spiritual beliefs" (Kubicek et al., 2009, p. 602). Further research is needed to explore how religious and spiritual beliefs and sexual and gender identity in later adulthood vary by religious traditions, cultural factors, and other personal attributes.

Ethnicity and Race (E)

The majority of research on LGBT older adults is limited to a Eurocentric perspective. Although one's ethnicity and race can influence his or her attitudes concerning sexual orientation and gender identity, researchers rarely consider these cultural attributes when attempting to understand the lived experiences of LGBT older adults. Likewise, the developmental process of identifying as LGBT may be influenced by ethnicity and race, but again little attention is paid to this in the literature (Meyer, 2010; Moradi, DeBlaere, & Huang, 2010). Limited research indicates that because in U.S. culture, older persons tend to be depicted as White, middle class, female, and heterosexual, the experiences of elders of color and LGBT elders of color are poorly accounted for in research. Although the United States has a growing population of non-Caucasian older adults, the vast majority of research has been conducted among Caucasians. Therefore, it is extremely important to recognize the significance of ethnicity and race when discussing the LGBT older population.

Socioeconomic Status (S)

Just as there is limited research on the racial and ethnic diversity of LGBT older adults, even less is known about their socioeconomic diversity. Socioeconomic status includes level of education, economic class, lifestyle, occupation, and living conditions. Limited research has suggested that older lesbians and gay men have a greater likelihood of living in poverty than their heterosexual counterparts (Appelbaum, 2008; Cahill et al., 2000). Additionally, some studies have indicated that LGBT elders are more likely to live in urban rather than rural areas and are more likely to live alone than heterosexuals of the same age. Generally, older adults in the United States live in their own homes or apartments, but many are choosing to live in continuing care retirement communities (CCRCs). Only a small percentage of the general older adult population (4.5%) resides in long-term-care facilities, but there is little demographic data on the number of LGBT older adults who reside there or in CCRCs (Hillman, 2012).

Sexual Orientation (S)

When researching or working with LGBT older adults, it is important to recognize that the current LGBT older adult population came of age when their sexual orientation was regarded as a form of mental illness and that sexual behaviors between individuals of the same sex were illegal and/or considered immoral (for a comprehensive review of LGBT and aging literature, see Kimmel, Rose, & David, 2006). Older adults who self-identify as LGBT have faced numerous challenges due to the prevailing heterosexist and homophobic attitudes within the culture. An exploration of the LGBT older adult population must take into consideration the similarities between the social construction of sexual orientation as a sexual minority status and the social construction of aging. Kimmel, Rose, Orel, and Greene (2006) indicated that both social categories are evaluated negatively and associated with flagrant acts of discrimination. Because it is possible to conceal sexual orientation and even chronological age to some extent, sexual orientation and age have similar social constructions. For example, "within an ageist and heterosexist culture, the phrase (and former policy) 'Don't ask, don't tell' is applicable and often applied to both older adults and LGBT persons by those who would prefer that *they* [older LGBT adults] remain invisible" (Orel & Fruhauf, 2013, p. 179).

An exploration of the LGBT older adult population must also take into consideration that LGBT persons are members of families and actively participate in family roles such as grandfather, grandmother, father, mother, son, daughter, sister, brother, niece, nephew, uncle, and aunt. Many LGBT older adults were forced to live secretive lives in which their sexual orientation was closeted, and this may have had profound implications for their familial relationships. The research on the familial roles that LGBT persons enact has increased within the past decade, with particular attention being given to lesbian mothers. Recently, researchers have documented the perceptions and experiences of lesbian, gay, and bisexual grandparents (Fruhauf, Orel, & Jenkins, 2009; Orel, 2006; Orel & Fruhauf, 2006).

Individualistic Life Experiences (I)

Each LGBT older adult has personal life experiences that have influenced her or his beliefs and attitudes and thus her or his ability to age successfully. Significant for LGBT older adults is their past and current history of managing disclosure. This includes a past history of stigma related to coming out to family members, employers, friends, and, with the broad reach of the Internet, coming out nationally. Although coming out nationally is rarely anyone's intent, with social media (e.g., Facebook) and extensive search engines, an older adult's sexual orientation may be "discovered" or assumed by the viewing public. LGBT older adults who have experienced enacted stigma also report heightened lifetime rates of exposure to violence and victimization (Fredriksen-Goldsen et al., 2011). For many LGBT older adults, these life-altering individualistic life experiences of violence, victimization, and trauma exact a tremendous psychological toll, and this in turn can jeopardize mental, physical, and social functioning and general well-being.

A significant event in the collective memories of most LGBT older adults was the 1981 report of a mysterious infection that was taking the lives of gay men living in San Francisco. Since the first report and labeling of "gay-related infectious disease," "the AIDS epidemic has evoked widespread fear and condemnation both of the disease and those afflicted by it" (Siegel, Lune, & Meyer, 1998, p. 4). Because AIDS was first associated with gay men and viewed as a "self-inflicted" disease, the resulting stigma, discrimination, social exclusion, and alienation experienced by gay men in the early 1980s have had lasting effects. The emotional impact of HIV and AIDS on the LGBT community cannot be understated. However, it is important to note that the LGBT community experienced resiliency in the face of this adversity. Its work in developing effective HIV-prevention education programs has been a model for the resilient ways in which LGBT individuals respond to stigma and discrimination. Although a lifetime of stigma can create insidious hardships for LGBT older adults, stigma can also be associated with the potential for growth, creative expression, and hardiness.

National Origin (N)

Attitudes toward sexual orientation and gender identity can be shaped by one's country of origin. What is considered "normal" or "deviant" within a particular culture depends on salient aspects of the culture. When considering the unique needs and concerns of LGBT older adults, it must be recognized that an LGBT older adult's self-identification may include identification as an immigrant or refugee. According to the 2010 American Community Survey of the U.S. Census, 60% of older immigrants are from racial and ethnic minority groups, compared with only 20% of the total older population being persons of color. In contrast, the nonelderly population is 38% persons of color. Immigration patterns have changed dramatically during the past century. Whereas in 1970, the vast majority (79%) of immigrants ages 65 and older in the United States was from Europe, in 2010, fewer than 30% of older immigrants were born in Europe. In 2010, 32% of immigrants were born in Latin America, and 25% were born in Asia. It is estimated that of the 8.5 million undocumented immigrants in the United States, a significant number are older adults from Mexico. More recently, refugees from Bosnia, Sudan, Somalia, and Afghanistan have been entering the United States, and it is imperative that national origin be considered whenever one works with an older adult population. Limited research has systematically explored cultural similarities and differences in beliefs and values related to sexual orientation and gender identity.

Gender (G)

Although gender is conceptualized in the ADDRESSING model as being distinct from sexual orientation, they are closely intertwined because, as research indicates, "the process of exploring gender identity invariably includes exploring sexual orientation as well" (Kaufman, 2008, p. 335). Gender identity is particularly salient for transgender individuals, who identify with a gender other than their biological or birth gender.

Dominant Discourse

In addition to recognizing these 10 cultural factors and personal attributes that influence aging, it is just as important to identify the *dominant discourse* within the culture that has an impact on each of these personal attributes. The dominant discourse is a particular way of conceptualizing or talking about a subject. In this discussion, the dominant discourse refers to biases that are held by a dominant group and, if reinforced by political, economic, and social power, lead to "isms" (e.g., ageism, sexism, racism).

For example, when conceptualizing the personal attribute of age, "youth" is the dominant discourse within the United States and within most countries because youth is glorified in mass media. The glorification of youth can lead to ageist attitudes and ageism. With regard to one's degree of physical and cognitive ability, the dominant discourse is "able-bodied." The assumption within most cultures is that "normal" individuals are able-bodied. Individuals with any type of physical or cognitive limitation face potential stigma. Collectively, the dominant discourses within the United States assume that "privileges" are available to individuals who are young, able-bodied, Christian, European American, middle class, heterosexual, American born, and male. Additionally, it is assumed that individuals will successfully engage in expected life course roles and encounter on-time or "typical" life experiences and events (Bengtson & Allen, 1993). Individuals with individualistic life experiences that are not typical or are considered "off-time" events for the majority of the population are often misperceived or viewed as being "different" or "odd" (Bengtson & Allen, 1993). These off-time events often bring increased stress and strain to individuals' lives. However, it is these individualistic life experiences that often play a tremendous role in defining an individual, and these experiences set processes in motion that may have long-term consequences over the life course. For example, many individuals experience life events as personal traumas (e.g., physical and sexual abuse, witnessing violence, unexpected death of family and friends). These traumatic events often have a significant impact on the individual and play a tremendous role in how she or he views the world (and herself or himself) over time, and especially as the individual ages.

THE CHAPTERS IN THIS BOOK

This book consists of 10 chapters. Chapter 2, by Karen I. Fredriksen-Goldsen, Charles P. Hoy-Ellis, Anna Muraco, Jayn Goldsen, and Hyun-Jun Kim, explores the health disparities of LGBT older adults and their caregivers. Attention is given to the complexity of family dynamics in the context of caregiving, as well as to the effects of health disparities on older LGBT adults who are receiving care from family and friends.

Chapter 3, by Brian de Vries, discusses the oppression and discrimination experienced by LGBT older adults and their families. De Vries eloquently explains the costs and consequences of stigma, oppression, and exclusion that many LGBT older adults have experienced across the life span and how this stigma and the resulting stress can adversely affect the cognitive ability and mental health of LGBT elders.

In Chapter 4, Douglas C. Kimmel applies theories of aging to LGBT older adults, explaining how LGBT persons develop crisis competency, or mastery of stigma, when faced with the challenges associated with aging. Specifically, being harassed for being LGBT, being limited by homophobic policies, facing overt discrimination, and coming out to family and friends enable LGBT individuals to develop a competency for dealing with other crises throughout the life span.

Chapter 5, by Cody Swartz, Morgan Bunting, Christine A. Fruhauf, and Nancy A. Orel, discusses spirituality and end-of-life issues among older LGBT adults and their families, with particular attention given to the multitude of needs, concerns, and experiences that can affect end-of-life decisions.

Chapter 6, by Shari Brotman, Ilyan Ferrer, Tamara Sussman, Bill Ryan, and Brenda Richard, discusses the accessibility of health and social care among LGBT older adults within a Canadian context. This chapter also eloquently highlights the practice-related implications for clinicians, policymakers, and practitioners from a life course perspective and emphasizes the concept of intersectionality.

Chapter 7, by Sean Cahill, discusses the particular kinds of community resources and access to government services that are needed by LGBT older adults. Cahill also reports the most current research illustrating the impact of socioeconomic status on the lived experiences of LGBT older adults and provides a comprehensive discussion of LGBT-specific senior services.

Chapter 8, by Kristin S. Scherrer and James P. Fedor, uses the life course perspective to contextualize the family lives of LGBT older adults. The authors convey the importance of examining the ways that family members' lives are linked.

Chapter 9, by Loree Cook-Daniels, describes in rich detail the intersection of aging and transgenderism from a life course perspective, highlighting the fact that the T is often omitted in research on LGBT older adults. A special emphasis has therefore been placed on information needed by practitioners when planning and providing services for aging transgender people and their families.

Chapter 10, by the volume editors, concludes the book by considering future directions in research, theory, and practice.

CONCLUSION

LGBT older adults have faced numerous challenges within a culture fraught with "isms" that reflect the dominant discourses. As this chapter illustrates, an investigation of the intersectionality of personal attributes and the dominant discourses leads to a more comprehensive exploration of the issues and concerns of the LGBT older adult population. The authors in this book all discuss the ways in which the life course approach, enhanced by an intersectionality perspective, can inform our views on a diversity of issues related to aging and aged LGBT adults. It is imperative that all practitioners and researchers adopt a broader view of the lived experiences of LGBT elders, and each author stresses the importance of considering the intersectionality of age, degree of physical and cognitive ability, religion, ethnicity and race, socioeconomic status, sexual orientation, individualistic life experience, national origin, and gender over the life course. Each dimension and the multiple ways in which they interact must be considered, and the interpersonal strengths and resiliency of the LGBT older adult population must be acknowledged and celebrated. The ADDRESSING framework can be helpful in reminding all practitioners of the importance of considering the strengths related to personal attributes as well as to minority group membership. Further research with LGBT older adults focused on intersectionality and the life course perspective would allow for a broader and more detailed analysis of the complex and diverse lived experiences of LGBT elders and the attributes that have led to their resiliency. Greater acknowledgment and understanding of resilience among LGBT older adults would inform practitioners in developing effective interventions, programs, and services (Fredriksen-Goldsen et al., 2013).

REFERENCES

Administration on Aging. (2010). *A profile of older Americans: 2010*. Washington, DC: U.S. Department of Health and Human Services.

Administration on Aging. (2012). *A profile of older Americans: 2012*. Washington, DC: U.S. Department of Health and Human Services.

Appelbaum, J. (2008). Late adulthood and aging: Clinical approaches. In H. Makadon, K. Mayer, J. Potter, & H. Goldhammer (Eds.), *Fenway: Guide to lesbian, gay, bisexual, and transgender health* (pp. 135–156). Philadelphia, PA: American College of Physicians.

Bengtson, V. L., & Allen, K. R. (1993). The life course perspective applied to families over time. In P. G. Boss, W. J. Doherty, R. Larossa, W. R. Schumm, & S. K. Steinmentz (Eds.), *Sourcebook of family theories and methods: A contextual approach* (pp. 469–504). New York, NY: Plenum Press. doi:10.1007/978-0-387-85764-0_19

Brennan-Ing, M., Seidel, L., Larson, B., & Karpiak, S. E. (2013). "I'm created in god's image, and god don't create junk": Religious participation and support among older GLBT adults. *Journal of Religion, Spirituality & Aging, 25*, 70–92. doi:10.1080/15528030.2013.746629

Cahill, S., South, K., & Spade, J. (2000). *Outing age: Public policy issues affecting gay, lesbian, bisexual, and transgendered elders*. New York, NY: The Policy Institute of the National Gay and Lesbian Task Force.

Carlat, D. J., Camargo, C. A., Jr., & Herzog, D. B. (1997). Eating disorders in males: A report on 135 patients. *The American Journal of Psychiatry, 154,* 1127–1132.

Carpenter, C. (2003). Sexual orientation and body weight: Evidence from multiple surveys. *Gender Issues, 21,* 60–74. doi:10.1007/s12147-003-0006-z

Cochran, S. D. (2001). Emerging issues in research on lesbians' and gay men's mental health: Does sexual orientation really matter? *American Psychologist, 56,* 931–947. doi:10.1037/0003-066X.56.11.931

Cochran, S. D., & Mays, V. M. (2000). Lifetime prevalence of suicide symptoms and affective disorders among men reporting same-sex sexual partners: Results using NHANES III. *American Journal of Public Health, 90,* 573–578. doi:10.2105/AJPH.90.4.573

Cochran, S. D., & Mays, V. M. (2006). Estimating prevalence of mental and substance-using disorders among lesbians and gay men from existing national health data. In A. Omoto & H. Kurtzman (Eds.), *Sexual orientation and mental health* (pp. 143–165). Washington, DC: American Psychological Association. doi:10.1037/11261-007

Cochran, S. D., & Mays, V. M. (2009). Burden of psychiatric morbidity among lesbian, gay, and bisexual individuals in the California Quality of Life Survey. *Journal of Abnormal Psychology, 118,* 647–658. doi:10.1037/a0016501

Cochran, S. D., Mays, V. M., Bowen, D., Gage, S., Bybee, D., Roberts, S. J., . . . White, J. (2001). Cancer-related risk indicators and preventive screening behaviors among lesbians and bisexual women. *American Journal of Public Health, 91,* 591–597. doi:10.2105/AJPH.91.4.591

Cohn, D., & Taylor, P. (2010, December). *Baby boomers approach 65—glumly.* Washington, DC: Pew Research Social & Demographic Trends. Retrieved from http://www.pewsocialtrends.org/2010/12/20/baby-boomers-approach-65-glumly

Daling, J. R., Weiss, N. S., Hislop, T. G., Maden, C., Coates, R. J., Sherman, K. J., . . . Corey, L. (1987). Sexual practices, sexually transmitted diseases, and the incidence of anal cancer. *The New England Journal of Medicine, 317,* 973–977. doi:10.1056/NEJM198710153171601

D'Augelli, A. R., Grossman, A. H., Hershberger, S. L., & O'Connell, T. S. (2001). Aspects of mental health among older lesbian, gay, and bisexual adults. *Aging & Mental Health, 5,* 149–158. doi:10.1080/13607860120038366

Denenberg, R. (1995). Report on lesbian health. *Women's Health Issues, 5,* 81–91. doi:10.1016/1049-3867(95)00030-8

Deputy, N. P., & Boehmer, U. (2010). Determinants of body weight among men of different sexual orientation. *Preventive Medicine, 51,* 129–131. doi:10.1016/j.ypmed.2010.05.010

Diamant, A. L., Schuster, M. A., & Lever, J. (2000). Receipt of preventative health care services by lesbians. *American Journal of Preventive Medicine, 19,* 141–148. doi:10.1016/S0749-3797(00)00192-6

Diamant, A. L., Wold, C., Spritzer, K., & Gelberg, L. (2000). Health behaviors, health status, and access to and use of health care: A population-based study of lesbian, bisexual, and heterosexual women. *Archives of Family Medicine, 9,* 1043–1051.

Dibble, S. L., Vanoni, J. M., & Miaskowski, C. (1997). Women's attitudes toward breast cancer screening procedures: Differences by ethnicity. *Women's Health Issues, 7,* 47–54. doi:10.1016/S1049-3867(96)00048-5

DuRant, R. H., Krowchuk, D. P., & Sinal, S. H. (1998). Victimization, use of violence, and drug use at school among male adolescents who engage in same-sex sexual behavior. *The Journal of Pediatrics, 133,* 113–118. doi:10.1016/S0022-3476(98)70189-1

Fergusson, D. M., Horwood, L. J., & Beautrais, A. L. (1999). Is sexual orientation related to mental health problems and suicidality in young people? *Archives of General Psychiatry, 56,* 876–880. doi:10.1001/archpsyc.56.10.876

Fredriksen-Goldsen, K., Kim, H. J., Emlet, C. A., Muraco, A., Erosheva, E. A., Hoy-Ellis, C. P., & Petry, H. (2011). *The aging and health report: Disparities and resilience among lesbian, gay, bisexual, and transgender older adults.* Seattle, WA: Institute for Multigenerational Health. Retrieved from http://caringandaging.org/index.php

Fredriksen-Goldsen, K. I., Emlet, C. A., Kim H. J., Muraco, A., Erosheva, E. A., Goldsen, J., & Hoy-Ellis, C. P. (2013). The physical and mental health of lesbian, gay male, and bisexual (LGB) older adults: The role of key health indicators and risk and protective factors. *The Gerontologist, 53,* 664–675. doi:10.1093/geront/gns123

Fredriksen-Goldsen, K. I., Kim, H. J., & Goldsen, J. (2011). *The health report: Resilience and disparities among lesbian, gay, bisexual, and transgender older adults—preliminary findings.* Seattle, WA: Institute for Multigenerational Health. doi:10.1037/e561402013-001

Fruhauf, C., Orel, N., & Jenkins, D. (2009). Grandfathers' perceptions of their adult children's influence on their coming out process to grandchildren. *Journal of Gay, Lesbian. Bisexual and Transgender Family Studies, 5,* 99–118.

Gates, G. J. (2011, April). *How many people are lesbian, gay, bisexual, and transgender?* Los Angeles, CA: The Williams Institute.

George, L. K. (2013). Age structures, aging, and the life course. In J. M. Wilmoth & K. F. Ferraro (Eds.), *Gerontology: Perspectives and issues* (pp. 149–172). New York, NY: Springer.

Hagestad, G., & Dannefer, D. (2001). Concept and theories of aging: Beyond microfication in social science approaches. In R. Binstock & L. George (Eds.), *Handbook of aging and the social sciences* (pp. 3–21). San Diego, CA: Academic Press.

Hays, P. (1996). Culturally responsive assessment with diverse older adults. *Professional Psychology: Research and Practice, 27,* 188–193. doi:10.1037/0735-7028.27.2.188

Hays, P. (2008). *Addressing cultural complexities in practice: Assessment, diagnosis, and therapy* (2nd ed.). Washington, DC: American Psychological Association.

Herek, G. M. (2008). Hate crimes and stigma-related experiences among sexual minority adults in the United States: Prevalence estimates from a national probability sample. *Journal of Interpersonal Violence, 24*, 54–74. doi:10.1177/0886260508316477

Hillman, J. (2012). *Sexuality and aging: Clinical perspectives.* New York, NY: Springer.

Hunter, S. (2007). *Coming out and disclosures: LGBT persons across the life span.* New York, NY: Haworth Press.

Institute of Medicine. (1999). *Lesbian health: Current assessment and directions for the future.* Washington, DC: National Academy Press.

Institute of Medicine. (2011). *The health of lesbian, gay, bisexual, and transgender people: Building a foundation for better understanding.* Washington, DC: National Academy of Sciences.

Jacobs, R. J., & Kane, M. N. (2012). Correlates of loneliness in older gay and bisexual men. *Journal of Gay & Lesbian Social Services, 24*, 40–61. doi:10.1080/10538720.2012.643217

Kaufman, R. (2008). Introduction to transgender identity and health. In H. Makadon, K. Mayer, J. Potter, & H. Goldhammer (Eds.), *Fenway guide to lesbian, gay, bisexual, and transgender health* (pp. 331–363). Philadelphia, PA: American College of Physicians.

Kimmel, D., Rose, T., & David, S. (Eds.). (2006). *Lesbian, gay, bisexual, and transgender aging: Research and clinical perspectives.* New York, NY: Columbia Press.

Kimmel, D., Rose, T., Orel, N., & Greene, B. (2006). Historical context for research on lesbian, gay, bisexual, and transgender aging. In D. Kimmel, T. Rose, & S. David (Eds.), *Lesbian, gay, bisexual, and transgender aging: Research and clinical perspectives* (pp. 2–19). New York, NY: Columbia University Press.

Koblin, B. A., Hessol, N. A., Zauber, A. G., Taylor, P. E., Buchbinder, S. P., Katz, M. H., & Stevens, C. E. (1996). Increased incidence of cancer among homosexual men, New York City and San Francisco, 1978–1990. *American Journal of Epidemiology, 144*, 916–923. doi:10.1093/oxfordjournals.aje.a008861

Koenig, H. G. (2002). A commentary: The role of religion and spirituality at the end of life. *The Gerontologist, 42*(special issue III), 20–23.

Koh, A., & Ross, L. K. (2006). Mental health issues: A comparison of lesbian, bisexual, and heterosexual women. *Journal of Homosexuality, 51*, 33–57. doi:10.1300/J082v51n01_03

Koh, A. S. (2000). Use of preventive health behaviors by lesbian, bisexual, and heterosexual women: Questionnaire survey. *The Western Journal of Medicine, 172*, 379–384. doi:10.1136/ewjm.172.6.379

Krause, N. (2003). Religious meaning and subjective well-being in late life. *Journal of Gerontology, Series B, Psychological Sciences and Social Sciences, 58B*, S160–S170.

Kubicek, K., McDavitt, B., Carpineto, J., Weiss, G., Iverson, E. F., & Kipke, M. D. (2009). "God made me gay for a reason": Young men who have sex with men's resiliency in resolving internalized homophobia from religious sources. *Journal of Adolescent Research, 24,* 601–633. doi:10.1177/0743558409341078

Meyer, I. H. (2003). Prejudice, social stress, and mental health in lesbian, gay, and bisexual populations: Conceptual issues and research evidence. *Psychological Bulletin, 129,* 674–697. doi:10.1037/0033-2909.129.5.674

Meyer, I. H. (2010). Identity, stress, and resilience in lesbians, gay men, and bisexuals of color. *The Counseling Psychologist, 38,* 442–454.

Meyer, I. H., & Northridge, M. E. (Eds.). (2007). *The health of sexual minorities: Public health perspectives on lesbian, gay, bisexual and transgender populations.* New York, NY: Springer. doi:10.1007/978-0-387-31334-4

Moradi, B., DeBlaere, C., & Huang, Y.-P. (2010). Centralizing the experiences of LGB people of color in counseling psychology. *The Counseling Psychologist, 38,* 322–330. doi:10.1177/0011000008330832

Orel, N., & Fruhauf, C. (2006). Lesbian and bisexual grandmothers' perceptions of the grandparent-grandchild relationship. *Journal of Gay, Lesbian, Bisexual, and Transgender Family Studies, 2,* 43–70.

Orel, N., & Fruhauf, C. (2013). Lesbian, gay, bisexual, and transgender (LGBT) grandparenting. In A. Goldberg & K. R. Allen (Eds.), *LGBT parent families: Innovations in research and implications for practice* (pp. 177–192). New York, NY: Springer. doi:10.1007/978-1-4614-4556-2_12

Orel, N., & Watson, W. (2012). Addressing diversity in sexuality and aging: Key considerations for healthcare providers. *Journal of Geriatric Care Management, 22,* 13–18.

Orel, N. A. (2006). Lesbian and bisexual women as grandparents: The centrality of sexual orientation on the grandparent–grandchild relationship. In D. Kimmel, T. Rose, & S. David (Eds.), *Lesbian, gay, bisexual, and transgender aging: Research and clinical perspectives* (pp. 175–194). New York, NY: Columbia University Press.

Orel, N. A. (2014). Investigating the needs and concerns of lesbian, gay, bisexual, and transgender older adults: The use of qualitative and quantitative methodology. *Journal of Homosexuality, 61,* 53–78. doi:10.1080/00918369.2013.835236

Ponce, N. A., Cochran, S. D., Pizer, J. C., & Mays, V. M. (2010). The effects of unequal access to health insurance for same-sex couples in California. *Health Affairs, 29,* 1539–1548. doi:10.1377/hlthaff.2009.0583

Porter, K. E., Ronneberg, C. R., & Witten, T. M. (2013). Religious affiliation and successful aging among transgender older adults: Findings from the Trans MetLife survey. *Journal of Religion, Spirituality, & Aging, 25,* 112–138.

Robertson, P., & Schachter, J. (1981). Failure to identify venereal disease in a lesbian population. *Sexually Transmitted Diseases, 8,* 75–76. doi:10.1097/00007435-198104000-00008

Salthouse, T. (2012). Consequences of age-related cognitive declines. *Annual Review of Psychology, 63,* 201–226. doi:10.1146/annurev-psych-120710-100328

Shippy, R. A., Cantor, M. H., & Brennan, M. (2004). Social networks of aging gay men. *Journal of Men's Studies, 13*, 107–120.

Siegel, K., Lune, H., & Meyer, I. H. (1998). Stigma management among gay/bisexual men with HIV/AIDS. *Qualitative Sociology, 21*, 3–24. doi:10.1023/A:1022102825016

Skinner, W. F., & Otis, M. D. (1996). Drug and alcohol use among lesbian and gay people in a southern U.S. sample: Epidemiological, comparative, and methodological findings from the Trilogy Project. *Journal of Homosexuality, 30*, 59–92. doi:10.1300/J082v30n03_04

Stall, R., & Wiley, J. (1988). A comparison of alcohol and drug use patterns of homosexual and heterosexual men: The San Francisco Men's Health Study. *Drug and Alcohol Dependence, 22*, 63–73. doi:10.1016/0376-8716(88)90038-5

Stall, R. D., Greenwood, G. L., Acree, M., Paul, J., & Coates, T. J. (1999). Cigarette smoking among gay and bisexual men. *American Journal of Public Health, 89*, 1875–1878. doi:10.2105/AJPH.89.12.1875

Tang, H., Greenwood, G., Cowling, D., Lloyd, J., Roeseler, A., & Bal, D. (2004). Cigarette smoking among lesbians, gays, and bisexuals: How serious a problem? *Cancer Causes & Control, 15*, 797–803. doi:10.1023/B:CACO.0000043430.32410.69

Tootelian, D., & Varshney, D. (2010). The grandparent consumer: A financial "goldmine" with gray hair? *Journal of Consumer Marketing, 27*, 57–63. doi:10.1108/07363761011012958

U.S. Census Bureau. (2000). *Statistical abstract of the United States.* Washington, DC: Government Printing Office.

U.S. Census Bureau. (2010). *American Community Survey.* Washington, DC: Government Printing Office.

Wink, P., & Dillion, M. (2001). Religion involvement and health outcomes in late adulthood. In T. Plante & A. Sherman (Eds.), *Faith and health* (pp. 75–106). New York, NY: Guilford Press.

Zaritsky, E., & Dibble, S. L. (2010). Risk factors for reproductive and breast cancers among older lesbians. *Journal of Women's Health, 19*, 125–131. doi:10.1089/jwh.2008.1094

2

THE HEALTH AND WELL-BEING OF LGBT OLDER ADULTS: DISPARITIES, RISKS, AND RESILIENCE ACROSS THE LIFE COURSE

KAREN I. FREDRIKSEN-GOLDSEN, CHARLES P. HOY-ELLIS, ANNA MURACO, JAYN GOLDSEN, AND HYUN-JUN KIM

Changing demographics, including an increase in diversity, is creating remarkable shifts in the U.S. older adult population. By 2050, more than 130 million Americans will be age 50 or older (U.S. Census Bureau, 2012); nearly 90 million will be age 65 or older, 42% of whom will be non-White (Vincent & Velkoff, 2010). The older adult population is increasingly diverse racially and ethnically, and lesbian, gay, bisexual, and transgender (LGBT) older adults are also becoming increasingly visible. The Williams Institute (2011) estimated that 3.5% of the U.S. adult population self-identifies as lesbian, gay, and bisexual and another 0.4% as transgender. These estimates increase to 8.2% when defined as lifetime same-sex behavior and to 11% when defined as lifetime same-sex attraction. The changing demographics will have a

Research reported in this chapter was supported by the National Institute on Aging of the National Institutes of Health under Award Number R01AG026526, Fredriksen-Goldsen, principal investigator. The content is solely the responsibility of the authors and does not necessarily represent the official views of the National Institutes of Health.

DOI: 10.1037/14436-002
The Lives of LGBT Older Adults: Understanding Challenges and Resilience, N. A. Orel and C. A. Fruhauf (Editors)
Copyright © 2015 by the American Psychological Association. All rights reserved.

profound impact on the social, political, and economic fabric of the U.S. population, as the number of LGBT older adults increases dramatically.

A better understanding of the range of health outcomes as well as the social and behavioral risks and resources that contribute to health disparities among LGBT older adults is essential. In this chapter, we use a life course perspective to better understand health and aging research among LGBT adults age 50 and older. Examining the existing health-related research and the risk and protective factors that influence LGBT older adults is a first step toward developing a comprehensive understanding of the health of LGBT older adults over the life course. Such a knowledge base is needed for developing services and interventions to improve health and well-being in these communities. We begin with an overview of health disparities among LGBT older adults and the life course perspective. Next, we discuss the influence of background characteristics and risks and resources on health and well-being in these communities. Finally, we consider future directions for policy, services, education, and research.

HEALTH DISPARITIES

Evidence demonstrates that older adults from disadvantaged populations are at elevated risk of poor health, disability, and premature death. The U.S. Department of Health and Human Services (2010) defined *health disparities* as follows:

> A particular type of health difference that is closely linked with social, economic, and/or environmental disadvantage. Health disparities adversely affect groups of people who have systematically experienced greater obstacles to health based on their racial or ethnic group; religion; socioeconomic status; gender; age; . . . *sexual orientation or gender identity*; geographic location; or other characteristics historically linked to discrimination or exclusion. (para. 5; italics added)

The National Institute on Aging (2011) is committed to reducing and eliminating health disparities. Costs related to health disparities are estimated to be more than $400 billion annually (Center for American Progress, 2010). Health disparities related to sexual orientation remain one of the most pronounced gaps in health research (Centers for Disease Control and Prevention [CDC], 2011a; Institute of Medicine, 2011). A greater understanding of health disparities in sexual minority communities is essential to developing efficacious and culturally sensitive interventions to improve health; yet most population-based health surveys do not include sexual orientation or gender identity measures.

LGBT older adults encounter obstacles in receiving health and aging services, including discrimination in health settings, limited access to formal services, and lack of legal protections for their partners and other informal caregivers (Fredriksen-Goldsen et al., 2011). To date, relatively little is known regarding the health and well-being of LGBT older adults, although an emerging body of work has begun to document health disparities in these populations. A population-based study using data from the Washington State Behavioral Risk Factor Surveillance System (WA-BRFSS) reveals that 44% of lesbian and bisexual older women and 38% of gay and bisexual older men report a disability, such as experiencing limited activities or having a health problem that requires the use of special equipment (e.g., wheelchair, special bed, or a special telephone); the disability prevalence rates for sexual minority older adults are significantly higher compared with 37% of heterosexual older women and 34% of heterosexual older men (Fredriksen-Goldsen, Kim, Barkan, Muraco, & Hoy-Ellis, 2013). According to the California Health Interview Survey (CHIS), 24% of gay and bisexual older men (adjusted odds ratio [AOR] 1.24, $p \leq .05$) and 31% of lesbian and bisexual women (AOR 1.32, $p \leq .05$) report substantial limitations in basic physical activities, such as walking, climbing stairs, reaching, lifting or carrying (Wallace, Cochran, Durazo, & Ford, 2011).

In terms of psychological distress and mental health in the WA-BRFSS, 16% of lesbian and bisexual older women and 13% of gay and bisexual older men report poor mental health (defined as 14 or more days of poor mental health during the previous 30 days); the prevalence rates are significantly higher compared with 9% of heterosexual older women and 7% of heterosexual older men (Fredriksen-Goldsen, Kim, et al., 2013). In the CHIS, 22% of gay and bisexual older men (AOR 1.45, $p \leq .05$) and 28% of lesbian and bisexual older women (AOR 1.35, $p \leq .05$) report psychological distress (Wallace et al., 2011).

According to analyses adjusting for background characteristics, the prevalence rates of poor physical health for gay and bisexual older men (17%) are significantly greater than those for heterosexual older men (13%; Fredriksen-Goldsen, Kim, et al., 2013). In addition, we found gay and bisexual older men are more likely to live alone (38%) compared with older heterosexual men (15%). No significant differences were found in poor physical health or living alone between lesbian and bisexual older women and heterosexual older women.

Transgender older adults appear to have even higher rates of adverse health outcomes than their nontransgender lesbian, gay, and bisexual (LGB) peers (Fredriksen-Goldsen, Cook-Daniels, et al., 2014). For example, transgender older adults have significantly higher rates of disability (62%) than nontransgender LGB older adults (46%) as well as elevated levels of psychological distress and lower levels of general physical health.

Limited evidence also documents heightened risks of specific chronic health conditions among LGB older adults, although inconsistently. Unlike findings that are fairly consistent across the literature in terms of poorer mental health outcomes for sexual minorities relative to heterosexuals of similar age, findings regarding physical health conditions are less consistent. On the basis of the WA-BRFSS data, we find that older lesbian and bisexual women have an elevated risk of cardiovascular disease (CVD; 11%; AOR 1.37, $p \leq .05$) and obesity (36%; AOR 1.42, $p \leq .001$) compared with older heterosexual women when controlling for background characteristics (Fredriksen-Goldsen, Kim, et al., 2013). CHIS data indicate that older gay and bisexual men are more likely to report hypertension (46%; AOR 1.17, $p \leq .05$) and diabetes (15%; AOR 1.28, $p \leq .05$) than their heterosexual counterparts (Wallace et al., 2011). Conron, Mimiaga, and Landers (2010), using the Massachusetts Behavioral Risk Factor Surveillance System, found no difference in rates of diabetes among LGB adults of all ages. The Women's Health Initiative study found that among women ages 50 to 79, lesbians and bisexual women are more likely to be obese and have higher rates of breast cancer than heterosexual women but that older lesbians may have a lower incidence of hypertension and stroke than bisexual and heterosexual older women (Valanis et al., 2000). Zaritsky and Dibble (2010) compared 42 pairs of lesbian–heterosexual sisters, at least one of whom was age 50 years or older, and found that the lesbian sisters had a higher risk of ovarian and endometrial cancer; unlike Valanis and colleagues (2000), they found no difference in the prevalence of breast cancer between lesbian and heterosexual women. Although across studies the findings are mixed, in the Zaritsky and Dibble's study, older lesbians had a lower risk of cervical cancer than their heterosexual sisters.

Such conflicting findings may result from multiple issues; for example, several of the population studies are based on regional or state-level samples, which may account for some variation when compared with other geographic locations. Some differences may also be attributed to differences in the operationalization of sexual orientation. Studies have also ranged in their definitions of sexual orientation, with some using self-identity (Fredriksen-Goldsen, Kim, et al., 2013), others incorporating a temporal dimension to identity, such as "lifetime lesbian" (Valanis et al., 2000), or as a behavior, such as in "homosexually experienced heterosexuals" (Cochran & Mays, 2007), or attraction (Sandfort, Bakker, Schellevis, & Vanwesenbeeck, 2006). There is a need for more consistent use of standardized measures to bring clarity to the nature and extent of health disparities. It is critical that such research also address gender identity and expression because emerging evidence suggests that transgender older adults experience health disparities associated with elevated rates of victimization

(Fredriksen-Goldsen, Cook-Daniels, et al., 2014). There is also concern that nonmedically supervised long-term use of hormones by some transgender individuals (among other health issues) may significantly increase the risk of age-related chronic conditions, such as osteoporosis and CVD (Witten & Whittle, 2004).

It is equally important to recognize the positive health and behaviors of LGBT older adults. For example, gay and bisexual older men have a lower likelihood of obesity than heterosexual older men (Fredriksen-Goldsen, Kim, et al., 2013). Gay men age 50 and older are more likely than heterosexual peers to have had a sigmoidoscopy or colonoscopy, which are screening examinations for colorectal cancers (Conron et al., 2010). In terms of preventive care, older gay men, lesbians, and bisexual men and women have a higher likelihood of receiving a flu shot and an HIV test, compared with older heterosexuals; however, bisexual older men are less likely than gay men to obtain an HIV test (Fredriksen-Goldsen, Kim, et al., 2013). Lesbian and bisexual older women are also at lower risk for sexually transmitted infections than heterosexual women (Valanis et al., 2000).

LIFE COURSE PERSPECTIVE

Life course theories provide a means for taking into consideration both the unique needs of LGBT older adults and the cohort effects that differentiate the experiences of younger and older adults (Institute of Medicine, 2011). According to Elder (1994, 1998), central to understanding the process of aging and development in the life course perspective are the interplay of historical times, the timing of social roles and events, the linked and interdependent nature of lives, and human agency. Life course theories identify an individual's life history as important in understanding later life health outcomes (Mayer, 2009). In particular, early life experiences and transitions influence health and well-being as people navigate the stresses and changes inherent in the life cycle (Elder, 1994, 1998). *Transitions* are events that signal a change from one stage of life to another or from one social role to another; they reflect patterned activities that unfold within specific social and historical contexts according to available human agency for social actors (Elder, 1998).

It is also important to attend to "age" itself, or age-cohort membership, as a variable when considering the relationships between intersectionality, health, and well-being. Gerontological studies often differentiate the general older adult populations by age group and/or cohort, such as the "young-old," the "old," and the "old-old"; yet LGBT adults are often grouped under the singular, homogenous rubric of "older," often as 50 and older. A body of evidence has found that different age cohorts of older adults have different physical- and mental health–related concerns. For example, although physical integrity appears to decline as a function of age, psychological well-being tends to increase with age, especially after age 65, based on data from large random samples, and this seems to occur for both women and men and among developed countries in Latin and North America, Europe, and Asia (Blanchflower & Oswald, 2008).

Situating LGBT older adults within the historical and social context of their lives, a key element of life course research, may help us to better understand the contemporary health needs they face as they age (Clunis, Fredriksen-Goldsen, Freeman, & Nystrom, 2005). With respect to the interplay of historical times, current cohorts of LGBT older adults are members of the Greatest and Silent Generations (those who are about 70 and older) who came of age during a time when same-sex relationships were criminalized and severely stigmatized and same-sex identities were socially invisible. The stigma endured by LGBT individuals was formalized by laws that criminalized homosexuality but also by mental health and medical diagnoses that considered a same-sex orientation to be an illness (Cain, 1993). The *Diagnostic and Statistical Manual of Mental Disorders*, which provides the standard diagnostic criteria used by mental health professionals, designated homosexuality as a mental illness until 1973 (Silverstein, 2009), a period when many of today's LGBT older adults were young adults. Baby boomers (those who are now about age 50–69) came of age and were forming identities in the post-Stonewall era of gay liberation, civil rights, and AIDS (Cain, 1993; Cronin & King, 2010).

The American Psychiatric Association also designated "gender identity disorder" as a disorder until 2013, when it replaced the category with gender dysphoria, "the emotional distress that can result from a marked incongruence between one's experienced/expressed gender and assigned gender" (American Psychiatric Association, 2013, p. 451). Although this change still has significant shortcomings given the continued pathologizing of transgender people, it is viewed by many as a step forward because it allows for treatment and care without the stigma of a "disorder."

Pathologizing and criminalizing same-sex identity and gender identity during such periods limits the agency of LGBT individuals to make decisions about how to build adult lives and likely has had lasting effects. The life course perspective incorporates the ways that social context, cultural meaning, and structural location, in addition to time, period, and cohort, affect aging processes, including health (Elder, 1994, 1998; Mayer, 2009). From a life course perspective, we will examine how background characteristics, risks, and resources influence the health and well-being of LGBT older adults.

INFLUENCE OF BACKGROUND CHARACTERISTICS ON HEALTH AND WELL-BEING

Health disparities among LGBT older adults may be partially accounted for by social determinants and other background characteristics, including sexual orientation and gender identity as well as age, sex, race and ethnicity, and socioeconomic status (Fredriksen-Goldsen, Cook-Daniels, et al., 2014; Fredriksen-Goldsen, Emlet, et al., 2013). Although some studies have found that sexual orientation itself is a determinant of health disparities among older adults, the intersectionality of other factors must also be considered. For example, gay and bisexual older adult men have comparable or lower incomes than heterosexual men of similar age, despite having higher levels of education and employment (Fredriksen-Goldsen, Kim, et al., 2013; Wallace et al., 2011). Transgender older adults have significantly lower incomes than their non-transgender heterosexual or LGB peers (Fredriksen-Goldsen, Cook-Daniels, et al., 2014; LGBT Movement Advancement Project & SAGE, 2010). Furthermore, LGBT older adults are also likely to have lower retirement incomes than heterosexual older adults, in part due to differential access to Social Security benefits related to same-sex marriage restrictions in place until June 2013 (Shankle, Maxwell, Katzman, & Landers, 2003).

Still, it is important to understand how and to what extent traditional social determinants are associated with physical and mental health among LGBT older adults. Caring and Aging with Pride (CAP), the first federally funded study of LGBT health and aging (http://caringandaging.org), gathered information from 2,560 lesbian, gay, bisexual, and transgender adults ages 50 to 95 from 11 community-based aging agencies across the country (Fredriksen-Goldsen et al., 2011). Almost half of the participants were 65 to 79 years of age, and more than 10% were 80 or older. This large number of sociodemographically diverse participants included 61% gay men, 33% lesbians, 5% bisexual men and women, and 7% transgender older adults. Thirteen percent were people of color, approximately 30% were at 200% of the poverty level or below, and 44% of the participants were partnered or married. We also found that participants had about two chronic conditions on average, including 45% with high blood pressure and 9% living with HIV disease. CAP included measures of physical and mental health, risk factors (e.g., experiences of discrimination and internalized stigma), resources (e.g., social support and religious and spiritual participation), and caregiving and care receiving.

CAP associations of lower income with poorer health among LGB older adults are consistent across studies. Among LGB older adults, poor mental health and physical health are associated with lower income (Grossman, D'Augelli, & O'Connell, 2002). LGBT older adults with lower levels of income are more likely to report poor physical health–related quality of life (QOL); poor general health; disability; and many chronic conditions, including high blood pressure, arthritis, CVD, osteoporosis, and diabetes. They are also more likely to report poorer mental health–related QOL as well as higher rates of depression, stress, loneliness, anxiety, and suicidal ideation (Fredriksen-Goldsen et al., 2011). The relationship between age and physical health is relatively linear among LGB older adults (Fredriksen-Goldsen et al., 2011). As age increases, the rates of poor physical health–related QOL, disability, chronic conditions (including high blood pressure, high cholesterol, arthritis, CVD, cataracts, osteoporosis, and cancer) also increase; exceptions are lowered rates of obesity and HIV. The relationship between age and mental health, on the other hand, appears nonlinear. LGBT adults ages 65 to 79 show better mental health–related QOL, lower depression, and lower stress than those ages 50 to 64 and ages 80 and older; overall, the rates of anxiety, suicidal ideation, and loneliness decrease with aging (Fredriksen-Goldsen et al., 2011).

In terms of gender, the CAP study found that while older sexual minority women are more likely than older sexual minority men to report poor physical health–related QOL, disability, arthritis, asthma, osteoporosis, and obesity, they report lower rates of high blood pressure, high cholesterol, CVD, diabetes, cancer, hepatitis, and HIV (Fredriksen-Goldsen et al., 2011). The relationship between gender and mental health seems to be inconclusive. The CAP study found lower rates of loneliness for women and a similar rate of suicidal ideation by gender (Fredriksen-Goldsen et al., 2011), and other studies found a similar rate of loneliness by gender and lower rates of suicidal ideation for women (D'Augelli, Grossman, Hershberger, & O'Connell, 2001; Grossman et al., 2002).

Partnership status also influences the health of LGB older adults, who are less likely to be married than their heterosexual age peers, although more likely to be partnered (Fredriksen-Goldsen, Kim, et al., 2013), which is likely a reflection of the fact that legal marriage between same-sex partners is not allowed in most states. In the general population, legal marriage confers benefits for both physical and mental health (Gay and Lesbian Medical Association, 2008), and the CAP study found that legal marriage is significantly associated with greater life satisfaction and fewer depressive symptoms than being partnered, yet unmarried, among LGB older adults (M. Williams & Fredriksen-Goldsen, 2013). Similarly, a recent study among older gay men found that legal marriage, but not legal domestic partnerships, is significantly associated with better mental health (Wight, LeBlanc, de Vries, & Detels, 2012).

These findings illustrate a component of Elder's (1994, 1998) life course perspective in that the current cohorts of LGB older adults were historically prohibited from legally marrying a same-sex partner, adopting children, and having access to other federal, state, and local laws that provide legal and economic protections. Because legal marriage affords numerous legal, policy, and economic benefits, historical prohibition of same-sex marriage is expected to have long-term effects on LGB older adults.

INFLUENCE OF RISKS ON HEALTH AND WELL-BEING

LGBT older adults face unique risks, such as the social and historical contexts in which current LGBT older adults have come of age and matured, that may jeopardize their mental and physical health including relatively high levels of gender identity– and sexual orientation–related stigma, discrimination, and victimization (Fredriksen-Goldsen, Cook-Daniels, et al., 2014; Fredriksen-Goldsen, Emlet, et al., 2013). The CAP study found that 82% of LGBT older adults have been discriminated or victimized at least once due to their sexual orientation, and more than 60% three or more times in their lifetime (Fredriksen-Goldsen et al., 2011). A study of 416 older American and Canadian LGB adults found that nearly 75% had been victimized because of their sexual orientation (D'Augelli & Grossman, 2001). Herek (2009) documented risk of internalized stigma for sexual minority individuals in which they accept and integrate negative societal values and attitudes.

Discrimination, victimization, and internalized stigma are significant predictors of adverse mental and physical health among LGB older adults; victimization and internalized stigma are associated with disability and depression, and victimization is also associated with poor general health (Fredriksen-Goldsen et al., 2011). Among transgender older adults, victimization and internalized stigma are associated with poor health outcomes (Fredriksen-Goldsen, Cook-Daniels, et al., 2014). LGB older adults who have been physically assaulted report more loneliness, poorer mental health, and more lifetime suicide attempts (D'Augelli & Grossman, 2001). Among midlife and older gay and bisexual men (ages 40–94), internalized stigma is an important factor that leads to increased loneliness (Jacobs & Kane, 2012), which may have negative impacts on health in various ways in later life. Among transgender older adults, risk factors, such as victimization and stigma, explained the highest proportion of the total effect of gender identity on health outcomes (Fredriksen-Goldsen, Cook-Daniels, et al., 2014). Furthermore, a literature review of 66 studies found that discrimination seriously affects LGBT older adults' access to health care; the quality of care received; and utilization of health care, housing, and social services (Addis, Davies, Greene, Macbride-Stewart, & Shepherd, 2009).

Chronic stress among racial and ethnic minorities has been found to be significantly associated with a variety of poor physical and mental health outcomes (Ahmed, Mohammed, & Williams, 2007; D. R. Williams, Neighbors,

& Jackson, 2003). As previously discussed, LGBT older adults evidence alarmingly high rates of psychological distress (Fredriksen-Goldsen, Cook-Daniels, et al., 2014; Fredriksen-Goldsen, Kim, et al., 2013; Wallace et al., 2011). Even at low levels, psychological distress is associated with premature emergence of chronic health conditions, such as CVD, and consequent premature death (Russ et al., 2012). The surfeit of psychological distress found in LGBT populations is theorized to result from their marginalized status (Huebner & Davis, 2007; I. H. Meyer, 2003; Szymanski, Kashubeck-West, & Meyer, 2008).

Ilan H. Meyer's (2003) minority stress model identifies stressors unique to sexual minority individuals in addition to the typical stressors of modern life (e.g., divorce, losing a job, economics). These stressors include external discriminatory conditions and events, and internal stressors such as internalized heterosexism and hiding one's nonheterosexual identity, often referred to as *concealment* or *being closeted*. Sex, age, and sexual orientation influence heightened risks of minority stressors. Studies found that LGB older men report significantly higher levels of discrimination and internalized stigma than LGB older women (Fredriksen-Goldsen et al., 2011). Older participants, compared with younger, report more internalized stigma but lower levels of discrimination and victimization (Fredriksen-Goldsen et al., 2011). Transgender older adults experience higher rates of discrimination and victimization than their nontransgender LGB peers (Fredriksen-Goldsen, Cook-Daniels, et al., 2014).

The link between health and concealment of one's sexual or gender identity is not clear. LGB individuals may attempt to hide their sexual orientation as a strategy to avoid victimization and discrimination (Kertzner, Meyer, Frost, & Stirratt, 2009; I. H. Meyer, 2003), but such efforts can deprive them of normative social interactions with like others (Herek, 2009). LGB older adults who disclosed their sexual identity more openly and were closeted for a shorter time were more likely to experience victimization (D'Augelli & Grossman, 2001). Individuals whose stigmatized identities can be hidden (i.e., LGBT) may benefit more from disclosure through associating with like others than those who have less concealable identities (i.e., some racial/ethnic minorities; Hatzenbuehler, Nolen-Hoeksema, & Dovidio, 2009). In the CAP study, 21% of LGBT older adults had not revealed their sexual orientation or gender identity to their primary physician (Fredriksen-Goldsen et al., 2011). The American Medical Association (2013) warned that physicians' failure to recognize, and patients' reluctance to disclose, can lead to failure to diagnose serious medical problems. Lack of disclosure prevents discussions about sexual health, risk of breast or prostate cancer, hepatitis, HIV risk, hormone therapy, and other risk factors.

Nondisclosure and its negative effects may be even more problematic for transgender people; 71% have attempted to conceal their gender identity, expression, or transition, whereas 57% have delayed transitioning in an attempt to evade discrimination (Grant et al., 2011). Fear of discrimination may explain why transgender older adults have higher rates of concealment than their LGB nontransgender counterparts (Fredriksen-Goldsen, Cook-Daniels, et al., 2014).

Intersectionality of diverse minority statuses and identities has to be considered in terms of the relationship between life stressors and health. The literature has raised the possibility that cumulative risks from multiple disadvantaged statuses among sexual minorities within racial and ethnic minority communities magnify health risks (Kim & Fredriksen-Goldsen, 2012). The consequences of multiple stressors such as racial and ethnic discrimination within sexual minority communities and antigay values within some communities of color may lead to an elevated risk of poor physical and mental health (Díaz, Ayala, Bein, Henne, & Marin, 2001; Díaz, Bein, & Ayala, 2006; Harper, Jernewall, & Zea, 2004). The CAP study found that Hispanic and Native American LGBT older adults are more likely to experience victimization than White LGBT older adults (Fredriksen-Goldsen et al., 2011). Native American LGBT older adults are more likely to experience verbal abuse from a partner, family member, or friend than Whites, whereas Asian/Pacific Islander LGBT older adults report higher levels of internalized stigma.

The CAP project revealed that more than one in 10 (13%) LGBT older adult participants reported being denied health care or provided with inferior health care because they were LGBT, and 15% of LGBT older adults fear accessing health care services outside the LGBT community (Fredriksen-Goldsen et al., 2011). According to a nationwide survey, although a third of agencies had provided their staff with some type of LGBT aging–related training, agencies have rarely offered LGBT-specific services or outreach (Knochel, Croghan, Moone, & Quam, 2010). Survey data from aging service providers in Michigan also indicate that few aging agencies provide services specific to LGBT older adults or have outreach to the LGBT community (Hughes, Harold, & Boyer, 2011).

As a result of such factors, LGBT adults often lack adequate access to aging services and health care (Conron et al., 2010; Dilley, Simmons, Boysun, Pizacani, & Stark, 2010), which may increase the risk of poor physical and mental health among LGB older adults. Other adverse health behaviors also increase the risk of many chronic health conditions. Compared with their heterosexual counterparts, LGB older adults are more likely to smoke and engage in excessive drinking (Fredriksen-Goldsen, Kim, et al., 2013; Valanis et al., 2000), both of which are leading causes of preventable deaths in the United States (CDC, 2010, 2011b; Substance Abuse and Mental Health Services Administration, 2010). Among LGB older adults, men are more likely to report alcohol abuse (D'Augelli et al., 2001) and drug use than women (Fredriksen-Goldsen et al., 2011). According to the CAP study findings, transgender LGB older adults are more likely to be engaged in smoking and excessive drinking than nontransgender LGB older adults (Fredriksen-Goldsen et al., 2011). The Women's Health Initiative study also found that lesbian and bisexual older women are less likely to consume fruits and vegetables than heterosexual women (Valanis et al., 2000).

Research shows that the desire to "age in place," close to support systems, may conflict with accessibility to health and long-term care, especially for LGBT older adults (King & Dabelko-Schoeny, 2006). For LGBT older adults, the ability to age close to one's community is related to health status, access to knowledgeable and responsive health care, transportation, affordability and fear of medical debt, and lack of coverage for same-sex couples. Issues such as isolation and lack of informal support make aging in place potentially more difficult for LGBT older adults, especially in rural areas (King & Dabelko-Schoeny, 2006).

Social isolation presents significant risks for health and well-being (Berkman, Glass, Brissette, & Seeman, 2000; Cornwell & Waite, 2009) and increases the risks of institutional care, nutritional deficiencies, and psychological distress (Blank, Asencio, Descartes, & Griggs, 2009). Living alone increases the risk of social isolation and loneliness (Perissinotto, Stijacic Cenzer, & Covinsky, 2012; Taube, Kristensson, Midlöv, Holst, & Jakobsson, 2013; Yeh & Lo, 2004), which in turn is a significant risk factor for premature morbidity and mortality (Cacioppo & Hawkley, 2003). For example, loneliness has been known to affect cardiovascular risks (Ong, Rothstein, & Uchino, 2012), sleep dysfunction (Cacioppo et al., 2002), physical disability (Perissinotto et al., 2012), poor mental health (Cacioppo, Hughes, Waite, Hawkley, & Thisted, 2006), and mortality (Perissinotto et al., 2012). In fact, a study found that LGB older adults living alone are more likely to evaluate their physical and mental health as poor than those who live with a partner (Grossman, D'Augelli, & Hershberger, 2000). Compared with their heterosexual counterparts, LGB older adults are more likely to live alone and be socially isolated (Grossman et al., 2002; Kuyper & Fokkema, 2010).

INFLUENCE OF RESOURCES ON HEALTH AND WELL-BEING

The social resources available to LGBT older adults, including social support and social networks, decrease the risk of disability, poor general health, and depression among this group (Fredriksen-Goldsen, Kim, et al., 2013). In research that focuses on aging in general, an increased number of social contacts, a larger social network size, and more social support are associated with better health and QOL among older adults (Fiori, Smith, &

Antonucci, 2007; Zaninotto, Falaschetti, & Sacker, 2009). According to the CAP project, many LGBT older adults have available social resources despite the discriminatory social environment in which they have lived. For example, 89% feel positive about belonging to the LGBT community. In terms of social support network, two thirds of LGBT older adult participants (67%) reported that they have someone to help with daily chores if they are sick, 82% usually have someone to turn to for suggestions about how to deal with a personal problem, 83% have someone with whom to do something enjoyable, and 71% have someone to love and make them feel wanted (Fredriksen-Goldsen et al., 2011). Religious and spiritual activities may also offer support. Of the CAP participants, 38% attended religious or spiritual services or activities at least once a month, with transgender older adults more likely to attend than LGB nontransgender older adults (Fredriksen-Goldsen et al., 2011).

Nonetheless, additional social resources are needed for many LGBT older adults. According to the CAP project, more than half of LGBT older adults reported that social events and support groups are needed in LGBT older adult communities (Fredriksen-Goldsen et al., 2011). These requests for additional community-level social resources may be related to a higher likelihood of social isolation for LGBT older adults. Social resources can be protective in the relationship between victimization and health among LGBT older adults (Fredriksen-Goldsen, Cook-Daniels, et al., 2014; Fredriksen-Goldsen, Kim, et al., 2013). Increased social support is associated with a lower level of loneliness among LGB older adults (Grossman et al., 2000), and members of this population report less loneliness when they have a larger network size (Grossman et al., 2002).

Grossman and colleagues (2000) found that the most common social support networks of LGBT older adults are close friends. Blank and colleagues (2009) deemed social supports crucial, especially for LGBT older adults struggling with chronic illnesses. The Metlife Market Institute found LGBT older adults to be heavily involved in caregiving, caring for mostly parents, partners, and friends (Metlife Mature Market Institute & American Society on Aging, 2010). Interestingly, the study also found that LGBT baby boomers report an expectation to be caregivers. Social relationships of LGBT older adults may differ from those of the general older adult population, especially because many LGBT older adults do not have children or legally recognized family members to help them (Fredriksen-Goldsen et al., 2011). Hence they reported heavy reliance on partners (married or unmarried) and friends of similar age to provide help and caregiving assistance as they age (Beeler, Rawls, Herdt, & Cohler, 1999; Fredriksen-Goldsen & Hoy-Ellis, 2007).

According to Shippy, Cantor, and Brennan (2004), older gay men (ages 50–87) are likely to maintain close relationships with their biological family members regardless of disclosing their sexual identity; still, they are less likely to turn to relatives for help. Among LGBT older adult caregivers, most (35%) are providing care to their partner or spouse, and nearly one third (32%) assist a friend. Among care recipients, the majority (54%) receives care from their partner or spouse, and nearly one quarter (24%) receive help from a friend (Fredriksen-Goldsen et al., 2011). The quality of the caregiving relationship, in terms of mutual understanding, closeness, and acceptance, is important for promoting mental health of caregivers and care recipients among LGB older adults (Fredriksen-Goldsen, Kim, Muraco, & Mincer, 2009). There may be limits in friends' ability to care over the long term, especially when decision making is required due to cognitive impairment of the older adult or other factors (Muraco & Fredriksen-Goldsen, 2011). In the absence of a caregiver, LGB older adults may experience stress related to decision making about care in later life or may simply go without adequate care.

In the CAP study, participants with a same-sex partner, whether legally married or not, were significantly more likely to report better health and fewer depressive symptoms compared with single LGB older adults (M. Williams & Fredriksen-Goldsen, in press). This is similar to research on marriage and cohabitation among older adults in the general population, which shows that they live longer than unmarried peers who live alone (Goldman, Korenman, & Weinstein, 1995; Manzoli, Villari, Pirone, & Boccia, 2007; Scafato et al., 2008; Tower, Stanislav, & Darefsky, 2002) and reported a lower frequency of depressive symptoms (Henderson, Scott, & Kay, 1986).

Although, as previously noted, greater levels of education do not appear to confer commensurate levels of income (Fredriksen-Goldsen, Kim, et al., 2013; Wallace et al., 2011), education can provide other nontangible resources, including higher levels of civic involvement, as well as fostering cognitive development (Madsen, Hanewicz, & Thackery, 2010). LGBT older adults' lifetime experiences of navigating often hostile social environments may provide a sense of mastery that is particularly salient to older adulthood and its attendant challenges—"crisis competence" (Kimmel, 1978). Kertzner et al. (2009) found that LGB adults ages 40 and older evidenced higher levels of social well-being than their younger counterparts. Age itself may also be an indirect resource for older transgender adults; older male and female bodies become more androgynous as they age, so phenotypic gender differences become less obvious (Witten, 2002).

After adjusting for background characteristics such as age, income, and education, LGB older adults do not appear to differ from their heterosexual counterparts in terms of having health care insurance; roughly 10% do not have such coverage (Fredriksen-Goldsen, Kim, et al., 2013; Wallace et al., 2011), which may reflect leveling as a result of access to Social Security and Medicare. They also do not appear to differ in rates of having a regular care provider or being unable to access such care when needed due to financial considerations. Another study found that lesbian and bisexual women ages 50 to 64 are less likely to have insurance than heterosexual women of similar age, whereas the rates by sexual orientation among women ages 65 and older are similar (Valanis et al., 2000). According to CHIS, lesbian and bisexual older women are more likely to report delaying care than older heterosexual women (Wallace et al., 2011).

WHERE DO WE GO FROM HERE?

Research findings illustrate that, compared with the general older population, lesbian, gay, bisexual, and transgender older adults are health-disparate populations. Although many LGBT older adults experience risks such as discrimination and stigma, they also display important strengths, including developing unique and responsive support systems. To address the aging and health needs of LGBT older adults, a comprehensive approach is warranted to transform public policies, services, education, and research.

Policy

As we move forward, the distinctive health and aging needs of LGBT older adults must be recognized and accounted for in future policy. Researchers are at the risk of addressing the needs of LGBT older adults as a homogenous group rather than fully investigating the unique needs of each group. It is essential that efforts be made to address the distinct needs of subgroups among LGBT older adults and to recognize that both bisexual and transgender older adults are critically underserved. It is vital to investigate changes in LGBT health across the life course and understand how differing types of social structures and life events affect aging and health in these populations over time.

As Adams (2011) succinctly pointed out, "good ideas and theory are not enough to induce policy change" (p. 14); a sustainable LGBT aging agenda that incorporates attention to policy advocacy will require "leadership backed by institutional capacity" (p. 17). We must also be open to innovation in coalition building as well as intervention design and implementation. We often think of policy change as the purview of the public sector, yet as the amicus curiae briefs submitted by 48 major corporations (e.g., Boeing, Microsoft, Xerox, Aetna, Time/Warner) on behalf of parties seeking to overturn the Defense of Marriage Act (DOMA) indicate (Phillip, 2012), the private sector can also be a major resource for leadership and capacity development as well as policy change.

In a major policy shift, the U.S. Supreme Court struck down Section 3 of DOMA in 2013, ruling it unconstitutional, thereby allowing federal recognition of state-sanctioned same-sex marriages and providing equal access to the more than 1,100 marital rights, benefits, responsibilities, and privileges that federally recognized marriage confers (General Accounting Office & Office of the General Counsel, 1997). Such federal benefits are now available to same-sex couples legally married in any state with marriage equality, regardless of the state in which they reside. As important as these benefits are to individual lives, equal recognition of same-sex relationships is an effective "upstream intervention" that may with time reduce discrimination and heterosexist attitudes, values, and beliefs at the societal level (Hatzenbuehler, Keyes, & Hasin, 2009; Riggle, Rostosky, & Horne, 2010).

Advocacy now needs to focus on local and state levels so that the protections of marriage will be available to all LGBT older adults. First, it is important to recognize that federal recognition only extends to civil *marriage*; civil unions and domestic partnerships remain unrecognized by the federal government. Second, the United States has a contentious history regarding states' rights versus federal rights and jurisdictions; it is likely that many states will continue to resist sanctioning same-sex marriages. Contrary to the to the "full faith and credit" clause of Article IV of the U.S. Constitution, under Section 2 of DOMA, which remains intact, states are not required to recognize same-sex marriages lawfully entered into in other states (Human Rights Campaign, 2013), although heterosexual marriages must be recognized under the "full faith and credit" clause of Article IV.

It is also essential to protect the safety and security of LGBT older adults by implementing policies that ultimately shift the social and historical contexts by combating discrimination, victimization, and stigma. It is crucial that hate crimes be fully prosecuted and that discrimination based on sexual orientation or gender identity not be allowed at any level in employment, housing, or public accommodations so that members of LGBT older adult communities feel safe and are equally protected under the law.

Steps are needed to expand the Older Americans Act to target social and health services and programs for vulnerable LGBT older adults and their caregivers. The economic security of LGBT older adults and their loved ones will be protected by maintaining entitlement and need-based programs, such as Social Security, Supplemental Security Income, Social Security Disability Insurance, Medicare, and Medicaid. State and federal Family Medical Leave Acts should be updated to include same-sex partners and LGBT family-of-choice members as covered caregivers. Advocacy efforts should also include partnering with the Department of Housing and Urban Development to amend regulations so that same-sex couples have a right to share private bedrooms in facilities.

Projections indicate that by 2015, more than half of the 1.2 million Americans living with HIV will be age 50 or older, yet older HIV-positive adults are often excluded from clinical and pharmaceutical trials (Tietz & Schaefer, 2011). Similarly, although nearly one in five new HIV diagnoses are among adults age 50 or older, there are minimal outreach and prevention efforts that target older adults. In addition, public health policy must be responsive to the fact that nearly one in four Americans living with HIV are women (CDC, 2013); this is relevant in that HIV policy in the United States targets primarily injection drug users and men who have sex with men, which perpetuates the myth that HIV is a "gay" or a "drug user's" disease. This myth is believed to be a significant contributory factor in the increasing incidence of HIV infection among heterosexual, bisexual, and lesbian women.

In addition to improving population health and reducing health disparities, Healthy People 2020 seeks to improve the QOL of all Americans (U.S. Department of Health and Human Services, 2010). The National Prevention Strategy mandated by the Affordable Care Act calls on both private and public entities to recenter health care in the context of wellness and prevention (CDC, 2011b). The Affordable Care Act also mandates the availability of culturally responsive and appropriate health care for LGBT people, including older adults.

Services

Comprehensive aging and health services for LGBT older adults are needed. Partnerships between LGBT aging agencies, services in the larger LGBT community, and mainstream aging and health service providers need to develop culturally relevant programs to meet the needs of LGBT older adults. Services that are developed to target LGBT older adults at most risk, such as those living alone without adequate services or support, are critical to reach this underserved population. It is particularly important to develop programs that target LGBT older adults who do not live in major metropolitan areas.

A planning process that secures resources and develops successful programs and policies to address the growing aging and health needs of LGBT older adults will include, at all levels, not only organizations and communities but also LGBT older adults themselves. LGBT older adults should be included in all advocacy efforts, and opportunities for their increased civic and volunteer engagement must be identified (LGBT Movement Advancement Project & SAGE, 2010).

Another service goal is to ensure that providers understand the different needs, challenges, and perspectives of LGBT older adult cohorts. It is likely that baby boomers will increasingly demand more inclusive and culturally competent services from providers, but the generation that precedes them should not be ignored. Attention must also be paid to heterosexist attitudes and behaviors that may be held by other consumers of services. Even when staff members are trained in culturally competent practices, other older adults using senior services can contribute to an unfriendly and unsafe environment, so they too may need additional education and training.

Education

As mandated by the Affordable Care Act, cultural competency training is needed in order for health care, human services, housing, and legal professionals to be responsive and equipped to meet the needs of LGBT older adults and their caregivers. Training-related competencies need to be developed and integrated into educational programs, including medicine, nursing, social work, and law, to ensure that the health and service needs of LGBT older adults and their families are addressed.

Social workers and other health care providers trained to provide culturally competent services for LGBT older adults must have the skills necessary to use up-to-date practice modalities and to advocate for policies that foster the dignity and worth of this population and the importance of their relationships and families. Such training should address the diversity in age, gender, gender identity, ethnicity, race, socioeconomic status, geographic location, and ability among LGBT older adult populations. These competencies should also include an understanding that LGBT older adults remain sexually active, like their heterosexual counterparts (Fredriksen-Goldsen et al., 2011; Lindau et al., 2007). As such, service providers must be comfortable with discussing sexuality with older adults, including sexual function and behavior. When needed, these discussions should also include reframing risk for sexually transmitted infections as a concern for sexually active older adults.

Cultural competency training must include awareness of the historical and structural factors that act as barriers to health care and community support services. Understanding why LGBT older adults may be reluctant to access such services will provide insights into how health care and community support agencies and services can create more welcoming environments. Additionally, health care providers must be educated about the unique needs of transgender older adults. A significant proportion of transgender older adults have not disclosed their gender identity to their primary care physician, which can have serious negative impacts on health outcomes (American Medical Association, 2008). Female-to-male (FTM) older transgender adults may be at heightened risk for breast cancer; male-to-female (MTF) transgender older adults may be at elevated risk for prostate cancer (Persson, 2009).

Both providers and LGBT older adults need to be educated and trained to effectively navigate existing laws and public policies to increase their agency over decision making. Legal planning is necessary and must include wills and durable powers of attorney for health care in addition to the use of advocates if no one is available to act in such a capacity. Legal recourse must also be available if privacy is violated under the Health Insurance Portability and Accountability Act and other regulations in health care settings. Staff members of skilled nursing facilities, as well as LGBT older adults themselves, must be educated about their respective rights and responsibilities under the Nursing Home Reform Act. LGBT older adults also should be educated in how to hold providers accountable for violations (LGBT Movement Advancement Project & SAGE, 2010).

In addition to providing competency training to mainstream service organizations regarding the unique needs and challenges that older LGBT adults face, it is equally important to educate LGBT organizations regarding the needs and the invisibility of LGBT older adults within LGBT communities (H. Meyer, 2011). Ageism within LGBT communities must be addressed and challenged. Some studies have illustrated the negative effects of ageism through stereotypes and perceptions of accelerated aging and its resistance in gay male communities (Berger, 1982; Slevin, 2008) and addressed the lack of attention to elder cohorts in previous research and policy recommendations, which have rendered older LGBT adults invisible. Although most LGBT older adults feel positive about belonging to their communities (Fredriksen-Goldsen et al., 2011), the sense of connection may be somewhat attenuated as a result of ageism within those same communities (Brotman, Ryan, & Cormier, 2003). Just as most mainstream aging services and organizations are designed for heterosexuals, most services and organizations in the LGBT community target younger age groups (Johnson, 2013; Slusher, Mayer, & Dunkle, 1996).

Research

To fully assess the health needs of LGBT older adults, sexual orientation, gender identity, and sexual behavior measures must be integrated into public health and aging-related surveys. Standard reporting of sexual identity, behavior, and attraction, and gender identity and expression is necessary if health disparities are to be measured and addressed. Some may hesitate to implement these important measures because of a mistaken belief that older adults are reluctant to provide this information. However, previous studies have shown that LGBT older adults are willing to self-identify (Fredriksen-Goldsen, Cook-Daniels, et al., 2014; Fredriksen-Goldsen, Kim, et al., 2013; Valanis et al., 2000; Wallace et al., 2011). Questions regarding sexual orientation and gender identity should also be included in health care settings (Institute of Medicine, 2011).

The development of innovative sampling methods to reach those most isolated and to obtain more representative samples of LGBT older adults is needed. LGBT older adults in rural locales may be particularly hard to reach and may face additional barriers to optimal health and aging services (One Colorado Education Fund, 2011). The development and evaluation of interventions designed to improve the health of LGBT older adults must pay attention to the diversity and heterogeneity of these populations.

Although many researchers include the terms *transgender* and *bisexual* in studies of LGBT populations, rarely are transgender and bisexual older adults actually included in samples. Gender, gender identity and expression, and sexual orientation are inextricably intertwined; yet they are distinct constructs that need additional attention in future research. Particular attention to transgender and bisexual health and aging issues is critical to better understand the reasons certain subgroups in these communities may experience even greater health disparities than others (Fredriksen-Goldsen, Kim, et al., 2011).

More work is needed to examine the interplay between resilience and the stressors associated with aging, and the mechanisms through which social contexts may have direct and indirect effects on the health of LGB older adults. Future research that more directly tests the relationship between transitions and trajectories through the life course and investigates the role of human agency in adapting to structural and legal constraints would provide a greater understanding of how life experiences affect later life health outcomes. Attention to cohort differences is also critical in understanding how historical legacies of institutional discrimination in the past continue to affect the health of older LGBT adults. Further exploration of crisis competence will also enhance our knowledge of resilience in the lives of LGBT older adults (Institute of Medicine, 2011).

In addition to attention to structural factors, much more research is needed to truly understand the complex, dynamic, multilevel pathways that link sexual orientation and gender identity to health disparities. Studies should also include biomarkers to examine the role of stress in health disparities among LGBT older adult populations (Lindau & McDade, 2007). Objective measures of allostatic load can be invaluable in contributing to our understanding of how experiences of stress become embodied, allowing older bodies to tell the stories that may be unknown, unable, or unwilling to be told (Krieger, 1999). The combination of objective and subjective measures can only increase our understanding of underlying causal pathways, which is necessary for the development and implementation of culturally sensitive, effective interventions (Institute of Medicine, 2011).

Because there may be less reliance on partners, spouses, and children among LGBT older adults, future research needs to investigate how differing types of social networks, support, and family structures influence health and aging experiences (Muraco & Fredriksen-Goldsen, 2011). Another area that warrants future research is the longitudinal study of health of LGBT older adults. Longitudinal research that uses a life course perspective would elucidate the ways that various life experiences that occur earlier, such as the diagnoses of chronic illnesses or the end of a romantic relationship through the breakup or death of a partner, affect health outcomes later in life.

CONCLUSION

Taking into consideration the shifting social contexts that LGBT older adults experience can provide an even greater understanding of how the entirety of the life course shapes contemporary health disparities. Using a life course perspective, this chapter has provided an overview of important health issues affecting LGBT older adults and identified risks (e.g., stigma, victimization, health-related behaviors) and protective factors (e.g., social support, community integration) that are associated with physical and mental health of LGBT older adults. Policies and services aimed at reducing stigma and victimization are critically needed to address and reduce health risks facing these populations. Furthermore, individual, family, and community support through their unique social support systems should be bolstered to address the distinct health and aging needs in these growing communities.

REFERENCES

Adams, M. (2011). Reflections on advancing an LGBT aging agenda. *Public Policy & Aging Report*, *21*, 14–18.

Addis, S., Davies, M., Greene, G., Macbride-Stewart, S., & Shepherd, M. (2009). The health, social care and housing needs of lesbian, gay, bisexual and transgender older people: A review of the literature. *Health & Social Care in the Community*, *17*, 647–658. doi:10.1111/j.1365-2524.2009.00866.x

Ahmed, A. T., Mohammed, S. A., & Williams, D. R. (2007). Racial discrimination & health: Pathways & evidence. *The Indian Journal of Medical Research*, *126*, 318–327.

American Medical Association. (2013). *AMA policies on GLBT issues: H-65.973. Health care disparities in same-sex partner households*. Retrieved from http://www.ama-assn.org//ama/pub/about-ama/our-people/member-groups-sections/glbt-advisory-committee/ama-policy-regarding-sexual-orientation.page

American Medical Association House of Delegates. (2008). *Removing financial barriers to care for transgender patients* (Resolution 122 [A-08]). Washington, DC: American Medical Association.

American Psychiatric Association. (2013). *Diagnostic and statistical manual of mental disorders* (5th ed.). Arlington, VA: Author.

Beeler, J. A., Rawls, T. W., Herdt, G., & Cohler, B. J. (1999). The needs of older lesbians and gay men in Chicago. *Journal of Gay & Lesbian Social Services, 9,* 31–49.

Berger, R. M. (1982). The unseen minority: Older gays and lesbians. *Social Work, 27,* 236–242.

Berkman, L. F., Glass, T., Brissette, I., & Seeman, T. E. (2000). From social integration to health: Durkheim in the new millennium. *Social Science & Medicine, 51,* 843–857.

Blanchflower, D. G., & Oswald, A. J. (2008). Is well-being U-shaped over the life cycle? *Social Science & Medicine, 66,* 1733–1749. doi:10.1016/j.socscimed.2008.01.030

Blank, T. O., Asencio, M., Descartes, L., & Griggs, J. (2009). Intersection of older GLBT health issues: Aging, health, and community life. *Journal of GLBT Family Studies, 5,* 9–34.

Brotman, S., Ryan, B., & Cormier, R. (2003). The health and social service needs of gay and lesbian elders and their families in Canada. *The Gerontologist, 43,* 192–202.

Cacioppo, J. T., & Hawkley, L. C. (2003). Social isolation and health, with an emphasis on underlying mechanisms. *Perspectives in Biology and Medicine, 46*(Suppl. 3), S39–S52.

Cacioppo, J. T., Hawkley, L. C., Crawford, L. E., Ernst, J. M., Burleson, M. H., Kowalewski, R. B., . . . Berntson, G. G. (2002). Loneliness and health: Potential mechanisms. *Psychosomatic Medicine, 64,* 407–417.

Cacioppo, J. T., Hughes, M. E., Waite, L. J., Hawkley, L. C., & Thisted, R. A. (2006). Loneliness as a specific risk factor for depressive symptoms: Cross-sectional and longitudinal analyses. *Psychology and Aging, 21,* 140–151. doi:10.1037/0882-7974.21.1.140

Cain, P. A. (1993). Litigating for lesbian and gay rights: A legal history. *Virginia Law Review, 79,* 1551–1641.

Center for American Progress. (2010). *Racial health disparities by the numbers: We still have a long way to go on racial equality.* Retrieved from http://www.americanprogress.org/issues/race/news/2010/01/15/7195/racial-health-disparities-by-the-numbers

Centers for Disease Control and Prevention. (2010). Vital signs: Current cigarette smoking among adults aged ≥18 years—United States, 2009. *MMWR. Morbidity and Mortality Weekly Report, 59,* 1135–1140.

Centers for Disease Control and Prevention. (2011a). *Chronic disease prevention and health promotion: Healthy aging: Helping people to live long and productive lives and enjoy a good quality of life, at a glance 2011.* Retrieved from http://www.cdc.gov/chronicdisease/resources/publications/AAG/aging.htm

Centers for Disease Control and Prevention. (2011b). Rationale for regular reporting on health disparities and inequalities—United States. *MMWR. Morbidity & Mortality Weekly Report, 60*(Suppl.), 3–10.

Centers for Disease Control and Prevention. (2013). *HIV among gay and bisexual men*. Retrieved from http://www.cdc.gov/hiv/topics/msm/pdf/msm.pdf

Clunis, D. M., Fredriksen-Goldsen, K. I., Freeman, P. A., & Nystrom, N. (2005). *Lives of lesbian elders: Looking back, looking forward*. Binghamton, NY: Haworth Press.

Cochran, S. D., & Mays, V. M. (2007). Physical health complaints among lesbians, gay men, and bisexual and homosexually experienced heterosexual individuals: Results from the California Quality of Life Survey. *American Journal of Public Health, 97*, 2048–2055. doi:10.2105/AJPH.2006.087254

Conron, K. J., Mimiaga, M. J., & Landers, S. J. (2010). A population-based study of sexual orientation identity and gender differences in adult health. *American Journal of Public Health, 100*, 1953–1960. doi:10.2105/AJPH.2009.174169

Cornwell, E. Y., & Waite, L. J. (2009). Measuring social isolation among older adults using multiple indicators from the NSHAP Study. *The Journals of Gerontology. Series B: Psychological Sciences and Social Sciences, 64B*(Suppl. 1), i38–i46.

Cronin, A., & King, A. (2010). Power, inequality and identification: Exploring diversity and intersectionality amongst older LGB adults. *Sociology, 44*, 876–892. doi:10.1177/0038038510375738

D'Augelli, A. R., & Grossman, A. H. (2001). Disclosure of sexual orientation, victimization, and mental health among lesbian, gay, and bisexual older adults. *Journal of Interpersonal Violence, 16*, 1008–1027.

D'Augelli, A. R., Grossman, A. H., Hershberger, S. L., & O'Connell, T. S. (2001). Aspects of mental health among older lesbian, gay, and bisexual adults. *Aging & Mental Health, 5*, 149–158. doi:10.1080/713650002

Díaz, R. M., Ayala, G., Bein, E., Henne, J., & Marin, B. V. (2001). The impact of homophobia, poverty, and racism on the mental health of gay and bisexual Latino men: Findings from 3 US cities. *American Journal of Public Health, 91*, 927–932.

Díaz, R. M., Bein, E., & Ayala, G. (2006). Homophobia, poverty, and racism: Triple oppression and mental health outcomes in Latino gay men. In A. Omoto & H. Kurtzman (Eds.), *Sexual orientation and mental health* (pp. 207–224). Washington, DC: American Psychological Association.

Dilley, J. A., Simmons, K. W., Boysun, M. J., Pizacani, B. A., & Stark, M. J. (2010). Demonstrating the importance and feasibility of including sexual orientation in public health surveys: Health disparities in the Pacific Northwest. *American Journal of Public Health, 100*, 460–467. doi:10.2105/AJPH.2007.130336

Elder, G. H. (1994). Time, human agency, and social change perspectives on the life-course. *Social Psychology Quarterly, 57*, 4–15.

Elder, G. H. (1998). The life course as developmental theory. *Child Development, 69*(1), 1–12.

Fiori, K. L., Smith, J., & Antonucci, T. (2007). Social network types among older adults: A multidimensional approach. *The Journals of Gerontology. Series B: Psychological Sciences and Social Sciences, 62B*, P322–330.

Fredriksen-Goldsen, K. I., Cook-Daniels, L., Kim, H. J., Erosheva, E. A., Emlet, C. A., Hoy-Ellis, C. P., . . . Muraco, A. (2014). Physical and mental health of transgender older adults: An at-risk and underserved population. *The Gerontologist, 54,* 488–500. doi:10.1093/geront/gnt021

Fredriksen-Goldsen, K. I., Emlet, C. A., Kim, H. J., Muraco, A., Erosheva, E. A., Goldsen, J., & Hoy-Ellis, C. P. (2013). The physical and mental health of lesbian, gay male, and bisexual (LGB) older adults: The role of key health indicators and risk and protective factors. *The Gerontologist, 53,* 664–675. doi:10.1093/geront/gns123

Fredriksen-Goldsen, K. I., & Hoy-Ellis, C. P. (2007). Caregiving with pride: An introduction. *Journal of Gay & Lesbian Social Services, 18*(3–4), 1–13. doi:10.1300/J041v18n03_01

Fredriksen-Goldsen, K. I., Kim, H.-J., Barkan, S. E., Muraco, A., & Hoy-Ellis, C. P. (2013). Health disparities among lesbian, gay male and bisexual older adults: Results from a population-based study. *American Journal of Public Health, 103,* 1802–1809. doi:10.2105/AJPH.2012.301110

Fredriksen-Goldsen, K. I., Kim, H.-J., Emlet, C. A., Muraco, A., Erosheva, E. A., Hoy-Ellis, C. P., . . . Petry, H. (2011). *The aging and health report: Disparities and resilience among lesbian, gay, bisexual, and transgender older adults.* Seattle, WA: Institute for Multigenerational Health.

Fredriksen-Goldsen, K. I., Kim, H. J., Muraco, A., & Mincer, S. (2009). Chronically ill midlife and older lesbians, gay men, and bisexuals and their informal caregivers: The impact of the social context. *Sexuality Research & Social Policy, 6,* 52–64. doi:10.1525/srsp.2009.6.4.52

Gay and Lesbian Medical Association. (2008). *Same-sex marriage and health.* Washington, DC: Author.

Goldman, N., Korenman, S., & Weinstein, R. (1995). Marital status and health among the elderly. *Social Science & Medicine, 40,* 1717–1730.

Grant, J. M., Mottet, L. A., Tanis, J., Harrison, J., Herman, J. L., & Keisling, M. (2011). *Injustice at every turn: A report of the national transgender discrimination survey.* Washington, DC: National Center for Transgender Equality and National Gay and Lesbian Task Force.

Grossman, A. H., D'Augelli, A. R., & Hershberger, S. L. (2000). Social support networks of lesbian, gay, and bisexual adults 60 years of age and older. *The Journals of Gerontology. Series B: Psychological Sciences and Social Sciences, 55B,* P171–179.

Grossman, A. H., D'Augelli, A. R., & O'Connell, T. S. (2002). Being lesbian, gay, bisexual and 60 or older in North America. *Journal of Gay & Lesbian Social Services, 13,* 23–40.

Harper, G. W., Jernewall, N., & Zea, M. C. (2004). Giving voice to emerging science and theory for lesbian, gay, and bisexual people of color. *Cultural Diversity and Ethnic Minority Psychology, 10,* 187–199. doi:10.1037/1099-9809.10.3.187

Hatzenbuehler, M. L., Keyes, K. M., & Hasin, D. S. (2009). State-level policies and psychiatric morbidity in lesbian, gay, and bisexual populations. *American Journal of Public Health, 99,* 2275–2281. doi:10.2105/AJPH.2008.153510

Hatzenbuehler, M. L., Nolen-Hoeksema, S., & Dovidio, J. (2009). How does stigma "get under the skin"?: The mediating role of emotion regulation. *Psychological Science, 20,* 1282–1289. doi:10.1111/j.1467-9280.2009.02441.x

Henderson, A. S., Scott, R., & Kay, D. W. K. (1986). The elderly who live alone. *Australian and New Zealand Journal of Psychiatry, 20,* 202–209.

Herek, G. M. (2009). Hate crimes and stigma-related experiences among sexual minority adults in the United States: Prevalence estimates from a national probability sample. *Journal of Interpersonal Violence, 24,* 54–74. doi:10.1177/0886260 508316477

Huebner, D. M., & Davis, M. C. (2007). Perceived antigay discrimination and physical health outcomes. *Health Psychology, 26,* 627–634. doi:10.1037/0278-6133.26.5.627

Hughes, A. K., Harold, R. D., & Boyer, J. M. (2011). Awareness of LGBT aging issues among aging services network providers. *Journal of Gerontological Social Work, 54,* 659–677. doi:10.1080/01634372.2011.585392

Human Rights Campaign. (2013). *Issue: Federal advocacy. Respect for Marriage Act.* Retrieved from http://www.hrc.org/laws-and-legislation/federal-legislation/respect-for-marriage-act?gclid=CN665JXGt7oCFSU6QgodMBIA6Q

Institute of Medicine. (2011). *The health of lesbian, gay, bisexual, and transgender people: Building a foundation for better understanding.* Washington, DC: The National Academies Press.

Jacobs, R. J., & Kane, M. N. (2012). Correlates of loneliness in midlife and older gay and bisexual men. *Journal of Gay & Lesbian Social Services, 24,* 40–61. doi:10.1080/10538720.2012.643217

Johnson, I. (2013). Gay and gray: The need for federal regulation of assisted living facilities and the inclusion of LGBT individuals. *Journal of Gender, Race and Justice, 16,* 293–321.

Kertzner, R. M., Meyer, I. H., Frost, D. M., & Stirratt, M. J. (2009). Social and psychological well-being in lesbians, gay men, and bisexuals: The effects of race, gender, age, and sexual identity. *American Journal of Orthopsychiatry, 79,* 500–510. doi:10.1037/a0016848

Kim, H.-J., & Fredriksen-Goldsen, K. I. (2012). Hispanic lesbians and bisexual women at heightened risk for health disparities. *American Journal of Public Health, 102,* e9–e15.

Kimmel, D. C. (1978). Adult development and aging: A gay perspective. *Journal of Social Issues, 34,* 113–130.

King, S., & Dabelko-Schoeny, H. (2006). Quite frankly, I have doubts about remaining: Aging-in-place and health care access for rural midlife and older lesbian, gay, and bisexual individuals. *Journal of LGBT Health Research, 5,* 10–21.

Knochel, K. A., Croghan, C. F., Moone, R. P., & Quam, J. K. (2010). *Ready to serve? The aging network and LGB and T older adults*. Retrieved from http://www.n4a.org/pdf/ReadyToServe1.pdf

Krieger, N. (1999). Embodying inequality: A review of concepts, measures, and methods for studying health consequences of discrimination. *International Journal of Health Services, 29,* 295–352.

Kuyper, L., & Fokkema, T. (2010). Loneliness among older lesbian, gay, and bisexual adults: The role of minority stress. *Archives of Sexual Behavior, 39,* 1171–1180. doi:10.1007/s10508-009-9513-7

LGBT Movement Advancement Project & SAGE. (2010). *Improving the lives of LGBT older adults*. Denver, CO; New York, NY: LGBT Movement Advancement Project & Services; Advocacy for Gay, Lesbian, Bisexual, and Transgender Elders (SAGE).

Lindau, S. T., & McDade, T. W. (2007). Minimally invasive and innovative methods for biomeasure collection in population-based research. In M. Weinstein, J. W. Vaupel, & K. W. Wachter (Eds.), *Biosocial surveys* (pp. 251–277). Washington, DC: National Academies Press.

Lindau, S. T., Schumm, L. P., Lauman, E. O., Levinson, W., O'Muircheartaigh, C. A., & Waite, L. J. (2007). A study of sexuality and health among older adults in the United States. *The New England Journal of Medicine, 357,* 762–774.

Madsen, S. R., Hanewicz, C., & Thackery, S. (2010). *The value of higher education for women in Utah* (Research and Policy Brief). Orem: Office of the Utah Women and Education Project, Utah Valley University.

Manzoli, L., Villari, P., Pirone, G., & Boccia, A. (2007). Marital status and mortality in the elderly: A systematic review and meta-analysis. *Social Science & Medicine, 64,* 77–94.

Mayer, K. U. (2009). New directions in life course research. *Annual Review of Sociology, 35,* 413–433. doi:10.1146/annurev.soc.34.040507.134619

Metlife Mature Market Institute & American Society on Aging. (2010). *Still out, still aging: The Metlife study of lesbian, gay, bisexual, and transgender baby boomers*. New York, NY: Metlife Mature Market Institute and American Society on Aging.

Meyer, H. (2011). Safe spaces? The need for LGBT cultural competency in aging services. *Public Policy & Aging Report, 21,* 24–27.

Meyer, I. H. (2003). Prejudice, social stress, and mental health in lesbian, gay, and bisexual populations: Conceptual issues and research evidence. *Psychological Bulletin, 129,* 674–697. doi:10.1037/0033-2909.129.5.674

Muraco, A., & Fredriksen-Goldsen, K. (2011). "That's what friends do": Informal caregiving for chronically ill lesbian, gay, and bisexual elders. *Journal of Social and Personal Relationships, 28,* 1073–1092.

National Institute on Aging. (2011). *Health disparities strategic plan: Fiscal years 2009–2013*. Retrieved from http://www.nia.nih.gov/AboutNIA/Health Disparities

One Colorado Education Fund. (2011). *Invisible: The state of LGBT health in Colorado*. Denver, CO: One Colorado Education Fund and Denver Health Level One Care for All.

Ong, A. D., Rothstein, J. D., & Uchino, B. N. (2012). Loneliness accentuates age differences in cardiovascular responses to social evaluative threat. *Psychology and Aging, 27*, 190–198. doi:10.1037/a0025570

Perissinotto, C. M., Stijacic Cenzer, I., & Covinsky, K. E. (2012). Loneliness in older persons: A predictor of functional decline and death. *Archives of Internal Medicine, 172*, 1078–1083. doi:10.1001/archinternmed.2012.1993

Persson, D. I. (2009). Unique challenges of transgender aging: Implications from the literature. *Journal of Gerontological Social Work, 52*, 633–646. doi:10.1080/01634 370802609056

Phillip, A. (2012). *Gay marriage advocates gain corporate support*. Retrieved from http://www.politico.com/news/stories/0612/77002.html

Riggle, E. D. B., Rostosky, S. S., & Horne, S. G. (2010). Psychological distress, well-being, and legal recognition in same-sex couple relationships. *Journal of Family Psychology, 24*, 82–86. doi:10.1037/a0017942

Russ, T. C., Stamatakis, E., Hamer, M., Starr, J. M., Kivimäki, M., & Batty, G. D. (2012). Association between psychological distress and mortality: Individual participant pooled analysis of 10 prospective cohort studies. *BMJ: British Medical Journal, 345*, e4933. doi:10.1136/bmj.e4933

Sandfort, T. G., Bakker, F., Schellevis, F. G., & Vanwesenbeeck, I. (2006). Sexual orientation and mental and physical health status: Findings from a Dutch population survey. *American Journal of Public Health, 96*, 1119–1125. doi:10.2105/AJPH.2004.058891

Scafato, E., Galluzzo, L., Gandin, C., Ghirini, S., Baldereschi, M., Capurso, A., . . . , & the Ilsa Working Group. (2008). Marital and cohabitation status as predictors of mortality: a 10-year follow-up of an Italian elderly cohort. *Social Science & Medicine, 67*, 1456–1464. doi:10.1016/j.socscimed.2008.06.026

Shankle, M. D., Maxwell, C. A., Katzman, E. S., & Landers, S. (2003). An invisible population: Older lesbian, gay, bisexual, and transgender individuals. *Clinical Research and Regulatory Affairs, 20*, 159–182. doi:10.1081/CRP-120021079

Shippy, R. M., Cantor, M. H., & Brennan, M. (2004). Social networks of aging gay men. *The Journal of Men's Studies, 13*, 107–120.

Silverstein, C. (2009). The implications of removing homosexuality from the DSM as a mental disorder. *Archives of Sexual Behavior, 38*, 161–163. doi:10.1007/s10508-008-9442-x

Slevin, K. F. (2008). Disciplining bodies: The aging experiences of older heterosexual and gay men. *Generations, 32*, 36–42.

Slusher, M. P., Mayer, C. J., & Dunkle, R. E. (1996). Gays and Lesbians Older and Wiser (GLOW): A support group for older gay people. *The Gerontologist, 36*, 118–123.

Substance Abuse and Mental Health Services Administration. (2010). *Increasing substance abuse levels among older adults likely to create sharp rise in need for treatment services in next decade*. Retrieved from http://www.samhsa.gov/newsroom/advisories/1001073150.aspx

Szymanski, D. M., Kashubeck-West, S., & Meyer, J. (2008). Internalized heterosexism—a historical and theoretical overview. *The Counseling Psychologist, 36*, 510–524. doi:10.1177/0011000007309488

Taube, E., Kristensson, J., Midlöv, P., Holst, G., & Jakobsson, U. (2013). Loneliness among older people: Results from the Swedish National Study on Aging and Care—Blekinge. *The Open Geriatric Medicine Journal, 6*, 1–10. doi:10.2174/1874827901306010001

Tietz, D., & Schaefer, N. (2011). The policy issues and social concerns facing older adults with HIV. *Public Policy & Aging Report, 21*, 30–33.

Tower, R. B., Stanislav, V. K., & Darefsky, A. S. (2002). Types of marital closeness and mortality risk in older couples. *Psychosomatic Medicine, 64*, 644–659.

U.S. Census Bureau. (2012). *The 2012 statistical abstract: Population. Estimates by age, sex, race/ethnicity: 9—Resident population projections by sex and age*. Retrieved from http://www.census.gov/compendia/statab/cats/population/estimates_and_projections_by_age_sex_raceethnicity.html

U.S. Department of Health and Human Services. (2010). *Foundation health measures: Disparities*. Retrieved from http://www.healthypeople.gov/2020/about/disparitiesAbout.aspx

U.S. General Accounting Office & Office of the General Counsel. (1997). *GAO/OGC-97-16—Defense of Marriage Act*. Washington, DC: United States General Accounting Office, Office of the General Counsel.

Valanis, B. G., Bowen, D. J., Bassford, T., Whitlock, E., Charney, P., & Carter, R. A. (2000). Sexual orientation and health: Comparisons in the Women's Health Initiative sample. *Archives of Family Medicine, 9*, 843–853.

Vincent, G. A., & Velkoff, V. A. (2010, May). *The next four decades, the older population in the United States: 2010 to 2050* (Current Population Reports, pp. P25–P1138). Washington, DC: U.S. Census Bureau.

Wallace, S. P., Cochran, S. D., Durazo, E. M., & Ford, C. L. (2011). *The health of aging lesbian, gay and bisexual adults in California*. Los Angeles, CA: UCLA Center for Health Policy Research.

Wight, R. G., LeBlanc, A. J., de Vries, B., & Detels, R. (2012). Stress and mental health among midlife and older gay-identified men. *American Journal of Public Health, 102*, 503–510. doi:10.2105/AJPH.2011.300384

Williams, D. R., Neighbors, H. W., & Jackson, J. S. (2003). Racial/ethnic discrimination and health: Findings from community studies. *American Journal of Public Health, 93*, 200–208. doi:10.2105/AJPH.93.2.200

Williams Institute. (2011). *How many people are lesbian, gay, bisexual, and transgender?* (pp. 1–8). Los Angeles, CA: The Williams Institute, UCLA School of Law.

Williams, M., & Fredriksen-Goldsen, K. I. (2013, November). *Marriage, health and the social integration of LGB older adults*. Paper presented at the Gerontological Society of America's 66th Annual Scientific Meeting, New Orleans, LA.

Williams, M., & Fredriksen-Goldsen, K. I. (in press). Same-sex partnerships and the health of older adults. *Journal of Community Psychology*.

Witten, T. M. (2002). Geriatric care and management issues for the transgender and intersex populations. *Geriatric Care Management Journal, 12*, 20–24.

Witten, T. M., & Whittle, S. (2004). Transpanthers: The graying of transgender and the law. *Deakin Law Review, 9, 503–522*.

Yeh, S., & Lo, S. (2004). Living alone, social support, and feeling lonely among the elderly. *Social Behavior and Personality, 32,* 129–138. doi:10.2224/sbp.2004.32.2.129

Zaninotto, P., Falaschetti, E., & Sacker, A. (2009). Age trajectories of quality of life among older adults: Results from the English Longitudinal Study of Ageing. *Quality of Life Research, 18,* 1301–1309. doi:10.1007/s11136-009-9543-6

Zaritsky, E., & Dibble, S. L. (2010). Risk factors for reproductive and breast cancers among older lesbians. *Journal of Women's Health, 19,* 125–131. doi:10.1089/jwh.2008.1094

3

STIGMA AND LGBT AGING: NEGATIVE AND POSITIVE MARGINALITY

BRIAN DE VRIES

An overarching, integrative framework tying together many of the experiences of lesbian, gay, bisexual, and transgender (LGBT) aging may be that of stigma. Over the course of their lives, LGBT people have been labeled as antifamily and immoral by religious groups and a security risk or morale threat by military leaders (Kochman, 1997). Additionally, expressions of love between same-sex individuals were "diagnosed" as a psychiatric disorder until 1973, and even today, committed lesbian or gay relationships are the subject of intense debate, with many states voting on their legitimacy and constitutionality (de Vries, 2008).

The costs and consequences of this oppression and exclusion are many and varied. The minority stress model, adapted by Meyer (2003), proposes that sexual and gender minorities experience chronic stress arising from the ongoing experience of stigma. The premise is that individuals experience an accumulation of stress (some implicit, some explicit) by living lives as sexual

DOI: 10.1037/14436-003
The Lives of LGBT Older Adults: Understanding Challenges and Resilience, N. A. Orel and
C. A. Fruhauf (Editors)
Copyright © 2015 by the American Psychological Association. All rights reserved.

minority persons in a heteronormative context. This stress accumulation may be seen in compromised physical and psychological well-being.

At the same time, there is a growing recognition of the resilience and strength of LGBT persons—and older adults in particular. Unger's (2000) work on positive marginality provides a framework for the consideration of such characteristics highlighting the many ways in which marginalized persons discover agency, purpose, and meaning through lives at the margins and resistance to stigma-related stressors. Such perspectives neatly align with notions of positive aging (e.g., Gergen & Gergen, 2001) claiming that a fuller awareness and appreciation of aging calls for a focus on more than just the decline and loss that are sadly seen as synonymous with later life; it mandates attention to growth, generativity, resilience, and hardiness. The study of LGBT later lives offers a window to the potential for positive aging under particular and particularly stigmatizing conditions.

An accounting of the costs of and responses to stigma shapes the text that follows. Herek's (2009) work on stigma is offered as a framework for the consideration of the many costs of stigma and ultimately minority stress. Unger's (2000) work on positive marginality conveys how stigma may be associated with a constructive reclaiming of identity and reframing of lives. A complete understanding of LGBT aging necessitates the recognition of both the hardships endured and the strengths developed over a lifetime living at the margins.

THE COSTS OF STIGMA

LGBT people experience three types of stigma from multiple, interacting sources and in multiple, interacting ways (Herek, 2009; Institute of Medicine [IOM], 2011): enacted stigma, felt stigma, and internalized stigma (Herek, 2009). *Enacted stigma* refers to explicit behaviors ranging from being ignored to being subjected to homophobic or transphobic slurs and even violence; these are acts of overt discrimination. *Felt stigma* derives from the effects of exposure to such experiences and may be seen in the modification of one's own behaviors in an effort to prevent future such encounters with stigma. This includes reticence to disclose one's gender orientation or gender identity (a reticence associated with both protections and costs) and related adaptive behaviors. *Internalized stigma* may be seen in the tacit acceptance of the legitimacy of society's negative regard for LGBT persons, more commonly identified as homophobia or transphobia. All of these forms are evident in the characterization of the lives of LGBT older persons and are discussed in this chapter to organize some of the literature on the experiences of aging as a member of a sexual or gender minority person.

Enacted Stigma

Enacted stigma comprises explicit acts of stigma and derives from multiple sources. The denial of federal marriage rights is a current and powerful example of enacted, institutional stigma. That vital components of the so-called Defense of Marriage Act were recently struck down will certainly mitigate this federal stigma; marriage remains under the jurisdiction of states, however, and the majority of states continue to deny marriage recognition to same-sex couples. Moreover, the checkerboard of recognition (e.g., where it is possible for same-sex couples to marry, where and when same-sex marriages are recognized) serves as a banner reminding all of unequal rights, treatment, and recognition.

In a related manner, a variety of studies have found that LGBT older adults (particularly among those who are not yet eligible for Medicare support), compared with heterosexual older adults, are less likely to have health insurance (IOM, 2011). This itself has a range of associated consequences; for example, LGBT persons are more likely to delay seeking health care (about twice as likely as heterosexual persons, although this could also be due to anticipated stigma, as noted later in the chapter); are more likely to receive health care in emergency department settings; and are more likely to delay or not receive needed prescriptions (which could also be a financial issue; Movement Advancement Project, 2010).

Enacted stigma is also sadly and perhaps most dramatically noted in a variety of studies in which LGBT older adults report high lifetime rates of exposure to violence and victimization (Balsam, Rothblum, & Beauchaine, 2005; Fredriksen-Goldsen et al., 2011). These reports include accounts ranging from homophobic or transphobic slurs to sexual and physical assault resulting in bodily harm, with the vast majority of assaults not reported to authorities. This reticence to report highlights the overlapping forms of stigma: the traumatic experience of the enacted stigma compounded by the felt stigma of the anticipated shame and fear of dismissal if an incident were to be reported, and the frequent decision to remain silent.

Felt Stigma

Felt stigma is reflected in behaviors that are undertaken as protection against anticipated acts of discrimination; these may be most acutely noted in the rates and forms of disclosure of sexual orientation or gender identity. The reality that decisions have to be made daily and even more frequently about such disclosure itself speaks to the ongoing life stresses of sexual minority men and women. In the national sample of LGBT boomers (i.e., ages 45–64), as previously described, about one quarter were not "completely" or "mostly" out to a wide range of others in their social environment. Among bisexual and transgender women and men, these percentages rose to more than 80% and 60%, respectively (MetLife Mature Market Institute, 2010). Even among their closest friends, more than 30% of bisexual boomers did not self-identify as such.

This guardedness extends to health care settings as well, an important limiting factor in securing sensitive and personal health care. Ponce, Cochran, Pizer, and Mays (2010) suggested that the significant disparities in health care access for gay men and lesbians, compared with heterosexuals, may best be understood in the terms of felt stigma—a type of nondisclosure as a pre-emptive strike against enacted, institutional stigma, as previously suggested.

A recent national study focused on LGBT issues in long-term care (National Senior Citizens Law Center, 2011). In this study, LGBT older persons age 65 and older, as well as their caregivers, health care providers, and others in such an environment, were asked about the extent to which LGBT people can be "out" in long-term-care settings. The evidence was clear: The vast majority—about 80% of all respondents, LGBT persons, caregivers, and providers—believed that LGBT older adults could not be out in long-term-care settings. This level of agreement is remarkable—and distressing.

Respondents were also asked about the issues that LGBT persons would likely encounter in long-term-care settings, and the evidence is again clear. The majority of respondents agreed that LGBT persons would likely encounter discrimination, isolation—from both residents and staff—and even abuse and neglect. These data clearly suggest that long-term-care settings are generally not regarded as safe places for LGBT older adults. Several authors have recently suggested that such appraisals may be associated with a return to the closet when institutional care is needed (e.g., National Senior Citizens Law Center, 2011).

Internalized Stigma

Internalized stigma may be best understood in terms of internalized homophobia: accepting the legitimacy of society's negative regard for the stigmatized group. In an explicit examination of this concept, Grossman, D'Augelli, and O'Connell (2001) found, with a sample of more than 400 older lesbians and gay men (ranging in age from 60 to more than 90), relatively low overall levels of internalized homophobia, although men reported higher levels than women; but internalized homophobia significantly increased with age. Internalized homophobia was also modestly and negatively related to income (as a measure of socioeconomic status), was higher among those with restricted or lower contact with others, and was higher among those who lived alone and were single.

Perhaps the associations between singlehood, living alone, reduced social contact, and internalized homophobia are multidirectional. That is, those with fewer social outlets have reduced opportunities to challenge homophobic assumptions and beliefs and may be disproportionately exposed to negative views through media and other portrayals of LGBT (later) lives. At the same time, homophobic beliefs and attitudes may preclude individuals from seeking companions, romantic and otherwise, reifying the institutional stigma and exclusion from formal partnership recognition.

Along such lines, a common finding in the literature on the lives of LGBT older adults is the high rate of singlehood (Adelman, Gurevitch, de Vries, & Blando, 2006; MetLife Mature Market Institute, 2010). In the MetLife sample of boomers (e.g., both LGBT and those from the general population), about 42% of the LGBT population identified their relationship status as single, far higher than the 27% of the general population. Even higher percentages of older lesbians and gay men, and especially the latter, identified as single—as many as 75% of gay men over age 65 stated that they were single in the Adelman et al. (2006) study, more than 3 times the U.S. national average. Moreover, within this relationship status, there were interesting significant sexual orientation differences. In particular, about 13% of gay men reported that they were "single, never partnered"—more than 4 times higher than any other group (and reminiscent of the gender difference in internalized homophobia). A sizable proportion of gay men (around 20%) and lesbians (about 30%) were also far more likely to have previously been in a relationship but currently identify as single. There are many paths to singlehood in mid and later life that have yet to be studied in-depth.

In a study focusing on those between the ages of 50 and 70 years in California (Wallace, Cochran, Durazo, & Ford, 2011), reported that about half of gay and bisexual men reported living alone compared with about 12% of heterosexual men in the state. For lesbians and bisexual women, the proportion was almost 30%, compared with just less than 20% of heterosexual women. Older gay men are thus much more likely to be both single and to live alone than either heterosexual persons or lesbians. This has important ramifications for the very later years, especially around issues of caregiving (Cantor & Mayer, 1979). In general, however, these rates of singlehood and living alone may be understood in terms of response to stigma—enacted stigma on the basis of exclusionary policies and laws as well as felt and internalized stigma on the basis of preemptively excluding oneself from partnerships.

Minority Stress

The many costs of stigma, contained in the foregoing accounts, may be seen as manifestations of minority stress—the tolls of living in an environment hostile to gay men and lesbians and others who fail to conform to heteronormative ideals (Meyer, 2003). These costs are further and more directly revealed in frequent findings of the impoverished health of LGBT older persons, relative to non-LGBT older adults.

A variety of studies have reported that LGBT people, particularly in the later years, rate their health more poorly than comparably aged persons in the general population (e.g., MetLife Mature Market Institute, 2010). LGBT older adults also report disabilities at alarming rates; in one recent national study, the disability rate was 45%, higher for women than for men (Fredriksen-Goldsen et al., 2011). In terms of specific conditions identified, gay and bisexual men have higher risk for anal cancer, for example, in part driven by a higher likelihood of exposure to human papilloma virus (Chin-Hong et al., 2004). Lesbian and bisexual women have higher rates of reproductive cancers probably associated with higher rates of nulliparity (e.g., never having been pregnant or bearing an offspring; Valanis et al., 2000). Gay and bisexual men as well as transgender men are at higher risk for HIV (Fredriksen-Goldsen et al., 2011), and all three groups seem to be at higher risk for diabetes and asthma (Adelman et al., 2006).

The higher rates of mental distress (D'Augelli & Grossman, 2001) and alarming rates of depression (e.g., Mills et al., 2004) among LGBT persons, including older adults, may be seen as a response to the multiple stigmatizing experiences endured. Maladaptive behaviors, as seen in higher rates of both alcohol and cigarette use (e.g., Gruskin, Greenwood, Matevia, Pollack, & Bye, 2007; Tang et al., 2004), may be similarly understood. The psychological weight of lives at the margins exacts a toll on mental health, in turn jeopardizing physical well-being in an oscillating fashion.

POSITIVE MARGINALITY

The dramatic, extensive effects of stigma, previously reviewed, merit—and have received—attention from researchers, policymakers, and service providers. However, not all LGBT older adults succumb to such illnesses, conditions, and states; some may be seen to overcome the adversity, and many demonstrate resilience and adaptability. Lee (1987) suggested that such life successes may be attributable to good fortune and the skillful avoidance of stress. Although such individual differences are clearly present and even likely, there is enormous variability in how stigmatized individuals and groups respond to experiences of stigma-related stress (Frost, 2011).

Unger's (2000) work on positive marginality offers an intriguing perspective on the ways individuals respond to stigma. She proposed that through their attempts to reduce stress and resist adversity, marginalized individuals can find meaning in their experiences of stigma; such meaning promotes a sense of agency and resilience and may allow individuals to thrive even in nonsupportive conditions and circumstances. Positive marginality supports the reframing of one's stigmatized characteristics as ultimately positive aspects of one's identity.

By example, approaches similar to this have been present in the literature in other forms as well. For instance, Folkman and Lazarus (1984) described the appraisals of stressors as loss, threat, or challenge, each of which may be associated with different approaches to the stressor and often different outcomes. A loss may precipitate grief; a threat may lead to retreat; a challenge may stimulate action. Responses to the stressor are dependent on the appraisal, some of which may lead to more agentic, self-enhancing, and self-affirming behaviors.

Another example may be found in work on stress-related growth. Tedeschi and Calhoun (2004) commented that stressful and potentially life-changing experiences affect individuals in many ways, one of which manifests in the disruption of assumptive worlds—rendering somewhat chaotic a world that was previously predictable. This is often seen in experiences of grief, but it can certainly also have applications in the face of stigma, discrimination, and violence. In the service of modifying or rebuilding one's world—of making it predictable, finding sense and imposing order—individuals can emerge with a newfound sense of strength, priorities, and relationships. Evidence of these efforts may be seen in the experiences of LGBT persons in general, and older members of the LGBT population in particular.

Stigma and Its Positive Consequences in LGBT Lives

A recent study by Meyer, Ouellette, Haile, and MacFarlane (2011) neatly and creatively reveals this perspective. A diverse, small ($N = 57$) sample of sexual minority women and men in the early to mid-adult years responded to the question "What do you think your life would be like without homophobia, racism, and sexism?" Participants imagined a world without inequalities and the implications of living in such a world. These imagined experiences included narratives that spoke of lost possibilities and accounts that focused on the lack of safety and acceptance; in the case of the former, participants reflected on how inequality has influenced them over the course of their lives depriving them of critical possibilities and resources; in the case of the latter, participants described a lack of safety and acceptance that focused more on the present and the future. That the life course was addressed without any probe reflects the broad and longitudinal impact of stigma in the lives of these older gay men and lesbians. Several participants noted that in a world without stigma, they would not know who they would be.

On further and deeper reflection, however, many of the participants reported that their ongoing and continuous confrontations with stigma (based not only on sexual orientation but also on race and gender) resulted in selves that they cherish and believe were better than they would otherwise have been. These reports yielded a third theme, more relevant to this discussion, in the analyses of Meyer et al. (2011) and one that focused on positive marginality. Participants attributed to stigma enhanced self-concepts and an appreciation for the many roles they have been called to play (including friend, neighbor, worker). Participants spoke of the communities that they formed in response to oppression and their efforts to fight for social justice and equality. This resolve and these outcomes are not without cost, but nor are they without a sense of contentment.

In a narrative analysis of relationship stories reported by 99 LGB persons (average age of 35 years), Frost (2011) presented illuminating accounts of the enhancing effect of stigma on intimacy. Amid dramatic accounts of the varying costs and weights of stigma, participants also reported the generative consequences of stigma and how stigma provided an opportunity for (re)definition of self, relationships, and life experiences. For example, Frost noted that more than one quarter of his LGB participants reported that living in a stigmatizing social environment motivated them to become activists around issues of same-sex marriage, provided them with coping mechanisms that they transferred to a variety of other domains of their lives, and served to make their relationships stronger. In a similar manner, a smaller proportion of participants commented on the exclusionary heteronormative definitions of relationships and availed themselves of opportunities to develop relationship trajectories of their own design and meaning.

Riggle, Whitman, Olson, Rostosky, and Strong (2008) asked a large group of lesbian and gay adults, ranging in age from 18 to 72, to identify the positive things about being an LGBT person. Interestingly, only 1% of the sample (of 553 lesbians and gay men) said that they did not believe there was anything positive about being a gay man or lesbian; less than 5% of the sample said there was nothing positive or negative about being lesbian or gay (e.g., reporting that it is just a part of them, nothing special). Three overarching themes emerged from the analysis of these qualitative data (collected through an online survey). These included issues of disclosure and social support (framed in terms of belonging to a community, creating families of choice, having strong connections with others, and serving as positive role models), insight into and empathy for self and others (e.g., authentic self and honesty, personal insight and sense of self, increased empathy and compassion for others, and social justice and activism), and freedom from societal definition of roles (e.g., freedom from gender-specific roles, exploration of sexuality and relationships, and egalitarian relationships, the latter exclusively identified by lesbians in the sample). The similarity of many of these themes to the findings discussed earlier highlight the pivotal role of stigma as a force in the lives of LGBT persons—and the positive derivative effects.

These same authors presented comparable research with samples of 157 bisexual (Rostosky, Riggle, Pascale-Hague, & McCants, 2010) and 61 transgender (Riggle, Rostosky, McCants, & Pascale-Hague, 2011) adults within similar age ranges. Many of the same themes emerged, although there were a few interesting differences. For example, transgender adults made more frequent reference to congruence of the self (congruence between inner feelings and outer appearance), an understanding of the limitations of binary appraisals of sex and gender, and a concomitant unique perspective on both sexes. Interestingly, about 10% of the transgender sample reported that there was nothing positive about being transgender—even as almost all of these same participants ultimately went on to identify positive aspects. Bisexual adults spoke more of understanding privilege and oppression and a freedom of sexual expression.

Stigma and Its Positive Effects Among LGBT Persons in the Second Half of Life

Evidence of positive marginality is also apparent in the growing area of LGBT aging research. This construct is often implicitly referenced in overall appraisals of well-being among LGBT older adults and framed in terms of crisis competence (Kimmel, 1978). For example, almost half of the sample of more than 1,200 in the MetLife study of LGBT boomers said that being LGBT had made aging more difficult. Yet, at the same time, almost three quarters of the sample reported that being LGBT had helped prepare them for aging (MetLife Mature Market Institute, 2010).

Perhaps this apparent incongruity may be explained along the lines of "that which challenges us ultimately makes us stronger." These respondents said that living with the stigma, having to fight your way through the world, needing to combat the stereotypes, and stress are what makes aging harder for LGBT persons. When asked what about being LGBT helps prepare them for aging, these respondents said that they fought their way through life, forged their own paths, and formed their own communities. LGBT boomers reported that they prepared themselves for aging by having become more accepting, resilient, and self-reliant, by taking nothing for granted, and by having learned how cruel society can be and developing coping resources for the discrimination they have confronted.

Such experiences, including the flexible ways in which gender is, and was, enacted over the course of their lives (Riggle et al., 2008), may provide for more adaptability and suppleness in response to the demands of aging. For example, Friend (1990) described the "successful aging" of LGBT older adults and suggested that being freed (or excluded) from the relative bounds of traditional gender role definitions have afforded gay men and lesbians the opportunity to engage in behaviors throughout their lives that heterosexuals rarely confront, perhaps until the death of a spouse. Along such lines, Ritter and Terndrup (2002) proposed that LGBT older adults may enjoy a broader array within a repertoire of age-related strategies for coping. Education is certainly a factor in this repertoire and may be reciprocally related to action, activism, and future planning, all of which may be similarly associated with a sense of community and care, as described next.

Education

A common demographic finding, reported in both national (e.g., Black, Gates, Sanders, & Taylor, 2000) and local (e.g., Adelman et al., 2006) surveys, is that LGBT boomers and older persons tend to be more highly educated than those of comparable age from the general population. Education may be seen as a proxy for problem solving, solution seeking, and action-taking, as Lopata (1993) suggested. As such, education may be seen as a resource for many older LGBT persons and may well underlie many of the positive attributes described here and yet to be articulated.

Activism and Action: AIDS

The early response to HIV/AIDS may be seen along these lines of confronting the problem, demanding solutions, and taking actions. LGBT older adults represent the cohort who created the organizations and communities of care for those with HIV/AIDS (even as there was not yet a name for this disease) at times when governments and others shamefully turned their backs. They were on the front lines of the battles with many health care institutions, and they were at the bedsides of their friends and colleagues who were sick and dying.

During these years, care plans and care programs were developed to address the disease, and care for those living with it, that are now replicated and widely applied by communities and districts around the world. This often involved dealing with the violence, ignorance, and stigma with which they were confronted by educating themselves and others—by coming out, taking stands, and becoming visible. Ironically, the attempts to silence and exclude LGBT people by a stigmatizing majority ultimately may have been the prompts that led to the successful creation of an LGBT community with a political presence. In many locales across the country—and beyond—these same LGBT communities whose origins lie in the earlier actions of these now older persons are turning their attention to services and support for older persons.

Future Planning

Education and the legacy of these early experiences with disease and death may also be seen to underlie the efforts undertaken by LGBT boomers, for example, in preparation for the later years. The MetLife study found that LGBT boomers were significantly more likely than were boomers in the general population to have completed living wills, durable power of attorney, informal caregiving arrangements, partnership agreements, and rights of visitation—the difference in completion rates were often 10 to 15 percentage points higher for the LGBT boomers (MetLife Mature Market Institute, 2010). This level of preparation (even if it remains the minority of the LGBT boomer population—i.e., completion rates of less than 40%) may be seen as an adaptive response to stigma manifested in the denial of such rights and exclusionary policies around marriage.

De Vries, Mason, Quam, and Acquaviva (2009) examined the completion of these documents by LGBT boomers who lived in states where their same-sex relationships were recognized and those who lived in states where those relationships were not recognized. The latter were more likely to have completed these documents—again with differences of about 10 percentage points, as if the lack of recognition spurred these boomers into action.

The MetLife study also included questions about the nature of discussions of end-of-life care and treatment that these boomers had had with others in their social environment (MetLife Mature Market Institute, 2010), including spouses or partners, friends, siblings, parents, other relatives, primary care providers, and adult children. The study found many similarities again across sexual orientations and gender identities, but LGBT people were more likely to have had such discussions overall and were more likely to have had them with their friends especially (22% vs. 11%) but also with some family members and their health care provider (although this latter was only 10%). Inadequate as these levels of preparation might be for all groups, the fact that LGBT persons in the middle years were more likely to have engaged in such activities stands as evidence of adaptive behaviors in response to stigma.

Caregiving

Such preparations for later life, perhaps building on the experiences in the early years of HIV/AIDS, may also be associated with the higher rates of caregiving among LGBT boomers than among those in the general population (MetLife Mature Market Institute, 2010). Recent research has revealed the impressive and high rates at which LGBT persons, most of whom are in the second half of life, provide care for another person (as many as 27%; Fredriksen-Goldsen et al., 2011). The MetLife study (2010) revealed that LGBT boomers are more likely to be caregivers than are those in the general population; moreover, they also provide a significantly greater amount of care.

In a study of more than 200 mostly gay male caregivers in the middle and later years (de Vries & Wardlaw, 2003), all of whom were bereft of the person for whom care was provided and all of whom responded to a general probe about how life turned out, participants identified a number of themes that referenced hardiness, thoughtfulness, resilience, and growth. Most prominently, for example, participants made frequent reference to increased self-awareness and a new or renewed commitment to and appreciation of life. Exemplary quotes (not previously published) include the following:

- "I think often [of] what I went through with [care-recipient]. It made me a lot more aware of what's important and in having a few good, close friends."
- "I've come to realize that . . . I'm closer to the kind of person that I had hoped I would be. Things I've admired in others, I see more in myself. . . . In a funny way, it was an empowering experience. It's all in how you perceive things. I've learned a lot."
- "It's a gift that [care recipient] gave me. AIDS changed my life and made it more meaningful."
- "I have a great measure of peace. I know I am human. It's easier to love people—humanity—now. I'm far more forgiving. Having this tragedy happen helped me to mature. I've learned about the value of other human beings, including myself."

Amidst accounts of all that was lost and the many and significant stressors of caregiving, many of these gay men who had provided so much revealed all that was given to them and all that was learned through the experience. Similarly, many made reference to the importance of community and connectedness along with the painful reminders of their deceased loved ones. Perhaps this speaks to the intimacy that is a part of caring for a dying loved one and the nature of the tasks undertaken by those in committed and caring relationships—and the gifts of caregiving (Goldman, 2002).

Friends and Chosen Families

There is a growing body of research on the positive contributions of friends to the well-being of older adults. Grossman, D'Augelli, and Hershberger (2000) suggested that such positive contributions should be even more strongly noted in the lives of LGBT older persons, given that friends and the support they provide "can serve a unique function in mitigating the impact of stigmatization" (p. 171). In analyses of caregiving and future planning, it has been found that LGBT persons are significantly more likely to turn to their friends (compared with those in the general population; MetLife Mature Market Institute, 2010).

In comparing the meaning of friendship among a group of older gay men and lesbians with a comparably aged group of heterosexual adults (between 50 and 88 years), de Vries and Megathlin (2009) found that the former described friends using a greater and more varied number of dimensions and attributes. In particular, gay men and lesbians were more likely to define friendship using terms such as *trust*, *shared values*, and *acceptance* (defined as measures of cognitive aspects of friendship) as well as terms such as *compatibility* and *care* (as measures of affective aspects of friendship). Frequency of contact and length of time known were also more prominent terms in the definition of friends for these lesbians and gay men. De Vries and Megathlin (2009) interpreted this finding as evidence of the richness of the construct of friendship in the lives of these respondents, as suggested by de Vries and Hoctel (2006) as well.

These friends are the likely constituents of the *families of choice* (also described as *chosen families* or *logical kin*, as described by Maupin, 2007, as a cleverly worded contrast to *biological kin*) reported in the lives of LGBT adults (e.g., MetLife Mature Market Institute, 2010). For example, in the boomer study, LGBT respondents were asked if they had a "chosen family," and more than two thirds reported that they did (MetLife Mature Market Institute, 2010). In the qualitative research of de Vries and Hoctel (2006), all but one of the 20 gay men and lesbians reported that they had a "chosen family." They described these relationships in multiple ways, in affective terms of significance ("I think we know that we can depend on each other for the kinds of things that families do") and acceptance ("To my family of choice, I am a whole person. I was invisible to my biological family"), as well as in more structural terms of breadth ("It's a different relationship; I do consider my friends an extended family") and presence ("I see my friends as my family, because I don't have any connections with my birth family").

The deeper consideration and/or redefinition of friendship and kinship may be seen as responses to stigma and exclusion. The costs of such marginalization are legion in the social lives of LGBT persons; the benefits may be similarly many and significant and may include, for example, opportunities to design and develop relationships with the potential for authentic connections to others of an individual's choice. When standard models do not apply, or are not offered, the potential exists for relationships to be structured around and best suited to the needs, desires, and goals of the participants.

CONCLUSION

Stigma, in its many and insidious forms, is a prominent factor in the lives of LGBT persons and the cause, both direct and indirect, of significant hardship in multiple domains; it is also associated with the potential for growth, creative expression, and hardiness. As Meyer et al. (2011) noted, "the challenge for researchers is to capture both aspects of stigma without neglecting either the negative experiences and conditions which are at the root of stigma, or the resilient ways in which individuals enact acts of survival and resistance" (p. 212). The study of LGBT aging offers the opportunity to meet this challenge—an opportunity that has only recently been visited, as revealed in the research summarized in this chapter and in this book.

Concomitantly, much remains to be discovered in this area. Our understanding of the lives of older LGBT persons is naturally rooted in cohort and time effects; younger LGBT persons are moving through a world rendered more inclusive, accepting, and open by the experiences of their elders. Even as dramatic challenges remain (as the distressingly high suicide rates among LGBT youth connote), younger LGBT people have models and a language for their lives and loves in ways that were not true for their elders. Challenges to binary conceptions of gender and sex are entering mainstream discourse, driven by the open questioning of familiar concepts of LGBT and allied persons. Many cities, some counties, and a few states recognize same-sex marriage; gay or lesbian television characters are almost commonplace in prime-time shows. How will LGBT lives be fashioned in this new reality?

A sincere examination of the intersection of sexual orientation, gender identity, and other relevant demographic (e.g., race, ethnicity), physical (e.g., different abilities), and psychosocial (e.g., cognitive and affective characteristics) attributes is just underway and represents a new frontier of LGBT research. These areas speak to understanding whole persons, defined by multiple identities, evolving over time and circumstance. Such recognition affords new questions to ask in studies of LGBT lives, including the consideration of older persons in the context of lives lived, losses endured, and challenges met.

LGBT aging is sorely understudied, which contributes to an imbalance in our understanding of the diversity of later life experiences. By studying LGBT older adults, we not only learn about a group "twice hidden" (Blando, 2001), we also learn about the effects of a lifetime of stigma, its many costs, and also its consequences, both negative and positive. We learn about different approaches to the world, the creation of different pathways, and the formation of different alliances—lives that have evolved against the grain. The study of LGBT aging challenges our heteronormative assumptions (de Vries & Blando, 2004), suggesting new questions to ask and new ways of relating—and perhaps even new ways of aging.

REFERENCES

Adelman, M., Gurevitch, J., de Vries, B., & Blando, J. (2006). Openhouse: Community building and research in the LGBT aging population. In D. Kimmel, T. Rose, & S. David (Eds.), *Lesbian, gay, bisexual, and transgender aging: Research and clinical perspectives* (pp. 247–264). New York, NY: Columbia University Press.

Balsam, K. F., Rothblum, E. D., & Beauchaine, T. P. (2005). Victimization over the life span: A comparison of lesbian, gay, bisexual, and heterosexual siblings.

Journal of Consulting and Clinical Psychology, 73, 477–487. doi:10.1037/0022-006X.73.3.477

Black, D., Gates, G., Sanders, S., & Taylor, L. (2000). Demographics of the gay and lesbian population in the United States: Evidence from available systematic data sources. *Demography, 37,* 139–154. doi:10.2307/2648117

Blando, J. A. (2001). Twice hidden: Older gay and lesbian couples, friends, and intimacy. *Generations, 25,* 87–89.

Cantor, M. H., & Mayer, M. (1979). Factors in differential utilization of services by urban elderly. *Journal of Gerontological Social Work, 1,* 47–61. doi:10.1300/J083V01N01_05

Chin-Hong, P. V., Vittinghoff, V., Cranston, R. D., Buchbinder, S., Cohen, D., . . . Palefsky, J. M. (2004). Age-specific prevalence of anal human papillomavirus infection in HIV-negative sexually active men who have sex with men: The EXPLORE study. *Journal of Infectious Diseases, 190,* 2070–2076.

D'Augelli, A., & Grossman, A. (2001). Disclosure of sexual orientation, victimization, and mental health among lesbian, gay, and bisexual older adults. *Journal of Interpersonal Violence, 16,* 1008–1027. doi:10.1177/088626001016010003

de Vries, B. (2008). Lesbian, gay, bisexual and transgender persons in later life. In D. Carr (Ed.), *Encyclopedia of the life course and human development* (pp. 161–165). Farmington Hills, MI: Gale.

de Vries, B., & Blando, J. (2004). The study of gay and lesbian lives: Lessons for social gerontology. In G. Herdt & B. de Vries (Eds.), *Gay and lesbian aging: Research and future directions* (pp. 3–28). New York, NY: Springer.

de Vries, B., & Hoctel, P. (2006). The family friends of older gay men and lesbians. In N. Teunis & G. Herdt (Eds.), *Sexual inequalities and social justice* (pp. 213–232). Berkeley: University of California Press.

de Vries, B., Mason, A., Quam, J., & Acquaviva, K. (2009). State recognition of same-sex relationships and preparations for end of life among lesbian and gay boomers. *Sexuality Research & Social Policy, 6,* 90–101. doi:10.1007/BF03165990

de Vries, B., & Megathlin, D. (2009). The meaning of friends for gay men and lesbians in the second half of life. *Journal of GLBT Family Studies, 5,* 82–98. doi:10.1080/15504280802595394

de Vries, B., & Wardlaw, L. (2003, October). *The consequences of care: Narratives of bereaved caregivers.* In P. Clark (Chair), Narrative gerontology: Theory, research, and application. Symposium conducted at the meeting of the Canadian Association on Gerontology, Toronto, Canada.

Folkman, S., & Lazarus, R. S. (1984). *Stress, appraisal and coping.* New York, NY: Springer Publishing Company.

Fredriksen-Goldsen, K. I., Kim, H.-J., Emlet, C. A., Muraco, A., Erosheva, E. A., . . . Petry, H. (2011). *The aging and health report: Disparities and resilience among lesbian, gay, bisexual, and transgender older adults.* Seattle, WA: Institute for Multigenerational Health. doi:10.1037/e561402013-001

Friend, R. A. (1990). Older lesbian and gay people: A theory of successful aging. *Journal of Homosexuality, 20,* 99–118. doi:10.1300/J082v20n03_07

Frost, D. M. (2011). Stigma and intimacy in same-sex relationships: A narrative perspective. *Journal of Family Psychology, 25,* 1–10. doi:10.1037/a0022374

Gergen, M. M., & Gergen, K. J. (2001). Positive aging: New images for a new age. *Ageing International, 27,* 3–23. doi:10.1007/s12126-001-1013-6

Goldman, C. (2002). *The gifts of caregiving: Stories of hardship, hope, and healing.* Minneapolis, MN: Fairview Press.

Grossman, A. H., D'Augelli, A. R., & Hershberger, S. L. (2000). Social support networks of lesbian, gay, and bisexual adults 60 years of age and older. *The Journals of Gerontology. Series B: Psychological Sciences and Social Sciences, 55B,* 171–179.

Grossman, A. H., D'Augelli, A. R., & O'Connell, T. S. (2001). Being lesbian, gay, bisexual, and 60 or older in North America. *Journal of Gay & Lesbian Social Services: Issues in Practice, Policy & Research, 13,* 23–40.

Gruskin, E. P., Greenwood, G. L., Matevia, M., Pollack, L. M., & Bye, L. L. (2007). Disparities in smoking between the lesbian, gay, and bisexual population and the general population in California. *American Journal of Public Health, 97,* 1496–1502. doi:10.2105/AJPH.2006.090258

Herek, G. M. (2009). Sexual stigma and sexual prejudice in the United States: A conceptual framework. In D. A. Hope (Ed.), *Contemporary perspectives on lesbian, gay, and bisexual identities* (pp. 65–111). New York, NY: Springer Science + Business Media.

Institute of Medicine. (2011). *The health of lesbian, gay, bisexual, and transgender people: Building a foundation for better understanding.* Washington, DC: The National Academies Press.

Kimmel, D. C. (1978). Adult development and aging: A gay perspective. *Journal of Social Issues, 34,* 113–130. doi:10.1111/j.1540-4560.1978.tb02618.x

Kochman, A. (1997). Gay and lesbian elderly: Historical overview and implications for social work practice. In J. Quam (Ed.), *Social services for senior gay men and lesbians* (pp. 1–10). New York, NY: Haworth Press. doi:10.1300/J041v06n01_01

Lee, J. A. (1987). What can homosexual aging studies contribute to theories of aging? *Journal of Homosexuality, 13,* 43–71. doi:10.1300/J082v13n04_03

Lopata, H. Z. (1993). The support system of American urban widows. In M. S. Stroebe, W. Stroebe, & R. O. Hansson (Eds.), *Handbook of bereavement: Theory, research, and intervention* (pp. 381–396). New York, NY: Cambridge University Press. doi:10.1017/CBO9780511664076.026

Maupin, A. (2007). *Michael Tolliver lives.* San Francisco, CA: HarperCollins.

MetLife Mature Market Institute. (2010). *Still out, still aging.* Westport, CT: Author.

Meyer, I. H. (2003). Prejudice, social stress, and mental health in lesbian, gay, and bisexual populations: Conceptual issues and research evidence. *Psychological Bulletin, 129,* 674–697. doi:10.1037/0033-2909.129.5.674

Meyer, I. H., Ouellette, S., Haile, R., & MacFarlane, T. (2011). "We'd be free": Narratives of life without homophobia, racism, or sexism. *Sexuality Research & Social Policy, 8,* 204–214. doi:10.1007/s13178-011-0063-0

Mills, T. C., Paul, J., Stall, R., Pollack, L., Canchola, J., Chang, Y. J., . . . Catania, J. A. (2004). Distress and depression in men who have sex with men: The Urban Men's Health Study. *The American Journal of Psychiatry, 161,* 278–285. doi:10.1176/appi.ajp.161.2.278

Movement Advancement Project. (2010). *Improving the lives of LGBT older adults.* Retrieved from http://www.sageusa.org/uploads/Advancing%20Equality%20 for%20LGBT%20Elders%20%5BFINAL%20COMPRESSED%5D.pdf

National Senior Citizens Law Center. (2011). *LGBT older adults in long-term care facilities: Stories from the field.* Washington, DC: Author.

Ponce, N. A., Cochran, S. S., Pizer, J. C., & Mays, V. M. (2010). The effects of unequal access to health insurance for same-sex couples in California. *Health Affairs, 29,* 1539–1548. doi:10.1377/hlthaff.2009.0583

Riggle, E. D. B., Rostosky, S. S., McCants, L. E., & Pascale-Hague, D. (2011). The positive aspects of a transgender self-identification. *Psychology and Sexuality, 2,* 147–158.

Riggle, E. D. B., Whitman, J. S., Olson, A., Rostosky, S. S., & Strong, S. (2008). The positive aspects of being a lesbian or gay man. *Professional Psychology: Research and Practice, 39,* 210–217. doi:10.1037/0735-7028.39.2.210

Ritter, K. Y., & Terndrup, A. I. (2002). *Handbook of affirmative psychotherapy with lesbians and gay men.* New York, NY: Guilford Press.

Rostosky, S. S., Riggle, E. B., Pascale-Hague, D., & McCants, L. E. (2010). The positive aspects of a bisexual self-identification. *Psychology and Sexuality, 1,* 131–144. doi:10.1080/19419899.2010.484595

Tang, H., Greenwood, G. L., Cowling, D. W., Lloyd, J. C., Roeseler, A. G., & Bal, D. G. (2004). Cigarette smoking among lesbians, gays, and bisexuals: How serious a problem? (United States). *Cancer Causes & Control, 15,* 797–803. doi:10.1023/B:CACO.0000043430.32410.69

Tedeschi, R. G., & Calhoun, L. G. (2004). Posttraumatic growth: Conceptual foundations and empirical evidence. *Psychological Inquiry, 15,* 1–18. doi:10.1207/s15327965pli1501_01

Unger, R. K. (2000). Outsiders inside: positive marginality and social change. *Journal of Social Issues, 56,* 163–179.

Valanis, B. G., Bowen, D. J., Bassford, T., Whitlock, E., Charney, P., & Carter, R. A. (2000). Sexual orientation and health: Comparisons in the women's health initiative sample. *Archives of Family Medicine, 9,* 843–853.

Wallace, S. P., Cochran, S. D., Durazo, E. M., & Ford, C. L. (2011). *The health of aging lesbian, gay and bisexual adults in California.* Los Angeles, CA: UCLA Center for Health Policy Research.

4

THEORIES OF AGING APPLIED TO LGBT OLDER ADULTS AND THEIR FAMILIES

DOUGLAS C. KIMMEL

Theorizing is a process of developing ideas that allow us to understand and explain empirical observations.

(Bengtson, Gans, Putney, & Silverstein, 2009, p. 4)

One of the most significant advances during the lifetime of today's older Americans is their increased life span, not only because of reduced childhood mortality, better health care, and safer workplaces but also because of the dramatic improvement in longevity after age 65. This improvement is not only in quantity of years; there has also been an astonishing delay in the onset of old age. When today's elders were children, old age began at age 65 or 70. The years between 65 and 85 were filled with chronic illness and impairment. Today these years are often relatively healthy ones, filled with activities and accomplishments of considerable satisfaction. The effect of the aging revolution has been to postpone the onset of old age so that not only have years been added to life, but life has been added to the years of longer life. With the electronic revolution combined with the aging revolution, the potential to remain actively involved in the important aspects of one's life has grown

DOI: 10.1037/14436-004
The Lives of LGBT Older Adults: Understanding Challenges and Resilience, N. A. Orel and C. A. Fruhauf (Editors)
Copyright © 2015 by the American Psychological Association. All rights reserved.

dramatically. Even if chronic illness or some impairment limits mobility or vision or hearing, one can often find accommodations to work around such limitations. Truly, the fact that someone is over age 65 tells almost nothing about their life circumstances today.

Another significant advance during the lifetime of today's elders is the social acknowledgment of the fact that there are lesbian, gay, bisexual, and transgender (LGBT) adults and elders. Knowing that someone is LGBT, however, similar to knowing that someone is over age 65, says little about his or her specific life circumstances. In a very real sense, LGBT aging is as unique as one's own biography, and thus describing a theory of LGBT aging in the 21st century is a challenging endeavor.

Early research on gay aging began shortly after the paradigm shift regarding homosexuality around 1969—from being an individual condition to a group identity—marked by the rebellion at the Stonewall Inn in New York City. In those days, it was thought that being gay might be fun when one is young, but old age for this population was filled with loneliness and gloom. This theme was portrayed in the media and writings of the time, in which the gay man or lesbian ended life in despair. Thus, if they did grow old, they were tragic figures. The gay bars of the time, often the only socializing environments for young gay men, had their share of older alcoholic men to personify this grim theme.

Lesbians and gay men had few positive older role models in those days; few individuals had family elders who could encourage and nurture their struggles. Marriage and children were seen as the source of satisfaction for adults, and grandchildren were the goals of their parents. Same-sex marriage, single-parent adoption, alternative fertilization, and coming out publicly were unimaginable in 1970. Bisexuality was considered an undesirable phase before one acknowledged being lesbian or gay, and there were few role models of bisexuality for either women or men. Transgender expression was associated with cross-dressing, butch dykes, and drag queens; no one imagined children choosing to change gender identities and finding support for and acceptance of their endeavors.

This chapter discusses how general theories on aging relate to the lives of older LGBT adults, in particular, the life stages theory of Erik Erikson from 1950 and the intersecting components that influence aging (physical health, social context, and individual characteristics). The chapter then goes on to propose three theories of LGBT aging: the cohort theory (growing old in parallel universes), the convoy model (grow old along with me), and the successful model (prevention, accommodation, positiveness, and crisis competence). The chapter concludes with a discussion of the characteristics of LGBT aging theory that are distinct from general theories of aging.

PSYCHOLOGICAL THEORY OF LGBT LIFE SPAN DEVELOPMENT

One of the most famous theories of life span development was proposed by Erik Erikson (1950) as a series of interlocking stages. The details are well known and described elsewhere (e.g., Kimmel, 1990). For this chapter, I look at these stages from the point of view of the LGBT person developing into adulthood during the past century. Although Erikson's model is connected with certain ages and emerging values for each stage, here I look how the conflicting dialectic struggles of each stage live on in LGBT people at any point in their psychosocial development.

Hope: Basic Trust Versus Mistrust

Whom can I trust? Will my family or friends understand or betray me if they know who I am and what I am becoming? This must be one of the most pivotal issues of my life, and if I have the good fortune of a secure and loving environment that fosters a sense of trust that is internalized, then perhaps my developing sense of being different will be manageable.

Will: Autonomy Versus Shame and Doubt

Shame is one of the most primitive human emotions, often associated with lack of self-control, being dirty and unacceptable. Most of the socializing information about homosexuality focused on its shamefulness and dirtiness. The risk of internalizing this shame may be reduced by an early sense of autonomy and independence from social pressures.

Purpose: Initiative Versus Guilt

Even if homosexuality is not unnatural, the socializing information says that homosexual behavior is wrong and should produce guilt. Guilt paralyzes the person and prevents taking active steps to affirm oneself. Finding the courage to take the initiative when appropriate is one of the hallmarks of the early pioneers in the gay movement during the 1970s. Nearly all gay people in the generation growing up during those times had to deal with the feelings of guilt and shame.

Competence: Industry Versus Inferiority

It is easy to sympathize with those gay men who hated gym class or the lesbians who wanted to play sports before Title IX allowed some equality for them. Finding a niche to be productive was challenging in a culture that valued gender-based stereotypes of achievement and success and that associated happiness with heterosexual families and children. It was easy to feel inferior, and often school bullies would sense this vulnerability and attack physically or verbally.

Fidelity: Identity Versus Identity Confusion

Sexual orientation and gender identity are only partial aspects of an individual's identity; but in the America of the 1970s, it was a major component of one's sense of self. For example, masculinity was always at risk, because it could be lost through a careless or thoughtless act that was less than 100% macho. Femininity was in the eye of the beholder, conjured up through makeup and dress. Although associated with adolescence, this stage often lasted well into adulthood for many LGBT people as they sought to understand their sexual orientation.

Love: Intimacy Versus Isolation

Learning how to date and how permeable the boundaries were between friendship and love were terrifying challenges for LGBT young adults. There were few (if any) positive openly gay role models. Friendship did not mean sexual intimacy would be accepted. Sexual intimacy with gay friends was often unacceptable, and networks of ex-lovers and friends made social relations complicated. For many, isolation was a much easier solution, especially if homosexuality was also linked with shame and guilt about being LGBT.

Care: Generativity Versus Stagnation

The struggle to advance in life despite one's hidden LGBT minority status, considering heterosexual marriage and family life, deciding whether to "come out," and fearing the consequences of disclosure were typical concerns for LGBT adults. A major theme of this dialectic struggle was to deal with the anger that resulted from the unfairness of social stigma and constraints: Did it fuel activism or depression? Many waited until after retirement to live openly as LGBT individuals. Others lived openly in the community, some with same-sex partners, and provided mentoring, nurturing, care, and solace to kin and friends in a network of mutual support.

Wisdom: Integrity Versus Despair

The frailties of old age caused some LGBT older adults to go back into "the closet" when they entered a retirement community or nursing home.

Many had to confront family conflicts over end-of-life plans or inheritance when a long-time companion or friend died. Most reflected on the past chapters of their life and often reinterpreted them in the positive or negative light of how it worked out. Some left a legacy of significant contributions to the remarkable change in social understanding of sexual orientation and gender identity. Others passed away with no one except their intimate friends being aware of their secret lives.

The lengthy period of adult life is the topic of this chapter. It currently stretches well past retirement age and continues as long as health and cognition are intact. The ongoing construction and reconstruction of one's personal past can sustain individuals in late life, until loss of cognitive abilities or actual death brings the end. In this chapter, we look at this period through several lenses focusing on those LGBT individuals who grew up in the 1970s and are at the forefront of the aging baby boom cohort today.

INTERDISCIPLINARY MODELS OF AGING

One useful way to discuss theories of aging is to focus on the intersecting components that influence aging in primary ways: physical health, life circumstances, social context, and individual characteristics. The relative contribution of each of these characteristics varies greatly from one individual to the next (Fredriksen-Goldsen et al., 2013). For some, failing physical health or impoverished life circumstances overwhelm the aging experience. For others, whose physical health and life circumstances are more benign, the social context of family and friends versus isolation and loneliness may be the overwhelming component that determines their aging experience. For the wealthy, life circumstances may provide such a resource that even the effect of physical health challenges can be minimized.

Given the relatively circumscribed influence of sexual orientation on an individual's daily life, one might think that it should have little effect on an individual's experience of aging. Sexual orientation and gender identity cut across all dimensions of physical health, life circumstances, and social context. In that sense, the fact that someone is LGBT provides limited information, parallel with the fact that someone is a particular age. Often we think that knowing someone is a 75-year-old lesbian provides important information. However, when we examine the actual information we think we know, it is mostly based on stereotypes and generalizations.

Sexual orientation and gender identity are not just an individual characteristic for many older LGBT persons, however. They influence many of the other dimensions of aging either directly or indirectly. For example, sexual orientation can affect health status for some older gay men who engage in sexual behavior at high risk for HIV infection; it may increase the risk of substance abuse and eating disorders for gay men and lesbians as a group; and it acts indirectly to reduce preventative diagnosis, treatment, and counseling through the lack of affirmative health care services in the community. Likewise, sexual orientation may directly affect the individual's life circumstances through discriminatory employment practices and lack of available health insurance and indirectly through frequent experiences of microaggressions or subtle acts of discriminatory behavior by others. Moreover, sexual orientation may directly affect the extent and kind of social supports the aging individual has available, as well as the person's connection with the LGBT community. Moreover, sexual orientation often affects the nature and extent of family support and indirectly affects the availability of a multi-generational support system typically provided by the family.

Therefore, on the one hand, sexual orientation and gender identity may be overwhelmed by the effects of physical health, life circumstances, and the social context in the later years of life. On the other hand, sexual orientation and gender identity are important individual characteristics because of the direct and indirect influences they have on the process of aging for LGBT individuals at the beginning of the 21st century in North America.

THEORIES OF AGING AND THE LGBT EXPERIENCE

The theories of LGBT aging discussed in this chapter include the cohort theory of aging (growing old in parallel universes), the convoy model of aging (growing old along with me), and the successful model of aging (prevention, accommodation, positiveness, and crisis competence). First, however, it is interesting to ask some basic questions.

Why do humans age, and why are there LGBT individuals? From a purely reproductive point of view, neither of these phenomena makes sense. Once a woman has reached menopause she can no longer pass on her genes; so after the children have been reared, her reproductive role is complete. Yet women not only live long past menopause but generally outlive men who are able to pass on their genes well into old age.

Mead (1970) explained this longevity from an anthropological perspective by theorizing that humans were able to survive as a community because some women and men lived long enough to remember where to go during prolonged drought to find water and possessed other rarely needed knowledge that could be valuable within the community. This knowledge allowed the genes of the community to be passed on and gave an enhanced survival advantage for those communities that had long-living members.

In a similar way, Wilson (1975) theorized that communities that included adults who had not produced their own biological children (such as LGBT adults) had a survival advantage. These adults could be surrogate parents, assist in rearing offspring from other adults, and provide resources for their nieces and nephews that would aid them in survival. This kinship survival would increase the likelihood of passing on the family's genes and thus promote the survival of those communities that contained these childless adults who did not directly pass on their individual genes. It might be added that these "LGBT" adults might also provide care for the elders, thus promoting their longevity and providing an additional survival advantage for their community.

Cohort Theory of Aging: Growing Old in Parallel Universes

The year in which an individual is born has lifelong influences on the person's life in subtle and often surprising ways. The period in which one is born is known as the *birth cohort* and may represent a few years (e.g., 5 or 10) or a longer demographic event, such as the baby boom cohort that was born following the end of World War II. When viewed as a population pyramid, one can notice the bulge in the birth cohort from 1946 to 1964 (ages 46–64 in 2010) with smaller cohorts before 1946 (and especially during the Great Depression of the 1930s). Naturally, as the population ages, the size of the cohort decreases from mortality, which gives the pyramid (Ortman, 2013) its classic shape (see Figure 4.1). This view of the population demographics informs decisions about social policy regarding aging services and points out the importance of attention to the growing number of older LGBT persons that are heading toward old age and have no plans to go back into the closet.

The relatively low-birth-rate cohort before the baby boom has lived in a world that is very different from that of the slightly younger baby boom cohort. Examples of this difference include relatively small classes in school versus overcrowded schools, relatively little competition for scholarships or employment versus high competition for every educational or occupational opportunity, and guaranteed Social Security and Medicare coverage versus threats that these benefits will be made insolvent by the sheer size of the baby boom cohort.

Other cohort differences reflect the historical events that were significant during the childhood and early adult periods of life. For example, the cohort born in the early 1940s was faced with scarce resources during the war, polio epidemics until a vaccine was developed in 1952, the fear of imminent nuclear war (with "duck-and-cover" drills in classrooms and visible signs for fallout shelters), as well as the fear of losing the race to the moon until 1969

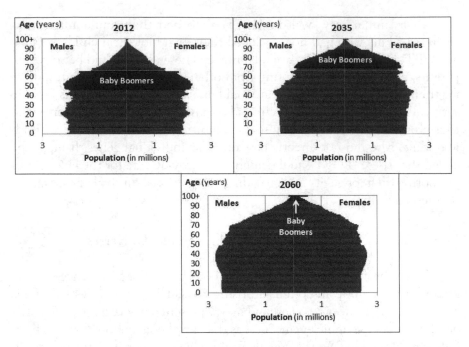

Figure 4.1. Population by age and sex: 2012, 2035, and 2060. From *U.S. Population Projections: 2012 to 2060,* by J. M. Ortman, 2013, Washington, DC: U.S. Census Bureau. In the public domain.

when Neil Armstrong stepped out of the landing capsule. This same year also marks the beginning of the modern gay movement, which occurred when the youngest of the pre–baby boom cohort was over age 24. In contrast, the baby boom cohort was between the ages of 9 and 23 in 1969. Thus, it may be obvious that these two cohorts came to sexual maturity as LGBT individuals in very different cultural environments.

Other significant differences between these two cohorts (who make up the population over age 55 in 2015) reflect the dramatic historical changes that have taken place between the 1930s and today. The pre–baby boom generation grew up when homosexuality was an illness, a crime, and a sin; people lost their jobs, their reputations, and sometimes went to prison or mental hospitals because of being homosexual. Variations of this stigma persisted until 1973, when homosexuality was dropped from the list of mental illnesses by the American Psychiatric Association, and until 2003, when the U.S. Supreme Court ruled that consensual homosexual behavior in private was not a crime. Today, for many Americans, it remains a sinful behavior that disqualifies individuals from equal treatment under the law (e.g., civil marriage, health care coverage, Social Security benefits, medical decisions by same-sex partners).

Therefore, to understand the individual characteristics in the aging model, one important fact to note is the year of birth, which reflects the cohort in which the individual has lived up to this point. It suggests the historical conditions that were present at the critical ages in the person's life. With regard to LGBT individuals, recalling the Erikson ages and stages model previously discussed, the school age years (*autonomy, initiative, industry*) and the adolescent years (*identity and intimacy*) were experienced in very different sociocultural environments for those born between the 1930s and 1960s compared with those born more recently. In that sense, these differing cohorts of LGBT individuals grew up in parallel universes. They live side by side today, but they experienced the dramatic changes related to sexual orientation and gender identity from very different perspectives.

Finally, the cohort theory of aging reminds us that those old LGBT individuals today are the *survivors* of their birth cohort. They are the ones who did not die from childhood illness, accidents, suicide, cancer, heart disease, or the AIDS epidemic. They are the survivors of their cohort and thus may be more resilient, lucky, or have better coping skills than those who did not grow old. In a later section, I discuss the positive aspects of resilience and aging.

Convoy Theory of Aging: Grow Old Along With Me

As the cohort grows older, it moves through the life cycle as a wave moves through a calm lake. Initially the entire cohort is large, but gradually it grows smaller as members die over the years. One's individual age-cohort friendship group likewise grows older and smaller over time. Often it is said that one of the worst things about aging is losing one's long-term friends, because they are impossible to replace. One can make new friends, but the 40 or 50 years of shared friendship is irreplaceable.

Generally the convoy model of aging focuses on the cumulative importance of social relations and friendship over the life span (Antonucci, Birditt, & Akiyama, 2009). One ages with one's support group of age mates. In the heterosexual world, this means that one's age peers entered the workforce, married, had children, managed child rearing and schooling, watched the children leave home, became grandparents, retired, and entered old age more or less in sync with their age mates. Neugarten (1968) referred to this timetable as the *social clock*. It set the expected time for the typical events and allowed individuals to determine whether they were on-time or off-time with regard to their age mates. The convoy of age mates provided role models, social support, and pragmatic advice and helped one to anticipate the expected life cycle events.

For LGBT individuals, of course, these social timetables were mostly irrelevant, and often problematic. Parents and peers urged everyone to follow the social clock, sometimes forcing LGBT youth to conform to gender roles and to marry and have children. Often this conformity was disastrous (Buxton & Piney, 2012). The image of a truck convoy with occasional wrecks alongside the road is an appropriate metaphor for many LGBT adults.

Some LGBT youth recognized their nonconformity with their convoy age mates and charted their own path. During the first half of the 20th century, before the Kinsey reports, these individuals were generally individual nonconformists: the bachelor uncle or maiden aunt, the old-maid schoolteachers who lived together, or the man who adopted a younger man as a son. Generally, their convoy of age mates passed them by silently and with perhaps a bit of pity, condescension, or compassion.

During the 1950s and 1960s, the Kinsey studies revealed that many men and women had same-sex experiences (Kinsey, Pomeroy, & Martin, 1948; Kinsey, Pomeroy, Martin, & Gebhard, 1953). Many women and men who had made contact with each other during World War II settled in Los Angeles, San Francisco, New York, and other urban centers. This coming together created a new convoy of LGBT age mates. They were beginning to form organizations that provided tangible social and emotional support for each other. They published (or mimeographed) newsletters; they held meetings and organized conferences; they found lawyers and bail bonds for those who were arrested in raids on homosexual bars; and they socialized in gay, lesbian, and transvestite bars (Katz, 1976). Hooker described attending a meeting of One, Inc., in Los Angles to recruit gay men for her groundbreaking study published in 1955 and attending transvestite performances at Finocchio's with her gay friends in the 1950s (Kimmel & Garnets, 2003). The members of this convoy of postwar LGBT pioneers are now in their 80s and 90s and have provided an impetus for building LGBT affirmative housing in San Francisco (Adelman, Gurevitch, de Vries, & Blando, 2006). They were the earliest of the marchers for nondiscrimination against homosexuals, motivated especially by Senator Joseph McCarthy's attacks on homosexual government workers and on gays in the armed forces (Katz, 1976).

The next convoy of LGBT aging came from the baby boom age cohort when young people were faced with being drafted into the Vietnam War and had learned techniques of civil disobedience from the civil rights movement. The Democratic Convention in 1968 was a disaster of broken glass, bloodshed, tear gas, and a "police riot" against protesters opposed to the war (Farber, 1988). Riots and fires raged on the west side of Chicago the night Martin Luther King was assassinated. Many college campuses around the world had experienced sit-ins and protests in 1969 and these were televised on the nightly news. So on the night of Judy Garland's memorial in New York City, the police attempted to conduct a routine raid on a gay bar in Greenwich Village called the Stonewall Inn (Duberman, 1993). Garland's role in *The Wizard of Oz* was legendary in the gay male community because many identified with the kid from Kansas who was suddenly transported to a Technicolor world where Judy and three misfits could have their dreams realized. (During the 1940s and 1950s, gay people adopted a term for themselves as "a friend of Dorothy"; and today cruise ships sometimes have a notice on the event schedule for a meeting of the "Friends of Dorothy.")

This convoy of LGBT people created a paradigm shift in the conceptualization of homosexuality. Before the riot that followed from the angry gay and transgender patrons of the Stonewall Inn, homosexuality was an individual pathology or private condition. After Stonewall, it became a minority group, a group identity that was proud and good (Hay, 1990). Many young people did not identify as a member of their minority group until well into adulthood, often after marriage and the child-rearing years had begun. Some had spent years in therapy trying to be "normal" (e.g., Duberman, 1991). Others became proponents of gay-affirmative programs and helped create the changes that followed (e.g., Silverstein, 2011). This convoy of aging LGBT adults is now in their 60s and 70s. They are role models for each other and often still more radical than either the convoy before them or the ones that follow.

Another important dimension of the convoy model of aging for the LGBT community is the fact that many in this aging convoy have survived and been personally affected by the HIV/AIDS epidemic. Many gay men who are now entering their 60s were in young adulthood when their convoy of same-age friends began to develop odd symptoms and, relatively quickly, become disabled and died. Beginning in 1981, before the HIV virus was identified, the disease first described as GRID (gay-related immune deficiency) caused many previously healthy gay men to die rapidly and horribly, frequently stigmatized and at risk for discrimination. In San Francisco, the gay newspaper was filled with obituaries; in New York, the Gay Men's Health Crisis (GMHC) was created, and later one of its founders, Larry Kramer, wrote a play, *The Normal Heart*, to dramatize the lack of federal attention to the disease (Kramer, 1985). The stigma was so great that even the *New York Times* refused to carry an article about a major fund-raising event by a circus for GMHC. A large number of gay leaders and pioneers were victims of the disease. Many of the survivors saw their friendship networks decimated. Some described attending a funeral more than once a week during the height of the epidemic. Others talked about their entire address book being wiped out. It was not until 1987 that a drug, AZT (azidothymidine), was approved for use. But AZT only slowed the virus; it did not prevent death. In 1996, the effective therapy known as highly active antiretroviral therapy, or HAART, became available. No longer was a diagnosis of HIV infection a death sentence, and today many older gay men are living with HIV (Emlet, Fredriksen-Goldsen, & Kim, 2013). However, the long-term effects of HAART are not known.

Gay and bisexual men in this convoy of young people in the 1980s, who were just coming out in a world they thought of as becoming increasingly gay-affirmative, were the LGBT persons most directly affected by the AIDS epidemic; however, lesbians and bisexual women were dramatically affected by it as well. Lesbians stepped in to fill the leadership positions emptied by AIDS, and they took up the struggle for funding, building, and creating the systems of care for persons with HIV/AIDS. Bisexual women not only took part in the struggle with their gay male and lesbian colleagues, they also found themselves at risk if they had unprotected sex with a bisexual man. Of course, no one was sure they were not at risk because the virus was unknown at first and was then found to be transmitted not only by sex but also by bodily fluids, needles, and during pregnancy. All LGBT persons therefore had to assess their risk factors for HIV and take precautions. This convoy of the survivors of the HIV epidemic is now in the aging pipeline. For example, some are entering their 60s, and others are older, having been older at the time of the epidemic. It is likely that many in this group lost a lover or many friends during this time.

Successful Aging and LGBT Experiences

Many theories of aging focus on adaptation to the biological decline and slowing of physiological responses, acceptance of physical losses and limitations, and accommodation to disabilities of the senses and mobility. A common theme is to "age gracefully" by acceptance of these inevitable changes and maintenance of a cheerful outlook on life. Often this theme is accompanied by plastic surgery, hair coloring, and clothing designed to hide signs of aging. The conceptualization of unsuccessful aging is one of a human object that was once attractive and useful that has become unattractive and useless with age.

Jean-Paul Sartre (1956) and Simone de Beauvoir (1952) offered extensive existential analysis on sex roles in Western society in which women and homosexual men were at risk for being defined as sexual and physical objects by the males to whom they sought to be attractive. The male role was seen as a "subject" whose eyes defined the standards of beauty by being socially and sexually dominant. Sartre (1963) expanded this idea in his existential psychoanalysis of Jean Genet:

> This priority, in the subject itself, of the object over the subject leads, as we see, to amorous passivity, which, when it affects a male, inclines him to homosexuality. . . . What he desires is to be manipulated passively by the Other so as to become an object in his own eyes. Any man who places his truth in his Being-for-the-Other finds himself in a situation which I have called pre-homosexual. (pp. 94–95)

To the extent this sweeping generalization is true for some gay and bisexual men, it also implies that lesbians may be less at risk of objectification than are gay and bisexual men or heterosexual women. It also implies that broad individual differences most likely exist in the extent to which a person's existential stance toward others in the world is as a subject or an "object" and the relative balance of each orientation in the present.

Viewing the process of aging through these existential lenses, it appears that aging as an object would be relatively negative—at risk for being devalued, ignored, and treated with a high degree of ageism. In contrast to the graceful acceptance of decline with aging, proponents of successful aging imply that many older adults can take an active or proactive stance toward the challenges of aging.

Zarit (2009), for example, noted that older adults in general (excluding those who have dementia) are happier and in better mental health than other age groups, despite losses and challenges. He cited several theories of aging to explain how this is achieved and proposed a model of primary prevention to allow individuals to compensate, overcome, and remain involved in life during old age. The characteristics involved "include good health habits, skills for managing chronic illness, good social skills, skills for managing emotions, good cognitive skills, leisure skills, good economic skills, and, finally, development of a sense of self-efficacy for the ability to change one's life" (Bengtson et al., 2009, p. 21). These skills Zarit discussed appear to be elements of what Sartre and de Beauvoir thought of as a *subject orientation:* that is, being active with regard to the challenges of life. Most important, these skills can be learned and practiced long before the person becomes chronologically old, and thus they do much to prevent or reduce some of the most serious correlates of aging.

In some ways, LGBT adults may be especially prepared to develop the skills of successful aging for the following three reasons. First, they are consciously creating their own models of relationships, choosing their own role models, and rejecting models that they view as dysfunctional. This process of *normative creativity* (Brown, 1989) allows, or even forces, LGBT individuals to make thoughtful choices about retirement planning, health care directives, relationship agreements, and wills.

Second, the gay community has promoted awareness of LGBT health disparities and risks that makes certain vulnerabilities more obvious and offers cultural support for reducing their impact. Examples include HIV education and screening, antismoking norms, support groups for eating disorders, and groups focused on physical activities such as dancing, bicycling, hiking, and bowling. In addition, the gym culture can reflect not only the objectification of the body but also good health and leisure skills through physical activity.

Third, several research studies have noted the potential for LGBT individuals to develop an ability I termed *crisis competence* (Kimmel, 1978) through which they discover or develop coping skills to manage crises early in life (Fredriksen-Goldsen & Muraco, 2010; Friend, 1990). Of course, the early experience of an emotional crisis is not desirable; but even today, and certainly in the past, being bullied and harassed for being gay, coming out to parents and friends, and being confronted by homophobic authorities are not uncommon experiences. To be sure, those young people who are confronted with a crisis they cannot manage may be at higher risk for suicide or long-term emotional distress. However, surviving such a crisis is empowering in ways that may bring long-term gains and skills for coping with the challenges of adulthood and aging or even thriving in old age.

One generic skill LGBT individuals have developed and use frequently, often when they first meet, is to tell their "coming-out story." For those who have survived the crisis of coming out, telling this story reaffirms their coping skills and provides a bond of social support that is important in many ways. My coming-out story is an illustration of crisis competence. My mother chanced to read over my shoulder a letter I was writing to my first lover just after I graduated from college. That night when my father arrived home, all hell broke loose, with lots of emotional crisis. I left home, taking refuge with a friend, supported by my few gay friends, and reading Sartre's book on Genet, which led me to write a treatise on homosexuality. Fortunately, I had a gay-affirmative therapist before the crisis hit, and I was going to graduate school in the fall, where I found more gay friends and a supportive environment. Four years later, the Stonewall event changed the paradigm of homosexuality, and eventually my parents resolved their conflict over it. Everyone's story is unique, and as LGBT people tell their stories, we each become the subject and can view how our coming out changed our lives. It may also help us remember that we are still writing the later chapters of our lives, potentially as subjects rather than as objects.

Unique Characteristics of LGBT Aging Theory

Two striking themes of LGBT aging have been noted in previous writing. The first theme is the notion of premature aging among gay men in which "old" is perceived to begin about age 40 (Bennett & Thompson, 1990). This phenomenon, insofar as it exists, is probably the result of gay and bisexual men's potential for being viewed as objects, as Sartre and de Beauvoir described sex roles—that is, being viewed through the eyes of men as attractive or unattractive. Much has been written on this topic for women, but little attention has been devoted to the situation for gay and bisexual men.

A second theme is the pervasive ageist (or age-conscious) attitudes within LGBT communities (Kimmel, 2002). Although ageism is frequently noted among gay and bisexual men for the same reasons as premature aging, it is also often reported among older lesbians and bisexual women and transgender elders. In our "throwaway" society that values newness and freshness in almost every realm, there is a danger that old people are more likely to be regarded as used up rather than as valued antiques.

Kimmel (2002, p. 31) observed numerous similarities and differences between ageism and heterosexism. Both old age and sexual minority sexual orientation

- have been the focus of an active search for biological origin, and possible cure, despite the fact that both are normal human characteristics;
- evoke irrational fear and avoidance in some people who tend to avoid close contact and physical touching with both groups;
- evoke confusion with associated conditions: aging with senility or death, sexual orientation with gender identity or promiscuity;
- operate as a master status that obviates other relevant social positions and characteristics;
- are perceived as being best to avoid if possible; they are both dealt with by "don't ask, don't tell" policies;
- are characterized more in terms of their perceived disadvantages than their advantages; losses are thought to exceed gains; strengths are seen only as compensations for weakness;
- are discriminatory views—ageism and heterosexism—that emphasize the importance of fertility and propagation as normative for everyone; and
- are conferred a special status in some cultures, in which the individuals may be seen as having special powers resulting from their minority status.

In contrast, there are four clear differences between ageism and heterosexism:

- Most people hope to become old one day; few hope to become a sexual minority.
- No one blames the individual's choice, or his or her mother, for becoming old.
- Families openly acknowledge and celebrate becoming older; few families celebrate their children coming out as lesbian, gay, bisexual, or transgender.
- Churches and moral guardians do not urge older persons to avoid acting old, but they often urge sexual minorities to avoid acting on their erotic or romantic attractions.

It will be interesting to see whether social media and electronic communities continue to reinforce ageist stereotypes and attitudes, or whether they will provide new opportunities for LGBT persons to interact across generations and cohorts more openly and honestly.

Finally, another paradigm shift may be underway currently—a shift from viewing sexual minorities only in terms of deserving equal rights and benefits to a minority group equal with heterosexuals in terms of love- and family-based commitments. It will be illuminating to see the impact of legalizing same-sex marriage on future cohorts of LGBT individuals. For example, as more LGBT parents and grandparents emerge in the community and the value of older mentors and role models becomes more salient for younger cohorts, we can envision some reduction in ageism in the LGBT community.

CONCLUSION

Within the lifetime of older adults alive today, the LGBT community has moved from a life condition that was illegal, immoral, shameful, sinful, and sick to a stigmatized minority group that is gaining recognition as equal to others in human value and rights. Through the events of history linked with the cohort of their birth, moving through their lives in a convoy of social support, and growing older as proactive elders, the stories of older LGBT adults are amazing. As individuals, these elders are as unique as any other group their age. But they have been on a journey, linked together by their individual shared stories and by their struggle against stigma and search for identity. They are conservative and progressive, healthy and disabled, and of all races and ethnicities. All have a history of discovery of their own sexual orientation and gender identity.

The goal of this chapter has been to provide some theoretical concepts to explain the empirical observations of older LGBT individuals contained in other chapters of this book. As with any theory, its strengths and weaknesses will be judged by those empirical observations.

REFERENCES

Adelman, M., Gurevitch, J., de Vries, B., & Blando, J. A. (2006). openhouse: Community building and research in the LGBT aging population. In D. C. Kimmel, T. Rose, & S. David, (Eds.), Lesbian, gay, bisexual, and transgender aging: Research and clinical perspectives (pp. 247–264). New York, NY: Columbia University Press.

Antonucci, T. C., Birditt, K. S., & Akiyama, H. (2009). Convoys of social relations: An interdisciplinary approach. In V. L. Bengtson, M. Silverstein, N. M. Putney, & D. Gans (Eds.), Handbook of theories of aging (pp. 247–260). New York, NY: Springer.

Bengtson, V. L., Gans, D., Putney, N. M., & Silverstein, M. (2009). Theories about age and aging. In V. L. Bengtson, M. Silverstein, N. M. Putney, & D. Gans (Eds.), *Handbook of theories of aging* (pp. 3–23). New York, NY: Springer.

Bennett, K. C., & Thompson, N. L. (1990). Accelerated aging and male homosexuality: Australian evidence in a continuing debate. *Journal of Homosexuality, 20*, 65–75.

Brown, L. S. (1989). New voices, new visions: Toward a lesbian/gay paradigm for psychology. *Psychology of Women Quarterly, 13*, 445–458. doi:10.1111/j.1471-6402.1989.tb01013.x

Buxton, A. P., & Piney, R. L. (2012). *Unseen—unheard: The journey of straight spouses.* Austin, TX: Creative House.

de Beauvoir, S. (1952). *The second sex* (H. M. Parshley, Ed.). New York, NY: Knopf.

Duberman, M. (1991). *Cures: A gay man's odyssey.* New York, NY: Dutton.

Duberman, M. (1993). *Stonewall.* New York, NY: Dutton.

Emlet, C. A., Fredriksen-Goldsen, K. I., & Kim, H.-J. (2013). Risk and protective factors associated with health-related quality of life among older gay and bisexual men living with HIV disease. *The Gerontologist, 53*, 963–972.

Erikson, E. H. (1950). *Childhood and society.* New York, NY: Norton.

Farber, D. (1988). *Chicago '68.* Chicago, IL: University of Chicago Press. doi:10.7208/chicago/9780226237992.001.0001

Fredriksen-Goldsen, K. I., Emlet, C. A., Kim, H.-J., Muraco, A., Erosheva, E. A., Goldsen, J., & Hoy-Ellis, C. P. (2013). The physical and mental health of lesbian, gay male, and bisexual (LGB) older adults: The role of key health indicators and risk and protective factors. *The Gerontologist, 53*, 664–675. doi:10.1093/geront/gns123

Fredriksen-Goldsen, K. I., & Muraco, A. (2010). Aging and sexual orientation: A 25-year review of the literature. *Research on Aging, 32*, 372–413. doi:10.1177/0164027509360355

Friend, R. A. (1990). Older lesbian and gay people: A theory of successful aging. *Journal of Homosexuality, 20*(3–4), 99–118.

Hay, H. (1990, April 22–28). Identifying as gay: There's the key. *Gay Community News, 5.*

Katz, J. (1976). *Gay American history: Lesbians and gay men in the U.S.A.* New York, NY: Thomas Y. Crowell.

Kimmel, D. C. (1978). Adult development and aging: A gay perspective. *Journal of Social Issues, 34*, 113–130. doi:10.1111/j.1540-4560.1978.tb02618.x

Kimmel, D. C. (1990). *Adulthood and aging* (3rd ed.). New York, NY: Wiley.

Kimmel, D. C. (2002). Aging and sexual orientation. In G. E. Jones & M. J. Hill (Eds.), *Mental health issues in lesbian, gay, bisexual, and transgender communities* (Review of Psychiatry Series, *21*(4), pp. 17–36.) Washington, DC: American Psychiatric Publishing.

Kimmel, D. C., & Garnets, L. D. (2003). What a light it shed: The life of Evelyn Hooker. In L. D. Garnets & D. C. Kimmel (Eds.), *Psychological perspectives on lesbian, gay, and bisexual experiences* (pp. 31–40). New York, NY: Columbia University Press.

Kinsey, A. C., Pomeroy, W. B., & Martin, C. E. (1948). *Sexual behavior in the human male*. Philadelphia, PA: Saunders.

Kinsey, A. C., Pomeroy, W. B., Martin, C. E., & Gebhard, P. H. (1953). *Sexual behavior in the human female*. Philadelphia, PA: Saunders.

Kramer, L. (1985). *The normal heart*. New York, NY: Plume.

Mead, M. (1970). *Culture and commitment: A study of the generation gap*. Garden City, NY: Doubleday.

Neugarten, B. L. (1968). Adult personality: Toward a psychology of the life cycle. In B. L. Neugarten (Ed.), *Middle age and aging* (pp. 137–147). Chicago, IL: University of Chicago Press.

Ortman, J. M. (2013). *U.S. population projections: 2012 to 2060*. Washington, DC: U.S. Census Bureau. Retrieved from http://www.gwu.edu/~forcpgm/Ortman.pdf

Sartre, J. P. (1956). *Being and nothingness* (H. E. Barnes, Trans.). New York, NY: Philosophical Library.

Sartre, J. P. (1963). *Saint Genet, actor and martyr* (B. Frechtman, Trans.). New York, NY: New American Library.

Silverstein, C. (2011). *For the ferryman: A personal history*. New York, NY: Chelsea Station Editions.

Wilson, E. O. (1975). *Sociobiology: The new synthesis*. Cambridge, MA: Belknap Press of Harvard University Press.

Zarit, S. H. (2009). A good old age: Theories of mental health and aging. In V. L. Bengtson, M. Silverstein, N. M. Putney, & D. Gans (Eds.), *Handbook of theories of aging* (pp. 675–691). New York, NY: Springer.

5

THE MEANING OF SPIRITUALITY IN END-OF-LIFE DECISIONS AMONG LGBT OLDER ADULTS

CODY SWARTZ, MORGAN BUNTING, CHRISTINE A. FRUHAUF, AND NANCY A. OREL

Spirituality and religion can be important components of end-of-life care, and care providers must be particularly sensitive to the unique challenges of the lesbian, gay, bisexual, and transgender (LGBT) population (Blevins & Werth, 2006). In particular, providers must understand the effects of stigma and discrimination on these individuals' health and well-being. For example, the historical religious scrutiny of the LGBT population has made many older LGBT adults hesitant to seek spiritual or religious services (Hughes, Harold, & Boyer, 2011). Outreach to this population is appropriate to overcome their possible distrust of providers.

Evidence shows that many providers do not provide such outreach. A study of Michigan aging-care service providers found that they were accepting of LGBT older adults and realized they had different needs that required different services; however, they were not offering such services or activities specifically related to the LGBT population (Hughes et al., 2011).

DOI: 10.1037/14436-005
The Lives of LGBT Older Adults: Understanding Challenges and Resilience, N. A. Orel and C. A. Fruhauf (Editors)
Copyright © 2015 by the American Psychological Association. All rights reserved.

Finding ways to encourage end-of-life care providers to promote outreach, including spiritual and religious care, for this population may benefit the LGBT community.

In this chapter, we present current research on end-of-life decisions and explain how spirituality may play an important role in the lives of LGBT older adults. We also discuss variations in spirituality among different cultures, religions, and care settings. Special attention is given to palliative care, otherwise known as hospice care, because a relatively new trend in the United States is to provide spiritual care in such settings to address end-of-life needs in a holistic manner. First, however, we consider the unique historical status of LGBT baby boomers and apply a life course perspective to understanding this population.

LGBT BABY BOOMERS

The baby boomer population includes all individuals who were born between 1946 and 1964; it is currently the largest cohort ever of older adults in the United States (U.S. Census Bureau, 2010). This group of individuals will need advanced medical and psychosocial care services. Along with the general older adult population, the population of LGBT older adults will increase. In a 2010 report by the National Gay and Lesbian Task Force (NGLTF), it was estimated that by the year 2030, the number of LGBT older adults over age 65 will be between 3.6 million and 7.2 million.

It is important not only to recognize the increasing LGBT older adult population in the United States but also to understand how this may affect society. For example, the MetLife study of aging gay and lesbian baby boomers (Metlife Mature Market Institute, 2006) describes the baby boomers as experiencing the greatest cultural shift within their cohort regarding LGBT individuals. Throughout their childhood, adolescence, early life, and midlife, LGBT older adults were subjected to an environment created by society in which homosexuality was considered sinful and LGBT persons did not have the same constitutional rights as others (Haber, 2009). Within this negative context, many were not "out" to family or friends. In today's society, however, many younger LGBT individuals are comfortable disclosing their sexual orientation without fear of backlash (Stein & Almack, 2012). Conversely, older LGBT adults may still be "in the closet" because of the negative repercussions they experienced when they were younger (Stein & Almack, 2012). All of the stigma and discrimination that LGBT baby boomers have faced thus far in their lives regarding their sexual orientation and gender identity may now be complicated with stigma and discrimination associated with advancing age. Ageism and homophobia, or discrimination based on a person's age or his or her sexual orientation, will impede an individual's access to care and possibly decrease the ability to access adequate health care in our current society (Macrae, 2010; Orel, 2004).

As society prepares for the influx of older adults generally, special consideration should be given to addressing the needs of the older LGBT population. While creating and introducing new ways to provide care, service providers should consider the challenges—such as homophobia and discrimination—that older LGBT adults have faced throughout their lives. Providers should take all of an LGBT patient's life experiences into consideration, as they would for any individual; but the manner in which these older adults' sexual or gender identities have colored their experience must be part of the overall picture. Applying care practices that address the unique needs of LGBT older adults promotes outreach to and improved care for this population.

The Life Course Perspective

The life course perspective is a popular theoretical model in the field of gerontology that is especially useful in the context of human development, life-span development, and social-historical development of families over time (Bengtson & Allen, 1993). According to Bengtson and Allen (1993), the major themes of the life course perspective include the appraisal of time (e.g., ontogenetic, generational, and historical timing), social context, the dynamic aspects of roles and relationships, and the heterogeneity in structures and processes that give meaning and importance to the linked lives of individuals within families across the life span. In essence, the life course perspective focuses on the development of individuals in the context of their families over time. Various life events shape an individual within a familial context, and for LGBT older adults, application of the life course perspective can provide insight into the lives and unique challenges they have faced.

A central feature of the life course perspective—time—is described in three parts; ontogenetic time, generational time, and historical time (Bengtson & Allen, 1993). *Ontogenetic time* refers to chronological age, but it reflects the unfolding of the life events or developmental processes of an individual's development. These form the basis that can shape or alter subsequent individual behaviors (Bengtson & Allen, 1993). *Generational time* refers to age groups or cohorts and is concerned with how individuals respond to societal events and how these events can influence interactions with others (Bengtson & Allen, 1993). These events often shape how individuals view their social roles as they progress through the life course. LGBT older adults have experienced homosexuality depicted in a negative context throughout their lives, and this may have shaped their views about coming out later in life to family or caregivers. Some LGBT older adults may find it more difficult to find their place in society because they believe they do not meet society's expectations. Finally, *historical time* refers to events within the broader social context, such as laws, political and social movements, and other large-scale events or changes, and how these affect the lives of individuals (Bengtson & Allen, 1993). Large-scale political and social movements within the past 60 years have had an effect on the current LGBT older adult population. For example, after the Stonewall riots of 1969 and the resulting gay rights movement, homosexuality was finally removed as a mental illness in the *Diagnostic and Statistical Manual of Mental Disorders* by the American Psychiatric Association in 1973. These events may have been liberating, encouraging some people to come out of the closet; for others, however, past or ongoing discrimination may continue to prevent them from disclosing their sexual orientation.

The social context has not been kind to the current LGBT older adult population. For example, members of this community have endured a plethora of negative comments and perceptions about sexual orientation and gender identity; the possible internalization of this experience may have shaped who they are today. Although some LGBT older adults may have become liberated, others may still struggle with their identities. Historical events and suppressed feelings can prevent LGBT older adults from expressing their identities and may inhibit end-of-life decisions that reflect their actual wishes.

Spirituality can be an outlet for LGBT older adults who have internalized their emotions as a result of discriminatory acts against them. When discussing spirituality and end-of-life decisions for LGBT older adults, it is important to consider historical timing and the impact of generational memories on their views and beliefs in relation to what society perceived at the time to be "normal." When discussing the importance and potential benefits of disclosing one's sexual orientation and gender identity with LGBT older adults, practitioners must be mindful of the painful generational memories that LGBT older adults may possess. It is important that both LGBT older adults and care providers find ways to confront any internalized negative beliefs concerning sexual orientation and gender identity to support the provision of care and to meet the needs of LGBT older adults; these efforts include the context of their spirituality.

Spirituality, Religiosity, and Their Significance for LGBT Older Adults

There is no universal definition for the term *spirituality* (Halkitis et al., 2009). Therefore, one definition could not encompass all individuals' views. As MacKinlay (2006) pointed out, spirituality is not necessarily synonymous with religion or religiosity. Spirituality is a realm of thoughts, practices, and ideas separate from any particular religious institution. One cannot assume that because someone is spiritual, he or she also follows a specific religious doctrine. Being spiritual is uniquely defined by the individual who identifies as such. Spirituality is one area of care that is particularly difficult for health care providers to address when designing care plans, such as those used in palliative care organizations. To provide adequate care services, practitioners must recognize that spirituality is defined by the individual.

In addition to spirituality, *religiosity* also needs to be defined. According to the Oxford English Dictionary Online (http://www.oed.com), the term is defined as a "religious belief" or simply a "belief." Many religious people look to a higher power for guidance and support while trying to create a bond with this higher power to guide these decisions (Larson, Swyers, & McCullough, 1998). Larson et al. (1998) identified at least three different historical designations of the term *religiosity:* (a) a supernatural power to which individuals must respond, (b) an emotional feeling in individuals who conceive of such a power, (c) and ritual acts carried out in respect of that power (as cited in Cohen, Holley, Wengel, & Katzman, 2012). Religiosity can be viewed as the degree in which people follow or practice a set of religious doctrines.

Accessing Care

As a normal part of aging, many older adults may face health challenges, and thus their need to access care increases. Care services can include anything that benefits older adults or helps them receive services that are beneficial for their quality of life, including (a) case and care management, (b) in-home care, (c) institutionalization, and (d) community-based services. For some, care is not solely restricted to their medical needs and services; spirituality can also play a substantial role. LGBT older adults may choose to use spirituality to practice their beliefs, due to traditional religious groups' condemning their sexuality. Robinson (1999) provided an online guide to religious groups' policies and practices regarding homosexuality. This guide covers major religions, such as Catholicism, various Christian faiths, and Judaism, and is useful in determining each religion's beliefs regarding homosexuality. It provides a good indication of how the various doctrines of these religions may be distasteful to an LGBT older adult; almost no support is provided to them in terms of religious guidance and acceptance. Tan (2005) pointed out that spirituality is often linked to or affiliated with religion. Thus, many would expect homosexuals to deny any desire for a spiritual life given the negative perceptions toward homosexuality held by many religions. This may push LGBT older adults away from religiosity and spirituality altogether. Yet Tan found that many of the gay and lesbian participants in his study led spiritually healthy lives. He concluded that many of his respondents may have been forced to look past traditional religion to find other sources of faith and meaning in their existence.

When practitioners work with older adults who do not consider themselves religious, as is the case for many in the older LGBT population, it can be beneficial to help them find spiritual meaning and thus an overall better sense of well-being in areas not typically considered religious. MacKinlay (2006) defined *spirituality* as the core meaning, deepest life meaning, and relationship that an individual has with another; this can be thought of as occurring through a relationship with God or one without God, which is more reliant on personal relationships with other people. MacKinlay posited that spirituality includes four domains: relationship, religion, environment, and the arts. The relationship domain includes one's intimacy with others, with God, or both and to what degree these relationships are held within the individual. The religion domain includes worship, prayer, reading of scriptures, and mediation. The environment domain includes nature, sea, mountains, and gardens. Last, the arts domain includes music, art, and dance as a way of guiding individuals through their spirituality (MacKinlay, 2006). Understanding the four domains of spirituality is useful when dealing with patients who state, "I'm not really religious" because such patients may still value their relationships, the environment, and the arts. By helping nonreligious patients enhance these other domains of their spirituality, practitioners can enhance such patients' well-being (MacKinlay, 2006).

Understanding the definitions of *spirituality* and *religiosity* can be useful when examining the connection between these concepts and self-identified sexual orientation or gender identity among LGBT older adults. Little is known about the degree to which LGBT older adults use religious or spiritual guidance in their lives as aids in decision making about life issues (Halkitis et al., 2009). Historically, the negative attitudes surrounding the topics of sexuality and homosexuality held by many religious denominations have imposed silence on the LGBT population and their religious or spiritual practices (Halkitis et al., 2009). Thus, there is little insight into the importance of spirituality and religion in their lives (Halkitis et al., 2009). Religious communities and individuals vary in their responses to the LGBT population. Acceptance of those in the LGBT community is determined by ideological practices, and these vary across religions. Some LGBT older adults may encounter negative reactions within certain religious denominations. Conversely, Halkitis and colleagues (2009) explained, those who are part of a welcoming community may face little or no conflict when it comes to their sexuality, sexual orientation, or gender identity.

When addressing religious issues and accessing care services, it is not uncommon for LGBT older adults to refer to their significant other, partner, or loved one as a roommate or sibling to avoid disclosure of their sexuality

(Services & Advocacy for GLBT Elders & Movement Advancement Project, 2010). If LGBT older adults do not disclose their sexual orientation, it prevents the health care practitioner from becoming more actively involved with patients and their partners, which may in turn impede their care. For example, because gay men engage in unprotected sexual practices at a higher rate than the general population, they are at risk for acquiring HIV/AIDS, and gay men are disproportionately affected by HIV/AIDS (Centers for Disease Control and Prevention [CDC], 2013). The CDC (2010) found that 60% of new sexually transmitted infections among older men were attributed to male-to-male sexual contact. One can conclude that if a gay older adult goes to the doctor because he is sick, a proper diagnosis may take longer if he does not disclose his sexual practices. A diagnosis of HIV/AIDS may not be his ultimate diagnosis, but obtaining a complete sexual history is necessary to rule out possible causes for his illness.

Religion-based messages that homosexuality is sinful can lead an LGBT person to remain in the closet, which hinders the delivery of appropriate care. The implications that spirituality, especially if religion-based, could have for an individual's health and well-being may be more dramatic for LGBT older adults than their heterosexual counterparts.

Dementia

A syndrome that is more prevalent among the older adult population is dementia, and there are many quality-of-life implications for an individual who is experiencing the signs and symptoms of dementia, regardless of one's sexual orientation or gender identity. However, the spiritual needs of individuals with dementia are important no matter how far the disease has progressed. MacKinlay (2006) noted that in late-stage dementia, the main form of communication may be through the fulfillment of spiritual needs; she maintained that cutting off spiritual opportunities for older adults with dementia can be equivalent to cutting the lifeline to their soul. This has huge implications, especially for institutionalized older adults, because staff members may assume that if a resident has dementia, he or she has no spiritual needs. Practitioners can help individuals with dementia by asking them about their spiritual needs or, if necessary, by asking friends or family about the individual's spiritual and religious practices before the dementia (MacKinlay, 2006). Practitioners may engage in this conversation with families or individuals as part of the initial interview process that occurs during institutionalization or when seeking services through an agency. Using the information will allow service providers to link available services to the individual that will meet his or her religious or spiritual needs. Depending on the level of disease progression, LGBT older adults with dementia, like their heterosexual counterparts, may experience more difficulty expressing their spiritual or religious needs because of their inability to effectively communicate with others.

Individuals with dementia not only face challenges associated with decline in mental ability but may also experience unique challenges related to end-of-life decisions. Ideally, those with dementia have made advanced directives for their health care needs either before their diagnosis or while they were still able to make decisions for themselves. For these individuals, an end-of-life decision may not include medical interventions but instead an acceptance of their prognosis, and they may put a "do not resuscitate" order in place. Upon accepting one's diagnosis, the greater process of acceptance can begin, and for some, spiritual or religious routines and practices may be appropriate and helpful.

Spiritual Reminiscence

MacKinlay (2006) described *spiritual reminiscence* as the process of expressing one's story, emphasizing aspects of joy, sadness, and the ultimate meaning of life. By emphasizing these aspects of an individual's story, spiritual reminiscence has been shown to be an effective way to speak to older adults about meaning in life, joy, sadness, and grief (Trevitt & MacKinlay, 2006). Through storytelling and life review, spiritual reminiscence addresses individuals' wants, hopes, and fears as well as other aspects of their spirituality that need to be addressed in their final years (MacKinlay, 2006; MacKinlay & Trevitt, 2010). Dementia can make finding meaning more difficult, but with caregivers carefully bringing up the subject and piecing together information, individuals' needs can be identified and communicated. Trevitt and MacKinlay (2006) also indicated that spiritual reminiscence may be an effective tool to help those with dementia cope with the diagnosis and in turn help them accept the lives they are currently living.

Caregivers must be vigilant to the spiritual needs of older adults and their importance in their lives. In an institutionalized setting, staff should be willing to ask residents about their spiritual needs rather than make assumptions, which may prove to be incorrect. MacKinlay (2006) pointed out certain assumptions that may be made, such as "the resident has dementia and thus no spiritual needs"; "the resident does not attend church services, therefore she has no spiritual needs"; and "the resident goes to church, therefore he has spiritual needs that are met" (p. 66). These assumptions are not strictly reserved for those in long-term-care settings, but for caregivers in the home or hospital as well. The search for someone's spiritual meaning is a challenge within itself, and for those who are LGBT, spiritual searching can be even more challenging. So in essence, it may be an even larger undertaking to uncover the true meaning of an individual's spirituality. Developing tools and practices to deter bias can help with these challenges in various health care settings.

PALLIATIVE CARE

Palliative care, also referred to as *hospice care*, is aimed at making an individual's experiences at the end of his or her life more peaceful, comfortable, and pain free. The World Health Organization (2014) defined palliative care as

> an approach that improves the quality of life of patients and their families facing the problems associated with life-threatening illness, through the prevention and relief of suffering by means of early identification and impeccable assessment and treatment of pain and other problems, physical, psychosocial and spiritual. (p. 1)

Traditionally, chaplains and pastors have been associated with, and considered solely responsible for, spiritual care of individuals nearing the end of their lives (MacKinlay, 2006). As this traditional assumption has faded, the general use of spiritual care during palliative care has increased. In the first author's experience as a hospice volunteer, the services provided by hospice organizations for their patients are nothing short of amazing, offering a full and diverse network of care providers including nurses, nurse aides, doctors, social workers, and chaplains. The care providers focus on gathering support from family, friends, and even volunteers from the community. For patients who receive palliative care, the social relationships they have developed over the course of their lives come together to serve as a network providing emotional support (Rawlings, 2012). Currently, the importance of spiritual care as a resource for those experiencing their end-of-life journey is evident. Palliative care was the first discipline to recognize this and include it in the services provided (Rumbold, 2006).

Providers of hospice care are not fully prepared to address the unique issues that LGBT older adults face. Although hospice professionals collect a comprehensive history on each individual, questions related to sexual health history can be intimidating and viewed as unnecessary. Therefore, this assessment may be overlooked or purposefully skipped, leaving the patient without his or her needs documented or addressed. This is evident in Rawlings's (2012) case study of end-of-life decisions for LGBT individuals. In the conclusion of her article, she states that those who provide palliative care do not fully understand the degree to which LGBT individuals have experienced hostility, violence, or rejection throughout their lives. These life experiences can provide a unique set of challenges for LGBT older adults in terms of seeking end-of-life care and how they experience this care. For example, LGBT older adults may not wish to speak about their sexuality openly for fear of retaliation by staff in the form of not providing care; they may also not want to endure harassment or other forms of abuse during the final journey of their lives. Rawlings's primary recommendation for palliative care providers is to focus on dignity, respect, and fairness. Following this recommendation has the potential to improve overall outcomes and quality of life.

Palliative care has the potential to be one of the most effective services to meet the unique needs of those members of the LGBT population nearing the end of life. This cannot be accomplished without many changes or without tolerance from those who work within the field. Awareness of LGBT adults' unique needs is vitally important and will help improve their end-of-life experiences.

CAUSES FOR LIMITATIONS TO CARE

A primary disadvantage that LGBT older adults face is the care and support available to them from their chosen families. Research from Blando (2001) indicates that LGBT older adults are more likely to live alone than their heterosexual counterparts or to be more closely associated with chosen families of the same age. Heterosexual older adults may rely on their children for their care needs as they age, relying less on their spouse if they are physically unable. Research has shown that LGBT older adults are more likely not to have children, and their chosen family is who they turn to for assistance. A large problem with this is that because these chosen family members are often in the same age group, they may not be able to offer the support a younger individual could (e.g., an adult child, a grandchild). Therefore, some LGBT older adults may face increased challenges as they age and may be more vulnerable to illness and premature death.

In the United States, the population is largely heterosexual. Gates (2012) analyzed all credible population-based surveys and concluded that only 3.8% of the U.S. population identifies as LGBT. Therefore, in our society, some may falsely assume that an individual is heterosexual and may be more prone to do so for those who are over age 65. Making such assumptions presents challenges for access and quality of care for older LGBT individuals, whether they are institutionalized or receiving outpatient or in-home services. Asking questions about one's past, including past and present sexual behaviors and experiences, can be crucial to providing adequate care.

But LGBT older adults sometimes go "back in the closet" if institutionalization is needed or they begin receiving other care services for fear of backlash from care providers. Haber (2009) pointed out that access to programs and services is hampered by the sexual orientation of older adults. Their inability to attend certain programs and services may be hindered by discrimination among providers or fellow participants, which can create an unwelcoming environment. Programs and services that may not be accessible to LGBT older adults include senior centers, congregate meal programs, public housing shelters, and many private counseling services. From a psychosocial perspective, the specific needs of older LGBT adults may be unmet if they hide their sexual orientation or gender identity. However, many LGBT older adults may hide their sexual orientation or gender identity because of fear of retribution (Shankle, Maxwell, Katzman, & Landers, 2003), and hence their needs may go unmet.

One event that had a significant impact on LGBT older adults was the Stonewall riots of 1969. For many years, patrons of gay bars were taken to jail because of their sexuality and conduct. Police would frequently raid the bars and take away patrons whom they perceived as "unusual." The bars were then fined but allowed to reopen if they paid the small fines. One evening at the Stonewall Inn, a raid took place that would change the gay community forever. As the raid was happening outside and arrests were being made, chaos erupted, and the police went inside the bar to continue their crusade. The bar patrons were attempting to show that they wanted to be treated equally and were not afraid to fight for equality. Riots and demonstrations continued for several days. These events are largely held to have prompted the gay rights movement.

Equal rights for the LGBT population have gradually improved since that time, but events and prejudices before the Stonewall riots may still play a significant role in the perceptions of the older LGBT population. Because of the discrimination by law enforcement and other officials, it is understandable that some LGBT older adults would want to remain in the closet. Historically speaking, disclosing one's sexuality may have had negative repercussions, and some may have decided to stay closeted to prevent negative responses. The Stonewall riots may have been a defining movement in the collective histories of current LGBT older adults, but with the reality that more progress is still necessary for equal rights, their hesitation to be forthcoming with their sexual identity is the continued result of prolonged discrimination. As stated earlier, past events and collective memories have shaped the spiritual and religious views of LGBT older adults, and their impact may be evident when end-of-life care is necessary. For instance, a negative religious or spiritual experience may cause individuals not to pursue end-of-life care for fear of backlash with regard to their sexuality. Fear of judgment from care providers or a chaplain because of one's sexuality can give rise to apprehension in choosing this type of care.

Halkitis and colleagues (2009) found that a majority of older LGBT adults in their study were raised in religious households, but only one quarter were currently members of any religious organization. The gay rights movement has been pivotal for LGBT adults, helping to liberate many and contributing to an overall more positive psychosocial well-being. This process may have included changes in religious and spiritual affiliations for older LGBT adults. Finding organizations that were more accepting of their sexual orientation or gender identity may have taken precedence in their quest to continue practicing religion and/or express their spiritually.

END-OF-LIFE DECISIONS

For LGBT older adults, the word *family* can have an entirely different meaning than it has for their heterosexual counterparts. This meaning is dependent in some cases on whether LGBT older adults have disclosed their sexual identity to family members or are still closeted, as well as the degree of their own acceptance of their disclosed identities. *Heteronormativity* is defined as the assumptions that normal gender roles coincide with biological sex and heterosexuality is the assumed sexual preference (Oxford English Dictionary Online, http://www.oed.com). Heteronormativity and discrimination on the basis of sexual orientation do not create a friendly environment for older LGBT adults who require care (Cartwright, Hughes, & Lienert, 2012). The challenges associated with family and end-of-life decisions can be stressful for anyone, but a conflict may exist between chosen families and biological families when an individual is incapable of making his or her own decisions and one of the groups must take responsibility. There may be tension between the two, even if the older adult is estranged from his or her biological family.

In the United States, the public largely believes that family is more than just a relationship defined by the legal system or the U.S. Census Bureau, and a life partner is not traditionally defined as a family member (Cahill & Tobias, 2007). A majority of policies define family as a legal unit consisting primarily of a man and woman who either have their own children or have adopted children (Cahill & Tobias, 2007). However, the family may be quite different for an LGBT older adult and could, therefore, vary greatly from the common societal view or legal definition. As a result, the potential for hostility and rejection by a person's biological family because of his or her sexual orientation and personal beliefs will affect who is considered family by an older LGBT adult (Stein & Almack, 2012). LGBT older adults may often rely on *chosen families*—selected individuals who are not biologically related to them but whom they consider family and often go to for support. Individuals in a chosen family are often selected because of a certain relationship or social tie (Stein & Almack, 2012). These individuals include past partners, partner's family, and friends of long standing. By having a chosen family, LGBT older adults are able to form relationships and a sense of community in a creative way that helps offset the negativity placed on them by society and family (Knauer, 2012).

End-of-life decisions can be tricky for LGBT older adults, especially if they are partnered. Not all U.S. states recognize same-sex marriages or domestic partnerships; therefore, LGBT elders' wishes may not always be respected or carried out, so having advance directives regarding health care and financial wishes is especially important. Current laws may not recognize a person's partner or chosen family as the next of kin, and this may hold true even if an LGBT older adult is estranged from his or her biological family. As a result, if there is no advance directive granting power of attorney to someone else, an LGBT elder's biological family members may be automatically granted the right to make decisions on his or her behalf. LGBT older adults, including those with general advance directives, should ideally have a comprehensive care plan that outlines their wishes in detail (Knauer, 2012). A detailed care plan will prevent the legal next of kin from making decisions contrary to what is on a traditional advance directive (Knauer, 2012). Detailed advance planning is essential for all individuals, but for LGBT individuals in states that do not recognize civil unions, domestic partnerships, or same-sex marriage, such planning is essential to ensure that the appropriate people are carrying out their wishes.

The laws that have been put in place to protect heterosexual older adults fail to adequately address the problems that LGBT older adults, partnered or single, face (Services & Advocacy for GLBT Elders & Movement Advancement Project, 2010). Awareness of the legal issues facing LGBT older adults should be focused on this area of "family" and how current laws can be changed to support LGBT elders. The ideal changes would include the recognition of a chosen family and LGBT older adults' ability to have the same rights and benefits as their heterosexual counterparts.

Since the November 2012 elections, more states have been added to the list of those that honor same-sex marriage. According to the NGLTF (2014), 17 states and the District of Columbia allow same-sex marriage. A number of other states offer domestic partnerships and civil unions, but with some limitations attached. These are huge steps forward for these states and for the country. LGBT older adults residing in these states may feel a little more at ease when preparing to make end-of-life decisions.

Addressing cultural, racial, and ethnic diversity is important when discussing end-of-life care. Different cultures have different values and beliefs, which can make it difficult to access appropriate care. Here we discuss issues of end-of-life care for African Americans and Hispanics because they represent a large proportion of the U.S. population. Furthermore, they face cultural challenges that have an even greater impact on those who also identify as LGBT.

A majority of African Americans face a unique set of challenges when it comes to receiving end-of-life care (Mouton, 2000). Mouton (2000) noted that the health care system in the United States is primarily run by Caucasians. He stated that some people of other races or ethnicities may have fears about the care they will receive, and as a result, they will not obtain care. The current cohorts of African American older adults lived through a historical time of racial disparities but today have gained more rights and freedoms compared with previous cohorts. *Double jeopardy*, as described by Ferraro and Farmer (1996), is the disadvantage that those who are of minority descent face in later life, which they described as being over age 65. As a result of double jeopardy, an African American older adult who is also LGBT would likely have faced even more institutional discrimination throughout his or her life, and therefore his or her willingness to seek out care would be even further diminished.

Hispanics are another large and rapidly growing segment of the U.S. population. It is important to remember that Hispanics come from a number of diverse countries. There are similarities among these subgroups, however; for example, a majority of them share a common language (with slightly different dialects), religion, and cultural attitudes toward familial relationships (Talamantes, Gomes, & Braun, 2000). Research has shown that in general, Hispanics are less likely to access the care they need. This could be due to language barriers, financial issues, mistrust of the health care system (or government-run systems), or certain religious preferences. Talamantes et al. (2006) also described the lack of knowledge among some health care providers regarding Hispanic belief systems, including familial, religious, and social roles. They also described the need for service providers to have a basic knowledge of the Spanish language or, ideally, to speak Spanish fluently because many Hispanic older adults may not be proficient in the English language. Talamantes et al. also suggested that as service providers gain increased knowledge and understanding of the Hispanic culture, Hispanic older adults may begin to trust the system and seek out services, but this process will take time. Hispanic older adults who identify as being LGBT may encounter even greater difficulty accessing adequate services.

ADDRESSING END-OF-LIFE GUIDANCE ISSUES

The purposes of end-of-life planning are to enable a person to express his or her final wishes and to provide valuable information to survivors. Many care services, including law firms, hospice organizations, and funeral homes, provide guidance for making such decisions. Reference guidelines for end-of-life planning, such as the Millhorn Law Firm's (2013) *Guide for End-of-Life Planning*, include topics related to general aspects of the average person's life, which offers the opportunity to thoroughly define one's wishes. Topics addressed in these guides, which are heteronormative in nature, include items such as (a) marital status (e.g., single, married, widowed, or divorced), (b) biological family relationships (e.g., parents, children, grandchildren, and brother/sister), and (c) religion (a specific affiliation). Furthermore, end-of-life planning guides instruct individuals on how to state their wishes, which are to be adhered to after death. These may include (a) disposition preference (e.g., burial or cremation), (b) memorial services, (c) financial information (e.g., safe deposit box, assets, life insurance), and (d) personal property disposition. Through these guides, wishes can be upheld after death with current laws dictating the powers that are awarded to chosen families and nonlegally recognized partners.

All information included in end-of-life planning is helpful for the general population. However, general guidelines almost always assume a heterosexual identity. For example, when addressing marital status, married, single, widowed, and divorced are typically the only options. Forms rarely recognize partnerships or civil unions. These statuses would more likely be used by the LGBT population in accordance with federal acknowledgment of homosexual relationships. The assumption that the deceased is heterosexual not only ignores partnered relationships and civil unions but also excludes the reality of chosen families. Again, some members of the LGBT aging population do not confide or interact with their biological family but rather depend on others as their chosen family. And again, the definition of *family* can be a substantial aspect of an individual's life. When the category of family includes only biological relationships, vital details about the deceased's life and wishes can be overlooked.

Another aspect assumed by end-of-life guidelines relates to religion. As previously explained, religion and spirituality are not necessarily synonymous (MacKinlay, 2006). Often, end-of-life planning guides, such as the Millhorn Law Firm's (2013) guide or the *Hastings Center Guidelines for Decisions on Life-Sustaining Treatment and Care Near the End of Life* (Berlinger, Jennings, & Wolf, 2013), ask for religious affiliations and various customs associated with any particular religion. The assumption that a person associates himself or herself with an organized religion eliminates the possibility that he or she may identify as spiritual and not religious. When all potential aspects of a person's life are included in end-of-life planning guides, one's wishes are more likely adhered to because they are known.

Changes to the standard end-of-life guidelines, as used by hospice organizations, to accommodate LGBT elders and other unique populations would be beneficial to providers, clients, and family members (including chosen family). For example, including partnership and civil union options for marital status acknowledges the LGBT population who are more likely to use these relationship categories because of current federal and state laws on same-sex marriage. Including this section would decrease heteronormativity and enable better data collection on the person planning for his or her end of life and thereby provide vital information to make the appropriate accommodations for each individual. Addressing chosen families and recognizing that these people may be as important to the individual—if not more so—than biological family members will also ensure that the wishes of the deceased are carried out accurately. Finally, religion and spirituality both need to be included when discussing customs and beliefs. Definitions of both terms are individually subjective, and therefore each topic needs to be addressed on its own to gain a well-rounded perspective on one's wishes during end-of-life planning.

CONCLUSION

LGBT older adults face a multitude of challenges stemming from years of oppression. Whether for their sexuality, gender identity, or religion, LGBT elders have encountered obstacles that their heterosexual counterparts have not. In today's society, being an LGBT person has become more socially acceptable in some parts of the United States, but the stigma still has an impact on both younger and older LGBT adults.

The challenges that LGBT older adults encounter may prevent them from accessing appropriate care and making accurate and effective end-of-life decisions. For example, many years of discrimination have left lasting impressions on the LGBT population, resulting in hesitation to come out to family, friends, and care providers. This has negative implications for health that could be prevented if these older adults had the opportunity to express themselves openly, without fear of discrimination.

Addressing spirituality as an alternative to religion allows for a wider perspective on how an older adult functions, acts, and thinks in response to a given situation. Openness and tolerance from care providers will also facilitate a stronger relationship with older adults who have unique needs, such as the aging LGBT population.

Society is gradually becoming more tolerant of the LGBT population. However, there remains a need for activism for LGBT rights, as well as more research on issues specifically affecting older adults who identify as LGBT. Continued research on LGBT older adults and their families, spirituality, and on the effects of federal law and social movements will have an impact on our progress in becoming a more tolerant society. The increased longevity and positive health outcomes resulting from this research will benefit the LGBT population and society as a whole.

REFERENCES

Bengtson, V. L., & Allen, K. R. (1993). The life course perspective applied to families over time. In P. G. Boss, W. J. Doherty, R. LaRossa, W. R. Schumm, & S. K. Steinmetz (Eds.), *Sourcebook of family theories and methods: A contextual approach* (pp. 469–504). New York, NY: Plenum Press. doi:10.1007/978-0-387-85764-0_19

Berlinger, N., Jennings, B., & Wolf, S. M. (2013). *The Hastings Center guidelines for decisions on life-sustaining treatment and care near the end of life: Revised and expanded* (2nd ed.). New York, NY: Oxford University Press. doi:10.1093/acprof:oso/9780199974566.001.0001

Blando, J. (2001). Twice hidden: Older gay and lesbian couples, friends, and intimacy. *Generations, 25*, 87–89.

Blevins, D., & Werth, J. L. (2006). End-of-life issues for lesbian, gay, bisexual, and transgendered older adults. In D. Kimmel, T. Rose, & S. David (Eds.), *Lesbian, gay, bisexual, and transgender aging: Research and Clinical perspectives* (pp. 206–226). New York, NY: Columbia University Press.

Cahill, S., & Tobias, S. (2007). *Policy issues affecting lesbian, gay, bisexual, and transgender families*. Ann Arbor: The University of Michigan Press.

Cartwright, C., Hughes, M., & Lienert, T. (2012). End-of-life care for gay, lesbian, bisexual and transgender people. *Culture, Health & Sexuality, 14*, 537–548. doi:10.1080/13691058.2012.673639

Centers for Disease Control and Prevention. (2010). *HIV among older Americans*. Retrieved from http://www.cdc.gov/hiv/risk/age/olderamericans/index.html

Centers for Disease Control and Prevention. (2013). *HIV among men in the United States*. Retrieved from: http://www.cdc.gov/hiv/risk/gender/men/index.html

Cohen, M. Z., Holley, L. M., Wengel, S. P., & Katzman, R. (2012). A platform for nursing research on spirituality and religiosity: Definitions and measures. *Western Journal of Nursing Research, 34*, 795–817. doi:10.1177/0193945912444321

Ferraro, K. F., & Farmer, M. M. (1996). Double jeopardy to health hypothesis for African Americans: Analysis and critique. *Journal of Health and Social Behavior, 37*, 27–43. doi:10.2307/2137229

Gates, G. J. (2012). LGBT identity: A demographer's perspective. *Loyola of Los Angeles Law Review, 45*, 693–714.

Haber, D. (2009). Gay aging. *Gerontology & Geriatrics Education, 30*, 267–280. doi:10.1080/02701960903133554

Halkitis, P. N., Mattis, J. S., Sahadath, J. K., Massie, D., Ladyzhenskaya, L., Pitrelli, K., . . . Cowie, S. E. (2009). The meanings and manifestations of religion and spirituality among lesbian, gay, bisexual, and transgender adults. *Journal of Adult Development, 16*, 250–262. doi:10.1007/s10804-009-9071-1

Hughes, A. K., Harold, R. D., & Boyer, J. M. (2011). Awareness of LGBT aging issues among aging services network providers. *Journal of Gerontological Social Work, 54*, 659–677.

Knauer, N. (2012). "Gen silent": Advocating for LGBT elders. *The Elder Law Journal*, *19*, 100–161.

Larson, D. B., Swyers, J. P., & McCullough, M. E. (1998). *Scientific research on spirituality and health. A report based on the scientific progress in spirituality conferences.* Rockville, MD: National Institute of Healthcare Research.

MacKinlay, E. (2006). Spiritual care: Recognizing spiritual needs for older adults. In E. MacKinlay (Ed.), *Aging, spirituality and palliative care* (pp. 59–71). New York, NY: Haworth Pastoral Press. doi:10.1300/J496v18n02_05

MacKinlay, E., & Trevitt, C. (2010). Living in aged care: Using spiritual reminiscence to enhance meaning in life for those with dementia. *International Journal of Mental Health Nursing, 19*, 394–401. doi:10.1111/j.1447-0349.2010.00684.x

MacRae, N. (2010). Sexuality and aging. In R. H. Robnett & W. C. Chop (Eds.), *Gerontology for the health care professional* (2nd ed., pp. 235–258). Sudbury, MA: Jones and Bartlett.

MetLife Mature Market Institute. (2006). *Out and aging: The MetLife study of lesbian and gay baby boomers.* Retrieved from http://www.metlife.com/assets/cao/mmi/publications/studies/mmi-out-aging-lesbian-gay-retirement.pdf

Millhorn Law Firm. (2013). *A guide for end-of-life planning.* Retrieved from http://millhorn.com/e-learning-center.php?elcId=1

Mouton, C. (2000). Cultural and religious issues for African Americans. In K. Braun, J. Pietsch, & P. Blanchette (Eds.), *Cultural issues in end-of-life decision making* (pp. 71–82). Thousand Oaks, CA: Sage.

National Gay and Lesbian Task Force. (2010). *FAQ sheet on LGBT elders & outing age 2010.* Retrieved from http://www.thetaskforce.org/downloads/release_materials/outing_age_2010_faq.pdf

National Gay and Lesbian Task Force. (2014). *Relationship recognition for same-sex couples in the U.S.* Retrieved from http://www.thetaskforce.org/downloads/reports/issue_maps/rel_recog_1_6_14_color.pdf

Orel, N. A. (2004). Gay, lesbian, and bisexual elders: Expressed needs and concerns across focus groups. *Journal of Gerontological Social Work, 43*, 57–77. doi:10.1300/J083v43n02_05

Rawlings, D. (2012). End-of-life care considerations for gay, lesbian, bisexual, and transgender individuals. *International Journal of Palliative Nursing, 18*, 29–34.

Robinson, B. A. (1999). *Policies of religious groups towards homosexuals and homosexuality.* Retrieved from http://www.religioustolerance.org/hom_chur.htm

Rumbold, B. (2006). The spirituality of compassion: A public health response to ageing and end-of-life care. In E. MacKinlay (Ed.), *Aging, spirituality and palliative care* (pp. 31–44). New York, NY: Haworth Pastoral Press. doi:10.1300/J496v18n02_03

Services & Advocacy for GLBT Elders & Movement Advancement Project. (2010). *Improving the lives of LGBT older adults.* Retrieved from http://lgbtagingcenter.org/resources/pdfs/ImprovingtheLivesofLGBTOlderAdultsFull.pdf

Shankle, M., Maxwell, C., Katzman, E., & Landers, S. (2003). An invisible population: Older lesbian, gay, bisexual, and transgender individuals. *Clinical Research and Regulatory Affairs, 20*, 159–182. doi:10.1081/CRP-120021079

Stein, G. L., & Almack, K. (2012). Care near the end of life: The concerns, needs, and experiences of LGBT elders. In R. Ward, I. Rivers, & M. Sutherland (Eds.). *Lesbian, gay, bisexual and transgender ageing: Biographical approaches for inclusive care and support.* New York, NY: Jessica Kingsley.

Talamantes, M., Gomez, C., & Braun, K. (2000). Advanced directives and end-of-life care: The Hispanic perspective. In K. Braun, J. Pietsch, & P. Blanchette (Eds.), *Cultural issues in end-of-life decision making* (pp. 83–100). Thousand Oaks, CA: Sage.

Tan, P. P. (2005). The importance of spirituality among gay and lesbian individuals. *Journal of Homosexuality, 49*, 135–144. doi:10.1300/J082v49n02_08

Trevitt, C., & MacKinlay, E. (2006). "I am just an ordinary person . . . ": Spiritual reminiscence in older people with memory loss. In E. MacKinlay (Ed.), *Aging, spirituality and palliative care* (pp. 79–91). New York, NY: Haworth Pastoral Press. doi:10.1300/J496v18n02_07

U.S. Census Bureau. (2010). *The next four decades: The older population in the United States: 2010–2050.* Retrieved from http://www.census.gov/prod/2010pubs/p25-1138.pdf

World Health Organization (2014). *WHO definition of palliative care.* Retrieved from http://www.who.int/cancer/palliative/definition/en

6

ACCESS AND EQUITY IN THE DESIGN AND DELIVERY OF HEALTH AND SOCIAL CARE TO LGBTQ OLDER ADULTS: A CANADIAN PERSPECTIVE

SHARI BROTMAN, ILYAN FERRER, TAMARA SUSSMAN,
BILL RYAN, AND BRENDA RICHARD

Inquiries into the lived experiences of lesbian, gay, bisexual, transgender, and queer (LGBTQ) older adults offer the potential to critically assess current social and health care systems, shedding light on the extent to which diverse populations have access to equitable services. Research on the older LGBTQ community has burgeoned within the past decade due in large part to the resistance, resilience, and advocacy work of LGBTQ seniors and their allies, whose collective lives have been captured only recently in gerontological literature (M. T. Brown, 2009; Fredriksen-Goldsen & Muraco, 2010). Although in terms of legal equality, particularly in Canada, there have been tremendous strides in acknowledging the histories of struggle and social marginalization within LGBTQ communities, themes of invisibility continue to serve as a crucial backdrop to their stories of aging. Health and social care services are implicated in the social exclusion and marginalization of

This chapter was developed with the financial support of the Centre de recherche et d'expertise en gérontologie sociale and the Centre de santé et de service sociaux Cavendish-Affilié universitaire.

DOI: 10.1037/14436-006
The Lives of LGBT Older Adults: Understanding Challenges and Resilience, N. A. Orel and C. A. Fruhauf (Editors)
Copyright © 2015 by the American Psychological Association. All rights reserved.

LGBTQ older adults through histories of discrimination in which heterosexism, homophobia, and transphobia were institutional, and gender expressions and sexualities beyond hetero- and cisnormativity[1] were pathologized.

ORGANIZATION OF THE CURRENT CHAPTER

In this chapter, we discuss the accessibility of health and social care to LGBTQ older adults within a Canadian context. We encountered several challenges in putting together this chapter. First, the Canadian literature continues to be sparse, requiring us to use a wider body of international (mostly U.S.-based) literature to explore the major themes that emerge in the research on service delivery. Although these themes are consistent across borders, we must not forget that current legal and policy arenas are markedly different, particularly when considering the jurisdictions of Canada and the United States. To contextualize our work, we begin with a short review of the historical context as well as recent legal and social policy developments in Canada. This will help to situate our recommendations for research, service delivery, and activism outlined at the end of the chapter. We target these recommendations at the level of institutions and professions, the primary repositories for current change making in Canada. Second, we call the reader's attention to the separation of issues of sexuality (sexual orientation, heteronormativity, and homophobia) and gender identity (cisnormativity and transphobia), particularly in the sections in which we review the literature. Although much activist work in recent years has brought lesbian, gay, bisexual, and transgender communities together to fight for social and institutional change, particularly in realms related to aging, social and legal histories as well as previous literature in social gerontology are markedly distinct for each community and require separate consideration and analysis. As well, much of the research on LGBTQ aging to date has excluded transgender people and their realities. To avoid compounding this omission, we have attempted to write distinct sections on access and equity in service delivery, focusing first on what we know in the context of lesbian, gay, and bisexual (LGB) populations and second on what we know specifically about transgender populations. Next, we discuss the gaps in the literature and the ways in which a life course approach, enhanced by an intersectionality framework, can bring diversity and multiple realities into the forefront of future LGBTQ research and practice. Finally, we discuss efforts to address inequities in health and social care access and service delivery in Canada by activists representing multiple perspectives across regions.

---

[1]Bauer et al. (2009) defined *cisnormativity* as the assumption that every individual assigned male at birth will always grow up to be men and those assigned female at birth will always grow up to be women.

As authors, we necessarily come to our work with our reflexive positions and social locations intact, and so we have chosen, in our research and writing, to engage in a way that calls attention to our experiences and identities. In the context of this chapter, we would like readers to know that, as professionals and activists, we have extensive knowledge on a range of issues related to aging and older LGBTQ adults, access, and equity (Brotman, Richard, Ryan, and Sussman), antioppression practice and intersectional analyses (Brotman, Ferrer, and Richard), long-term-care (Brotman and Sussman), and immigration and migration (Brotman and Ferrer). Although we represent a mixed team of LGBTQ people and their allies who engage in research, scholar-activist, and advocacy work, we cannot claim to represent the voices of many of those whom we discuss in this chapter, most notably transgender people or older adults themselves. This chapter has offered us an opportunity to reflect on our work and to combine our respective analytical lenses to critically assess and analyze the health and social care issues that face aging and aged LGBTQ adults. Where relevant, we use examples from our various research projects undertaken over the past 10 years to highlight emerging themes and incorporate the voices of those older adults and activists who have spoken with us and to whom we are grateful for their participation and their efforts toward change.

KEY ISSUES WITHIN THE LGBTQ COMMUNITY: PROGRESS AND PERILS WITHIN THE CANADIAN CONTEXT

The generational and cohort experiences that LGBTQ adults have faced over the past century offer a nuanced and diverse perspective on aging in Canada. Having lived through some of the most conservative and politically repressive climates, LGBTQ persons have gone through experiences characterized by intense vulnerability, oppression, and discrimination in all realms of their social lives, including employment, housing, health care, and social and family life (Brotman, Ryan, & Cormier, 2003; Donahue & McDonald, 2005; Namaste, 1999, 2009). Most of these experiences can be attributed to the prevailing social climate, which lasted well into the late 20th century—perpetuating the hegemony of heteronormativity and cisnormativity through the pathologizing of individuals and communities. Together, heterosexism, homophobia, and transphobia have defined the social mores within Canadian society (Fone, 2000). For example, in 1967, in an article in *Canadian Nurse* titled "Homosexuality Among Women," Rancourt and Limoges described being lesbian as an "addiction" and as a "retarded social development." These views were shared by health care professionals who publically problematized and pathologized sexual minority status and gender nonconformity as deviance. McLeod (1996) also reported that a leading psychiatrist at the University of Toronto stated that homosexuals would never be "well-adjusted people" (p. 39). This hegemony informed and directed academic and public discourse to focus on finding the cause and cure for homosexuality.

From a social policy and legal standpoint, Canada has witnessed tremendous change, beginning in 1967, when then Justice Minister Pierre Trudeau introduced Bill C-150 in the House of Commons to remove homosexuality, previously a crime, from Canada's Criminal Code. This occurred at a time when the momentum of progressive movements began to be felt with mass mobilization among advocacy groups in North America founded thanks to the National Gay Rights Coalition (1964) and the Stonewall Rebellion in New York City (1969), among other local events. These had a galvanizing impact on LGBTQ activists in Canada and around the world. Still, it was not until decades later that changes began to fully take shape in Canada. In 1977, Québec became the first jurisdiction in Canada, and the second in the world, to extend human rights protection to LGB citizens. Ontario became the second province in 1985. Then, in the landmark case of *Egan v Canada* (1995; 2S.C.R. 513), the Supreme Court of Canada declared that sexual orientation was an analogous ground of discrimination (Egale Canada, 2004, pp. 2–3). The provinces and territories were, as a result, required to recognize sexual orientation as a basic human right enshrined in their Human Rights Acts, thereby including it as a prohibited ground of discrimination. By 1998, all provinces, territories, and the federal government prohibited discrimination on the basis of sexual orientation. Additional changes were included in the Civil Marriage Act passed by Parliament on July 20, 2005, thus permitting same-sex partners to marry. Given the lengthy struggles for human rights in Canada, LGB people of all ages could be said to have achieved a high degree of legal and policy recognition. The situation for transgender individuals continues to lag behind. A recent report released by Egale Canada (2012) Human Rights Trust highlights how laws that prohibit discrimination on the basis of gender identity vary considerably across jurisdictions.[2] Until such recognition is acknowledged at the federal level, transgender people will continue to have their rights undermined by state-imposed restrictions and regulations (Egale Canada, 2012).

Although the rights and welfare of many LGBTQ people are being acknowledged by law and social policy changes, it is important to note that the task of dismantling the multiple forms of social and institutional

---

[2]The Northwest Territories has protected gender identity since 1999, Ontario and Manitoba since 2012, and Nova Scotia since 2013. Currently, legislation is pending before the Federal Parliament that would extend protection to transgender people in the Canadian Human Rights Code.

discrimination still often falls on individuals, their allies, and groups of LGBTQ activists themselves (Brotman et al., 2003; Egale Canada, 2012; Haber, 2009; McLeod, 1996; Ryan, 2003). Despite the advances that have been made, much work needs to be done at the institutional level, where practices within health and social care systems still hold general biases that problematize the social complexity LGBTQ persons have had to navigate all their lives. This is particularly true for older LGBTQ adults, who have lived through the social and political transitions of LGBTQ rights and liberation but may not have reaped the benefits. For instance, the necessary strategies for survival over the life course among today's older members of LGBTQ communities required that sexual minority status and transgender identity be subverted and that traditional social engagement be limited to subcultural status (Bonneau, 1998; Cronin, Ward, Pugh, King, & Price, 2011; Fredriksen-Goldsen & Muraco, 2010; Haber, 2009). Individuals were effectively forced into the "closet" where, marginalized from mainstream activity, LGBTQ older adults were required to live outside sites of hetero- and cisnormative privilege and service. The painstaking means taken to be "in the closet" or "out of the closet" were arranged in pursuit of safety, security, and peace. For those older LGBTQ adults who were born before the development of the gay liberation movement in Canada or who lived in regions in which there was little opportunity to develop a sense of gay community, "keeping things private" (the term many of the participants in several of our studies used to describe their reality) is still a commonly adopted survival strategy. Much research has documented that today's cohort of LGBTQ seniors may neither self-identify as LGBTQ nor feel a sense of belonging within the LGBTQ community. This makes older LGBTQ adults more vulnerable to invisibility and marginalization within the health, social, and community care arenas. As activists and allies, we must pay particular attention to ensure that access and equity initiatives take into account these unique lived experiences.

WHAT WE KNOW FROM THE LITERATURE: ISSUES IN PROVISION, DELIVERY, AND ACCESS IN LONG-TERM-CARE AND RESIDENTIAL SETTINGS

In the Context of Lesbian, Gay, and Bisexual Aging

In a scan of peer-reviewed literature within the past 25 years, Fredriksen-Goldsen and Muraco (2010) suggested that research on sexual orientation and age can be characterized by four waves. The earliest studies focused on challenging negative stereotypes as they related to mental health (depression) and maladjustment to aging, contesting widely held beliefs that older gay men and lesbians were alone, isolated, and depressed. The second and third waves were focused on positive psychosocial functioning despite structural inequality and discrimination and the transition to identity development over time (Fredriksen-Goldsen & Muraco, 2010). More recent research has focused on examining the social support and community-based needs and experiences of older adults through access to housing, health, and caregiving services. It is important to note, however, that although research addressing sexual orientation and age has blossomed considerably over the past decade, the vast majority of this work addresses only gay men and lesbian women. Except in a few rare cases, bisexual older adults continue to be subsumed within the umbrella of LGB without much attention paid to their unique needs and realities (Dworkin, 2006; Kingston, 2002; Rodriguez-Rust, 2012). The following review of literature draws on the fourth wave of work to address the main thematic areas of research from the past two decades.

Access and Invisibility

With respect to access, much research has documented the experience of discrimination and invisibility as particularly relevant in the determination of LGB older adults to seek care (Brotman et al., 2003; M. Hughes, 2005; Orel, 2004). Although many LGB older adults expect their health to become an increasingly serious problem as they age, there is consistent distrust of health care providers and fear of antigay bias or overt discrimination, based on past and concurrent experiences of prejudice (City and County of San Francisco, 2003; Heaphy, Yip, & Thompson, 2003; M. Hughes, 2005; Kirby, 1997; McFarland & Sanders, 2003; Orel, 2004; River, 2006). As such, LGB older adults often delay seeking support from the health and social care system and only approach the system in situations of significant distress (Brotman et al., 2003; L. B. Brown, Alley, Sarosy, Quarto, & Cook, 2001). This is particularly problematic given the range of studies on the health impacts of managing stigma in environments of discrimination and invisibility over the life span (Brotman et al., 2003). For example, high rates of depression (Rawls, 2004) and substance use difficulties have been identified as significant mental health concerns for older LGB people (Grossman, D'Augelli, & O'Connell, 2001).

Research has documented the lived experience of homophobia and heterosexism in health and social care facing LGB people over the life course and into old age. Manifestations of discrimination against LGB people have been and continue to be widespread in Canadian society. People have been physically and sexually assaulted and abused because of their sexual orientation by both strangers and people known to them (Balsam & D'Augelli, 2006; Brennan, Hellerstedt, Ross, & Welles, 2007; Demczuk, 1998; Hequembourg, Bimbi, & Parsons, 2011; Hequembourg, Parks, & Vetter, 2008; T. L. Hughes, Johnson, & Wilsnack, 2001). Verbal, emotional and psychological abuse, the more common forms of homophobia, have frequently been experienced by LGB people (Demczuk, 1998; Hequembourg et al., 2008, 2011; Hightow-Weidman et al., 2011). LGB people have faced considerable discrimination in health and social care service systems as well. Because LGB people have historically been socially defined in medical terms as being mentally ill, the health care system has been one of the primary arenas through which control over their lives was exerted. In 1973, the American Psychiatric Association removed homosexuality from the *Diagnostic and Statistical Manual of Mental Disorders*, and in 1992, the World Health Organization removed homosexuality from its list of mental disorders. Despite this, many health care professionals who were educated during the time period preceding these changes, as well as those influenced by social heteronormativity, continue to consider same-sex sexual orientation under the broader rubric of pathology (Balsam & D'Augelli, 2006; Bauer et al., 2009; Jones & Gabriel, 1999; Tomsen, 2006).

LGB people of all ages have reported a range of negative reactions from service providers, including rejection of the patient or exhibition of hostility, harassment, excessive curiosity, pity, condescension, ostracism, refusal of treatment, avoidance of physical contact, and breach of confidentiality (Brotman et al., 2003; Coon, 2007; Daley, 2006; Kauth, Hartwig, & Kalichman, 2000; Meezan & Martin, 2009). Although many of these studies document the health care experiences of LGB people regardless of age, it has been recognized that discrimination in health care is particularly salient for today's LGB older adults (Cahill, South, & Spade, 2000; Concannon, 2009; Cronin et al., 2011; D'Augelli & Grossman, 2001). Indeed, aging services have often been found to be discriminatory environments in which LGB older adults come into contact with much of the same discrimination faced by all LGB people in the health care system (Brotman et al., 2003). In addition, sectors of the aging network in which seniors work or gather (voluntary or social support organizations) or live alongside each other (congregate housing) can expose LGB older adults to further marginalization from contemporaries who hold homophobic and heterosexist attitudes, although the extent to which this is experienced by LGB people is underdocumented in the research.

In recent years, overt discrimination has often been replaced by an atmosphere of silence. This form of neglect must also be seen as an important component of discrimination. Older LGB people are rarely visible in mainstream senior networks, in health care institutions, and in society generally. Health and social care professionals often overlook the importance of addressing sexual orientation. This oversight serves to further marginalize older adults and their caregivers by failing to incorporate lived experiences into assessments, significantly limiting the capacity of service providers to account for important aspects of identity and social location in care planning. The invisibility of LGB older adults in the health care and social service systems also creates important barriers to the development of a social and political voice. Historically, LGB older adults have been excluded from discussion, planning, and programming processes in both mainstream senior networks and LGBTQ community organizations. When the unique needs of these seniors are raised, the most prominent reaction is one of discomfort (Brotman, Ryan, & Cormier, 2002).

Similar to the general older adult population, a vast majority of LGB seniors want to "age in place," remaining in their home and community for as long as possible (Hubbard & Rossington, 1995; McFarland & Sanders, 2003; National Gay and Lesbian Task Force, 2005). This highlights the importance of addressing homophobia and heterosexism in homecare provision. Although some LGB older adults would be unequivocally out to homecare providers, many others have expressed fears of having to hide books, pictures, and other "indicators" of their sexual orientation in their own home to avoid discrimination or being "preached at" (Brotman, Ryan, & Meyer, 2006; Orel, 2004; Stein & Beckerman, 2010; Zodikoff, 2006). For example, our study on access to care for lesbian and gay seniors living in the community found that homecare was an area in which exposure to homophobia and heterosexism was particularly problematic. For older cohorts of seniors who experienced particularly acute forms of violence and oppression in their younger adult lives, before the advent of the gay liberation movement, home was often the only space in which they could live out their identities and relationships in safety and security. Requiring homecare services meant, for many, losing the only space in which they could be themselves in an environment free from discrimination (Brotman et al., 2003). Research on homecare services calls for increasing education and evaluation of homecare providers to address this often neglected area of health and social care, recognizing that the low pay, lack of training, and high turnover of domiciliary staff result in particular systemic barriers to sensitivity training efforts (National Gay and Lesbian Task Force, 2005; River, 2006).

LGB seniors have been called the "most invisible of an already invisible minority group" (Blando, 2001, p. 87). This invisibility has important ramifications for front-line workers, who find it difficult to identify or reach out to such a hidden population (Brotman et al., 2002; City and County of San Francisco, 2003; Porter, Russell, & Sullivan, 2003; River, 2006) and often ignore or disregard patient or client attempts to disclose by donning "cultural blindfolds" (Harrison, 1999, p. 33). Discomfort with and ignorance of issues regarding sexual orientation are also reflected at the highest levels of organizations (Brotman et al., 2003; de Saxe & Lovett, 2004), reinforcing the assumption that either LGB older adults do not exist or their needs are exactly the same as those of their heterosexual peers, despite their opinions to the contrary (Kirby, 1997; River, 2006).

Research assessing attitudes of health care professionals have generally shown consistent lack of awareness when confronted with queries about LGB older adults—a reality that has a detrimental impact on access and equity in health and social care systems and on the building of trusting relationships between service providers and their LGB patients and clients. A majority of professionals have stated, for instance, that they had never had a gay or lesbian senior as a client or resident and did not believe they would have special needs (Opening Doors Thanet, 2003). Many organizations pointed to "equal opportunities" policies and expressed that they "treated everyone the same," reflecting liberal humanist attitudes that may "mask a more oppressive tolerance towards lesbian women and gay men" (Langley, 2001, p. 926). Phillips and Marks (2006) reviewed brochures for elder care facilities and found a complete absence of gay and lesbian representation, communicating systemic heterosexism to any potential resident. A catch-22 situation ensues in which heteronormative environments discourage LGB older adults to openly self-identify and organizations are able to claim that, because they have no identified LGB clients, they do not have to adapt the environment to respond to their unique needs.

Caregiving and Social Support

In terms of community support, the research suggests that cohort distinctions exist with respect to where LGB older adults want to receive care and support. Older LGBTQ adults who grew up before the gay liberation movement or who live in more isolated regions often prefer to receive their support and socialization services in the mainstream system, whereas those seniors who grew up during the gay liberation movement or lived in regions with visible and active gay communities are more likely to seek out social support and activities from gay, lesbian, and bisexual communities. It is important to emphasize that this is not always the case, and personal preference varies (Brotman et al., 2007). It should come as little surprise, then, that most research has found a strong desire to engage the mainstream system in change making while concurrently working to create organizations or programs tailored specifically to the social needs of LGB seniors (Brotman et al., 2007; Chamberlain & Robinson, 2002).

Informal support in terms of family and friend relationships is positively correlated with life satisfaction, including advocacy and protection against discrimination, and a multitude of sources—including friends, current and former partners, and pets—have been identified as sources of strength and resilience for LGB older adults (L. B. Brown et al., 2001; Clunis, Fredriksen-Goldsen, Freeman, & Nystrom, 2005). More than any other source, however, the literature indicates that partners are the most sought after sources of support (Butler & Hope, 1999; Heaphy et al., 2003; Van de Ven, Rodden,

Crawford, & Kippax, 1997). This support is especially important for couples less attached to gay, lesbian, and bisexual communities, who often socialize mainly with other couples (M. Hughes, 2005; Seabold, 1997).

The importance of biological families to LGB older adults is a complex issue that varies greatly from individual to individual, depending on a number of circumstances. Although some studies have found that out gay and lesbian seniors have limited support from or contact with their biological families (City and County of San Francisco, 2003; Comerford, Henson-Stroud, Sionainn, & Wheeler, 2004; Langley, 2001; W. R. Moore, 2002; Porter et al., 2003), other studies have indicated that the relationship with the biological family is probably more important than previously suggested (Heaphy et al., 2003). Furthermore, many studies have consistently reported that roughly half of all gay and lesbian older adults have children from previous heterosexual relationships (Langley, 2001; Peacock, 2000), providing accounts of issues faced by lesbian mothers or gay fathers with their children, as well as the fluidity and complexity of these relationships (Brotman et al., 2007; Heaphy et al., 2003). However, as Tasker (2013) noted in her assessment of the literature on lesbian and gay parenting after heterosexual divorce, additional research focused on intersectionality and the life course is needed to understand the complexities of "parental sexual orientation with cultural variation and the plurality of identity positions that LGBT parents may occupy over time" (p. 16). With regard to grandparenting, Orel and Fruhauf (2013) provided a historical and life course overview of lesbian motherhood/grandmotherhood and gay fatherhood/grandfatherhood, noting the sociopolitical and social cultural contexts of coming out and caring. Although research on these relationships has begun to emerge, Orel and Fruhauf advocated for a closer examination of the complexities and nuances of gendered familial relationships, roles, and expectations within LGBT grandparenting. Overall, however, many LGB older adults do find themselves without the support of children or other immediate family, and, considering that seniors in general receive most of their informal support from children and other relatives (Turcotte & Schellenberg, 2007), the importance of "families of choice" is especially worth highlighting. Unfortunately, for those older adults without close friends or family, isolation is a particularly serious threat to their well-being. The effects of isolation are magnified for those LGB seniors living alone, which by most accounts is a significant portion[3] (Heaphy et al., 2003; Rosenfeld, 1999, 2003), with even higher rates for the older cohort of seniors (Whitford, 1997) and persons with a disability (Brotman et al., 2003; Brotman, Watkins, & Ryan, 2010; River, 2006).

---

[3]A published report from the lobby group Stonewall (2011) asserted that in Britain as many as 41% of LGB older adults live alone.

Homophobic and heterosexist discrimination in health and social care also extends to the family members who provide informal care to LGB older adults. Research has documented how same-sex spouses and partners have been disregarded in health care planning and have been treated with intolerance and judgment by health care providers (Balsam & D'Augelli, 2006; Brotman et al., 2003). In addition, research we undertook between 2001 and 2006 showed that spouses and children of LGB older adults also have a difficult time accessing services to meet their own needs. For example, participants we interviewed spoke to us about the heterosexist and homophobic reception they received when attempting to participate in caregiver support groups and other activities in the mainstream health and social care sector. They also feared and experienced the stigma attached to their LGB loved ones (Brotman et al., 2007).

Residential Care

Although most older adults want to stay at home for as long as possible, statistics indicate that about 2% of those ages 65 to 74 live in institutional care, with the number jumping to 32% for those ages 85 and older, and even higher for women (Turcotte & Schellenberg, 2007). Note, however, that the views of older adults in their 80s and beyond (and thus most at risk of institutionalization) are underrepresented (Addis, Davies, Greene, Macbride-Stewart, & Shepherd, 2009; Brotman et al., 2010; Dworkin, 2006; Keppel, 2006). This fact is acknowledged by LGB seniors (Clunis et al., 2005; Hubbard & Rossington, 1995), although many express dread at the prospect of entering a nursing home or other residential care facility, the main stated concerns being loss of independence (which has been identified as a particularly salient fear for previously autonomous lesbian women; Cook-Daniels, 1997; River, 2006) and fear of discrimination in a vulnerable state (Butler & Hope, 1999; Chamberlain & Robinson, 2002; M. Hughes, 2005; Kirby, 1997; Langley, 2001; McFarland & Sanders, 2003). Relying on others for health care is a frightening enough experience for most older adults, but this is compounded for LGB seniors because of their distrust in the institution and fear of being forced back into the closet due to fears of discrimination (Brotman et al., 2003) or abuse (River, 2006). Unfortunately, fears are given credence by the fact that few facilities have implemented antidiscrimination policies related to sexual orientation (Cahill & South, 2002). A lack of government accountability mechanisms, as well as an increasing shift toward privatization may further challenge efforts to make change, although in Canada, long-term-care homes are provincially regulated, making public policy advocacy a potentially useful strategy among LGBTQ activists and their allies (Chamberland & Paquin, 2008; Harrison, 1999; Phillips & Marks,

2006; Porter et al., 2003). It is evident, however, that changes in policy or standards will do little to improve the situation unless the attitudes of staff and residents are addressed as well (Greene, 2002; Langley, 2001; W. R. Moore, 2002).

In the Context of Transgender Aging

It is important to reiterate that existing research on LGBTQ aging tends to emphasize the gay and lesbian community and often neglect the unique realities of transgender people (Fredriksen & Muraco, 2010) or simply subsume their issues under the broader rubric of "LGBT" (Bauer et al., 2009; Cook-Daniels, 2006; Witten & Eyler, 2012). The appropriation of transgender issues into the broader discourse of LGBQ aging can lead to problems in the development of knowledge. For example, although the term *coming out* has been used for the LGBTQ community, the *process of transition* is a more meaningful term for the transgender community because it encapsulates the changing of gender identity (Cook-Daniels, 2006). Because much of what we know of transgendered aging comes from studies that address only (or mostly) lesbian and gay seniors, terms such as *coming out*, which are readily accessible to LGBQ populations, are assumed also to be relevant to transgender populations—a reality that may contribute to misrepresentations of transgender seniors in aging and other literature (e.g., writings on and about the body, sexuality, and health by feminist researchers; Namaste, 2009). The few studies that address transgender aging note how transgender older adults face similar concerns of loneliness, poor health, and low income as their cisgender counterparts but encounter additional layers of concern that include fear of rejection by family and adult children, transphobia, dating difficulties, legal and employment concerns, marginalization from gay and lesbian communities, and discrimination from heterosexual communities and providers (Cook-Daniels, 2006; Persson, 2009; Witten & Eyler, 2012). Regarding health care for transgender persons in middle to late life, privacy of health records is an additional pervasive concern given that the need for medical services increases in late life (Witten & Eyler, 2012). Moreover, access to and maintenance of various hormone therapies are considerations in health assessment (Witten & Eyler, 2012). Our work on residential care settings has shown that issues facing transgender residents are particularly salient. Older adults whose bodies and physical features are not congruent with their expressed gender put them at significant risk when moving into a residential setting. The self-protective strategy of nondisclosure may be impossible when receiving health care in these environments, exposing them to discrimination in the forms of rejection, ridicule, and hostility from staff and other residents. The fears of rejection and discrimination lead to transgender residents hiding their care needs, declining needed assistance, and retreating from social interactions (Sussman et al., 2012). The fears of disclosure are not surprising given past models and experiences of discrimination in the health care system and the transphobic climate many older transgender Canadians have lived through.

WHAT IS MISSING FROM THE LITERATURE?

In this section, we elaborate further on our view that the overreliance on homogenous samples in current research on LGBTQ populations (including in our own work) has resulted in the perpetuation of stereotyping, invisibility, and exclusion of many diverse members of LGBTQ communities in educational, community, and research initiatives. Research in the past two decades has tended to address only those members of communities who are active, vocal, and identify themselves to both researchers and health care systems. Although such information has provided a degree of visibility to some members of gay and lesbian communities, others have remained invisible, most notably transgender and bisexual people, people of color, and those without privileges of citizenship, including LGBTQ immigrants, migrants, and refugees (Lee & Brotman, 2011). Although there has been attention to institutional change, it has been for the benefit of individuals already at least partially privileged by multiple social locations based on race, class, gender, age, citizenship, and ability.

Research has identified that although the existing literature represents an important base from which to understand experiences of aging in LGBTQ communities, the generalizability of past research must be questioned, mainly because of the heavy reliance on snowball sampling and on the recruitment of an extremely homogeneous sample of gay and lesbian older adults that can be characterized as predominately White, urban, educated, middle-class, able-bodied, noninstitutionalized, self-identifying as gay or lesbian, and with high community involvement (see Orel, 2004; Peacock, 2000). Although several studies have reported their subjects as "self-identified" gay and lesbian seniors (see McFarland & Sanders, 2003), older seniors appear more likely to self-define as "homosexual" (Rawls, 2004) or "bisexual" (Rodriguez-Rust, 2012) or not ascribe to any label (Brotman et al., 2007). These nuances question the wisdom of recruiting middle-aged subjects (Calasanti & Slevin, 2001) and generalizing their experiences to older cohorts and others who do not self-identify based solely on their sexual orientation (Boxer, 1997).

Class concerns seem to be especially glossed over in studies despite existing literature suggesting that a number of older adults placed their financial situation as more important to their life satisfaction than anything related to their sexuality (Beeler, Rawls, Herdt, & Cohler, 1999; Jacobs, Rasmussen, & Hohman, 1999; Witten, 2012), and as many as 70% stated that they are not financially prepared to face aging (McFarland & Sanders, 2003). Only a small number of published studies have addressed the experiences of poorer and working-class seniors (Comerford et al., 2004; Porter et al., 2003), for whom welfare cuts and lack of private insurance (often due to an inability to be covered under a partner's plan) have been stated as serious barriers to wellness (Cahill, South, & Spade, 2000). Older adults without a disposable income are also unable to participate in most programs offered within LGBTQ communities (Greene, 2002; Porter et al., 2003) and are almost certain to be unable to access private senior residences currently being developed, despite their greater need for housing (Cahill & South, 2002; Kirby, 1997; River, 2006).

Finally, the interlocking nature of considerations of class, gender, and race are especially important: Older women in general are often in a more financially vulnerable state than are men, and older lesbian and transgender women are no exception (Heaphy et al., 2003; Nystrom & Jones, 2003; Orel, 2004). In addition, with 7.2% of Canadian seniors indicating a visible minority status and half of newly immigrated seniors unable to speak either English or French (Turcotte & Schellenberg, 2007), the importance of linguistic and cultural accessibility cannot be overlooked (L. B. Brown et al., 2001; City and County of San Francisco, 2003).

Although the investigative lens within the LGBTQ community has tended to focus on White, privileged, and able-bodied members, researchers have begun to consider the ways in which racialized communities, as well as members of immigrant, migrant, and refugee populations, have been misrepresented and underrepresented within the wider LGBTQ community (Brotman & Lee, 2011; LaViolette, 2007; Miller, 2005; O'Brien et al., 2004; Rehaag, 2008). Giwa and Greensmith (2012) noted how intergroup racism and broader systemic racism are embedded in the mainstream and White dominant LGBTQ community, rendering invisible the lived experiences of LGBTQ communities of color in Canada. Finally, some research has identified how multiply marginalized LGBTQ communities, particularly those not represented by dominant queer ideology and culture, and who as a result stand outside and against Western manifestations of "queer community" and "queer discourse," are often the targets of multiple forms of discrimination in both LGBTQ communities and mainstream health and social care service delivery systems (Dauvergne & Millbank, 2003; Fairbairn, 2005; Jenicek, Lee, & Wong, 2009; Lee & Brotman, 2011; Ryan, Brotman, & Baradaran, 2008). However, it is important to note that although this analysis is emerging in research on the broader LGBTQ population, it has rarely been taken up in the context of aging.

The lack of consideration for diversity within LGBTQ communities in aging research and activism has implications for the ways in which institutional and programmatic responses, where they exist, are shaped. Anecdotal evidence in the field suggests that change making has focused on the most identified people—likely those who have some vestiges of privilege in which to situate themselves as vocal agents of change, enabling them to contest unfair treatment; these are likely to be financially secure, White gay men and those younger senior cohorts for whom identity recognition is positioned as a social and human right (Giwa & Greensmith, 2012; Riggs, 2007a, 2007b). We know that the current cohort of older adults, who grew up in a time period before universal health care coverage in Canada, are less likely to make demands on the system at least partially because of fears of losing much-needed services (Brotman et al., 2007). For LGBTQ older adults for whom this potential reality is amplified, remaining silent and invisible is a key self-care strategy (Ward, River, & Fenge, 2008). Still, because research and activism are largely based on the expressed needs and demands of mainstream, privileged LGBTQ community members, what we know about diverse groups of LGBTQ older adults is significantly compromised. As a result, the kinds of changes we advocate for in health and social care access and service delivery address only a fraction of the complexities of aging in these communities.

INCORPORATING A LIFE COURSE AND INTERSECTIONALITY FRAMEWORK INTO LGBTQ AGING RESEARCH AND PRACTICE

Considering the experiences of those outside the dominant Western LGBTQ communities and discourse can advance our understanding, both in terms of the unique needs and realities of multiply marginalized older people and of how interlocking systems of oppression work to limit access and equity in health and social care services. A conceptual framework that brings into focus the interactions of multiple identity and structural oppression would allow for specific attention to be placed on the unique and varied stories and experiences of diversity in LGBTQ communities. A first step is to articulate a framework that would account for these diversities and complexities. However, the challenge remains of how we then translate this into adapted practice among researchers, service providers, and activists. We end by discussing our emerging framework and how we envision future research in consideration of the concepts and theories introduced in the previous section. In our most current work, we have begun to think about how a framework that incorporates the concepts of the life course and intersectionality can be articulated and implemented. The next section addresses the challenges and benefits of incorporating such a perspective into our research on LGBTQ aging.

DISTINGUISHING BETWEEN THE LIFE COURSE AS A CONCEPT, AND THE LIFE COURSE PERSPECTIVE

The *life course* is a general concept that focuses on sequences (and consequences) of life events as they are organized, connected, and evaluated as meaningful (Dannefer & Settersten, 2010; Grenier & Ferrer, 2010; Hockey & James, 2003). More specifically, the life course refers to a fluid and interpretive process that occurs throughout an individual's life and encompasses a host of factors that form the context for lived experience (Dannefer & Settersten, 2010; Grenier, 2012). The most common application of the life course emphasizes individual development and life events and takes into consideration the various historical and cohort effects that shape experiences within the life span. The methodological approach used to query the life course is known as the *life course perspective* (Grenier, 2012). The life course perspective has been increasingly used as an analytical frame, with its intellectual base drawn from the contributions of psychology (life-span development) and sociology (cohort analysis). As such, the life course is not grounded with a unifying theory. Researchers have recently used the life course in two types of inquiries or approaches (see Dannefer & Settersten, 2010; Grenier, 2012). The first approach, as Dannefer and Settersten (2010) suggested in their genealogy of the life course, is one that focuses on the *personalogical paradigm*, as articulated by Glen Elder's (1994) publication "Time, Human Agency, and Social Change: Perspective on the Life Course" and George's (1993) "Sociological Perspective on Life Transitions." This type of approach, which draws heavily on Elder's work, tends to focus on explanations that examine late-life outcomes for individuals and populations based on early life course experiences. Elder (1975) and George investigated the ways in which roles, statuses, and transitions shift over time and consequently affect individual identities and behaviors. Rather than focusing on segmented parts of the life span, a life course perspective provides a multilevel account of the social stratification, personal, and social forces that shape life course and development. Contributions of life-span psychology and cultural and intergenerational models of change have provided the impetus for the life course perspective to examine ongoing issues that affect individuals and groups (Grenier, 2012). The fluid construct of age, as analyzed through a life course perspective, provides an explanation of how behaviors, status, and roles can change across the life span (Elder, 1975).

Although the majority of research has used the life course perspective as a research approach, Dannefer and Settersten (2010) noted that a second life course approach, the *institutional paradigm*, has been the focus for a number of researchers interested in emphasizing structural and institutional components of the life course. Works that provide inquiries into the social and political construct of the life course as they are created, reinforced, and legitimated by policies and the social and behavioral sciences have been seen particularly in Europe (Grenier, 2012). Our understanding of the institutional paradigm is that it is informed by a structural position that distinguishes it from the personal and individual model more commonly used in social gerontology to examine physical and health outcomes for the purposes of asserting a "successful" or "healthy" aging paradigm. Given more recent developments of the life course as a framework for sociological inquiry, there is significant potential in applying this theoretical and analytical lens to LGBTQ research that seeks to move beyond homogeneity to account for the ways in which structural and historical events can affect the development of identity.

An institutional approach to the life course has often been implicitly used in LGBTQ research on aging to partially explain cohort experiences of health and social care. The most notable of these is the connection between historic discrimination faced by preliberation era LGBTQ older adults compared with those who grew up during or after the civil rights movements, as previously described in this chapter. Although this *cohort effect* is an important consideration for both research and practice, the fact that this analysis is relevant mostly to Western, White, and relatively privileged members of LGBTQ communities has been underconsidered. In addition, although social gerontologists have made meaningful contributions to an understanding of the social and cultural differences of LGBTQ aging (drawing on social and cultural diversity to account for and emphasize the inequalities experienced by LGBTQ older adults), existing research is limited in its capacity to acknowledge the complexities and intersections of people's lives, identities, and realities (Cronin & King, 2010). We recommend that the structural life course approach be invested with a framework that challenges privilege and accounts for diversity as a core component of analysis, both for the development of theory on LGBTQ aging and for enhancing practice models in mainstream and LGBTQ health and social care systems. To engage in the kind of critical theorizing that includes in its analytical frame multiple forms of power and privilege, we suggest the use of the concept of intersectionality alongside that of the structural life course.

Intersectionality first emerged in the work of feminist and critical race scholars working within a legal framework who identified the particular burdens placed on Black women when they were forced to identify along a single identity category, either gender or race, when documenting experiences of discrimination within the law (Crenshaw, 1995). Although the existence of distinct categories of oppression (e.g., race, class, gender, sexuality, ability) is acknowledged, intersectionality asserts that these social locations and concomitant experiences of social domination cannot be separated out from each other (Brotman & Ryan, 2004; Crenshaw, 1995; Mullaly, 2010). Crenshaw

(1995) pointed to the fact that intersectional subordination does not necessarily result from the intentional practices of systems and institutions but is "frequently the consequence of the imposition of one burden interacting with predisposing vulnerabilities to create yet another dimension of disempowerment" (p. 359). Recently, a number of Canadian scholars have examined the complex role of social relations of dominance in the everyday realities of LGBTQ people of color. Through this work, they have advanced a critical analysis that moves beyond the dyad of gender and sexuality to include multiple intersections of race, class, religion, ethnicity, language, and citizenship (see, e.g., Hulko, 2009; O'Brien et al., 2004; Ryan et al., 2008; Wane & Massaquoi, 2007). This has served to render visible the subtle yet powerful ways in which histories of settler colonialism, imperialism, and White supremacy within the North American context have informed the dominant assumptions and worldview embedded within the majority of the previous literature related to health and social care practice with these populations. To this end, we follow the suggestion of Cronin and King (2010) and Koehn, Neysmith, Kobayashi, and Khamisa (2012), who called for the incorporation of an intersectional lens in aging research and practice. The potential of an intersectional analysis, incorporated into a structural life course approach, would allow for a richer consideration of the complex biographies of communities, a broader and more detailed analysis of the dynamics of power, and an accounting of the fluid nature of identity embedded within time, context, and space/place.

MAKING IT HAPPEN

In considering how to move forward with a research and practice agenda that pays attention to diverse intersections of LGBTQ aging across the life course, we want first to consider from where we came and where we are now both as researchers and members of a broader advocacy community. Canadian research and activism have transformed over the past decade with increased levels of activity evident across several sectors. As we stated in the introduction to this chapter, Canada has witnessed much legal and social policy movement. It is important to note, however, a considerable lag in developments within gerontological health and social care environments. Gerontological research funding and mainstream service delivery has been slow to recognize LGBTQ older people. And LGBTQ communities are themselves beginning to recognize the necessity of developing educational initiatives and service options within the community. For example, there are significant efforts being made in the urban centers of Toronto and Vancouver where there exists some institutional infrastructure to support LGBTQ aging specific programs.[4] Efforts are also being made in other geographic locations across the country to engage in localized research and education projects and to encourage consideration of LGBTQ issues in the planning and activities of LGBTQ health organizations. These are important efforts.

Considering Practice and Service Delivery

Turning our attention to practice, we begin by noting that the implications for practice are profound. Most important, the reality of vulnerability and invisibility seems paramount. LGBTQ older adults in particular are today vulnerable in ways yet to be described because their stories have not been captured (and, we might also add, these older adults are resilient in ways not yet identified). This has particular resonance in terms of working responsibly with seniors in community settings and in long-term-care settings. By *community settings*, we refer to the multitude of communities to which diverse older LGBTQ people belong, including those connected to their racialized[5] communities and the localized geographic communities of friends and neighbors on which most seniors rely in the lived experience of the everyday across Canada.

In terms of service delivery, we note some of the most common recommendations made to address concerns regarding access and equity in the design and delivery of health and social care services. These include mandatory training for staff (Cahill, South, & Spade, 2000; Donahue & McDonald, 2005; Opening Doors Thanet, 2003); increased support and outreach to gay, lesbian, bisexual, and transgendered staff (Brotman et al., 2003; City and County of San Francisco, 2003; Langley, 2001); provision of more information about relevant issues to professionals (McFarland & Sanders, 2003); and more representative material available and visible within organizations and institutions (Opening Doors Thanet, 2003; Zodikoff, 2006).

In a recent environmental scan we conducted that included 31 long-term-care homes and retirement facilities in Ontario, Quebec, and British Columbia considered to be sensitive to LGBTQ issues, 20 had engaged in some forms of staff training, seven made efforts to outreach to the LGBTQ community, and only four had adapted materials by using more inclusive language or ensuring

---

[4]See the Older LGBT Services of the 519 Community Centre: http://www.the519.org/programsservices/olderlgbt (Toronto) and the QMUNITY Generations Project: http://www.qmunity.ca/older-adults/ (Vancouver).
[5]The term *race* is understood as a socially constructed (thus the term *racialized*), rather than biologically determined, concept or category espoused by colonial and White supremacist epistemologies in which skin color and other visible, socially selected traits are used to classify groups hierarchically (Ryan et al., 2008). We use the term *racialized* as an umbrella category to include those who identify as visible minorities, mixed race, biracial, ethnoracial, and racialized. This term serves as a political tool in explicitly identifying race and calling attention to the ways in which racial hierarchies have been sociohistorically produced by processes of colonialism, imperialism, and racism.

more representative symbols within their homes (Sussman et al., 2012). This suggests that we are still a long way away from implementing many practice recommendations appearing in the literature, even in the most progressive of organizations. Although staff training is an important first step in the development of LGBTQ diversity strategies, and recommendations for increased sensitivity training of health care workers are near universal (e.g., Brotman et al., 2003; L. B. Brown et al., 2001; City and County of San Francisco, 2003; Comerford et al., 2004; M. Hughes, 2005; River, 2006), we believe that education of frontline staff alone is not sufficient to foster the environmental safety and openness many older LGBTQ persons require to feel that their LGBTQ status will not compromise their care. Rather, a multilevel approach in which openness is communicated throughout the organization through images, forms, policies naming LGBTQ status as a formal right, outreach to and connections with LGBTQ communities, and hiring policies will go much further toward fostering an LGBTQ-positive environment (D. Moore, 2009; Toronto Long Term Care Homes and Services, 2008). It is important to note that our recent scan with "sensitive" long-term-care home and residential facilities also revealed that one of the main barriers to implementing more organization-level change was service providers' perceptions that other residents would resist more changes. We were able to locate one rather dated study reporting on older adults' attitudes toward sexuality in general and sexual orientation in particular. Although homophobic attitudes were present, findings also revealed that most older adults believed that staff members should be open and tolerant of residents' sexual orientation (Walker & Ephross, 1999). Furthermore, the few facilities in our scan that made more organizational changes reported residents to be open and accepting of the implemented changes. Seemingly, staff's ageist perceptions of older adults as "rigid" and "closed-minded" may be more of a barrier to comprehensive implementation than residents' actual attitudes.

Finally, another consideration that many researchers have already suggested is the creation of LGBTQ-only residential institutions (Chamberlain & Robinson, 2002; Hamburger, 1997; Kirby, 1997; Nystrom & Jones, 2003; Orel, 2004), particularly among baby boomers who have been out since the 1960s and 1970s (Bergling, 2004) and among lesbians who desire a lesbian- or women-only commune-like atmosphere (Clunis et al., 2005; Harrison, 2005; M. Hughes, 2005; Phillips & Marks, 2006). This recommendation is far from universal, however, and participants have pointed out concerns related to safety issues around establishing a known gay-only residential institution (Hubbard & Rossington, 1995), prohibitive costs that put private sector services out of the reach of most LGBTQ older people (Brotman et al., 2003), and the "stultifying" effect of living only with other gay people (Bergling, 2004, p. 187; M. Hughes, 2005; River, 2006). Also, these recommendations assume a level of choice that may not be available to the oldest or most disabled members of the community, for example, those who require more care and therefore may be forced due to medical circumstance to relocate from an LGBTQ-friendly home to a public long-term-care facility. It would appear, then, that adapting existing services while also developing new LGBTQ-only services seems to offer the most choice to LGBTQ older adults, resulting in better overall access to care (Brotman et al., 2003; Cahill & South, 2002).

Considering Research

Turning our attention back to research, we begin by stating that our own work in LGBTQ aging suffers from the challenge of resisting homogeneity. To consider new ways of doing research, we look to our work in other areas for ideas and new directions. For example, most of us have already undertaken projects outside of the field of aging using an explicit framework of intersectionality—theorizing the intersections of race, class, and gender as part of design, data collection, and analysis (e.g., in studies on migration and the social determinants of health). To that end, strategies such as engaging in participatory action research approaches and using OCAP (Ownership, Control, Access, and Possession) principles[6] have ensured a greater degree of engagement with affected communities and diversity of voices in the research process and outcomes. We believe this type of approach to research is also possible in the field of social gerontology. For example, our work on access to homecare (Brotman et al., 2002) incorporated a networking component in which LGBTQ health and senior care activists and mainstream health and social care service policymakers sat together to exchange experiences, giving older members of the community a rare opportunity to address their concerns directly with those in the mainstream system who knew little about their realities and experiences. Developing creative ways to engage LGBTQ residents within long-term-care institutions in a similar model of research exchange is essential and may require the concomitant development of a connection to and understanding of the particular culture established in each long-term-care facility and of the particular communities providing support to the senior resident, as was done with the Diversity Project of Toronto Long Term Care Homes and Services (Toronto Long Term Care Homes and Services, 2008). Research efforts with multiply marginalized seniors will require longer term relationships of engagement on a number of fronts to finally make room for the voices of those seniors who have been silenced.

Finally, we believe that one of the only ways to ensure real diversity in our studies is to begin rethinking the large-scale projects in which many of us are or have been engaged. Although large representative samples are often

---

[6]OCAP principles are the four pillars by which ethical research practices are regulated by First Nations communities in Canada. See First Nations Centre (2007).

sought to ensure representation, identity fluidity among older LGBTQ people and those who do not subscribe to Western identity labels will challenge how we recruit participants, conduct outreach, and understand those who are outside mainstream gay discourse. As such, our next projects will likely focus on smaller scale, localized projects using narrative and life history approaches to make room for the possible multiple intersections of aging tied to region, age, gender, race, ethnicity, class, migration, and citizenship. We believe that individual stories across the life course (using a structural life course approach infused with an intersectionality framework) can do much to illuminate the varied, complex, and diverse experiences of aging in Canada (and beyond).

REFERENCES

Addis, S., Davies, M., Greene, G., Macbride-Stewart, S., & Shepherd, M. (2009). The health, social care and housing needs of lesbian, gay, bisexual and transgender older people: A review of the literature. *Health & Social Care in the Community, 17,* 647–658.

Balsam, K. F., & D'Augelli, A. R. (2006). The victimization of older LGBT adults: Patterns, impact, and implications for intervention. In D. Kimmel, T. Rose, & S. David (Eds.), *Lesbian, gay, bisexual and transgender aging: Research and clinical perspectives* (pp. 110–130). New York, NY: Columbia University Press.

Bauer, G. R., Hammond, R., Travers, R., Kaay, M., Hohenadel, K. M., & Boyce, M. (2009). "I don't think this is theoretical: This is our lives": How erasure impacts health care for transgender people. *JANAC: Journal of the Association of Nurses in AIDS Care, 20,* 348–361.

Beeler, J., Rawls, T., Herdt, G., & Cohler, B. (1999). The needs of older lesbians and gay men in Chicago. *Journal of Gay & Lesbian Social Services, 9,* 31–49.

Bergling, T. (2004). *Reeling in the years: Gay men's perspectives on age and ageism.* Binghampton, NY: Southern Tier Editions, Harrington Park Press.

Blando, J. A. (2001). Twice hidden: Older gay and lesbian couples, friends, and intimacy. *Generations, 25,* 87–89.

Bonneau, M. (1998). L'affirmation lesbienne en milieu regional: Une visibilité problematique [The affirmation of lesbian identities in regional areas: A problematic visibility]. In I. Demczuk (Ed.), *Des droits à reconnaître—Les lesbiennes face à la discrimination* [Understanding rights—Discrimination against lesbian women] (pp. 167–192). Montreal, Quebec, Canada: Les Éditions du Remue-ménage.

Boxer, A. (1997). Gay, lesbian and bisexual aging into the twenty-first century: An overview and introduction. *Journal of Gay, Lesbian, and Bisexual Identity, 2,* 187–196.

Brennan, D. J., Hellerstedt, W. L., Ross, M. W., & Welles, S. L. (2007). History of childhood sexual abuse and HIV risk behaviors in homosexual and bisexual men. *American Journal of Public Health, 97,* 1107–1112.

Brotman, S., & Lee, E. O. J. (2011). Exploring gender and sexuality through the lens of intersectionality: Sexual minority refugees in Canada. *Canadian Social Work Review, 28*, 151–156.

Brotman, S. & Ryan, B. (2004) An intersectional approach to queer health policy and practice: Two-spirit people in Canada. *Canadian Diversity, 3*, 59–64.

Brotman, S., Ryan, B., & Cormier, R. (2002). Mental health issues of particular groups: Gay and lesbian seniors. In National Advisory Council on Aging (Ed.), *Writings in gerontology: Mental health and aging* (Vol. 2, pp. 55–65). Ottawa, Canada: National Advisory Council on Aging.

Brotman, S., Ryan, B., & Cormier, R. (2003). The health and social service needs of gay and lesbian elders and their families in Canada. *The Gerontologist, 43*, 192–202.

Brotman, S., Ryan, B., & Meyer, E. (2006). *The health and social service needs of gay and lesbian elders: Final report.* Montreal, Quebec, Canada: McGill University School of Social Work.

Brotman, S., Ryan, W., Collins, S., Chamberland, L., Cormier, R., Julien, D., . . . Richard, B. (2007). Coming out to care: Caregivers of gay and lesbian seniors in Canada. *The Gerontologist, 47*, 490–503.

Brotman, S., Watkins, J., & Ryan, B. (2010). *City of Toronto Long-Term Care Homes and Services Division: LGBT Diversity Initiative Documentation Project.* Montreal, Quebec, Canada: McGill University.

Brown, L. B., Alley, G. R., Sarosy, S., Quarto, G., & Cook, T. (2001). Gay men: Aging well! *Journal of Gay & Lesbian Social Services, 13*, 41–54.

Brown, M. T. (2009, December). LGBT aging and rhetorical silence. *Sexuality Research & Social Policy, 6*, 65–78.

Butler, S. S., & Hope, B. (1999). Health and well-being for late middle-aged and old lesbians in a rural area. *Journal of Gay & Lesbian Social Services, 9*, 27–46.

Cahill, S., & South, K. (2002). Policy issues affecting lesbian, gay, bisexual, and transgender people in retirement. *Generations, 26*, 49–54.

Cahill, S., South, K., & Spade, J. (2000). *Outing age: Public policy issues affecting gay, lesbian, bisexual, and transgender elders.* New York, NY: The Policy Institute of the National Gay and Lesbian Task Force.

Calasanti, T. M., & Slevin, K. F. (2001). *Gender, social inequalities, and aging.* Walnut Creek, CA: AltaMira Press.

Chamberlain, C., & Robinson, P. (2002). *The needs of older gay, lesbian and transgender people, a report prepared for the ALSO Foundation.* RMIT University, Melbourne, Australia. Retrieved from http://www.rainbowvisions.org.au/resources/The NeedsofOlderGLTPeople.pdf

Chamberland, L., & Paquin, J. (2008) Le défi de l'adaptation des services résidentiels aux besoins des lesbiennes âgées [The rejection of adaptation of residential services to the needs of lesbian elders]. Montreal, Quebec, Canada: Réseau des lesbiennes du Québec.

City and County of San Francisco, Human Rights Commission and Aging and Adult Services Commission. (2003). *Aging in the lesbian gay bisexual transgender communities*. Retrieved from http://www.sfgov.org/site/uploadedfiles/sfhumanrights/docs/finalreport.pdf

Clunis, D. M., Fredriksen-Goldsen, K. I., Freeman, P. A., & Nystrom, N. (2005). *Lives of lesbian elders: Looking back, looking forward*. New York, NY: Haworth Press.

Comerford, S. A., Henson-Stroud, M. M., Sionainn, C., & Wheeler, E. (2004). Crone songs: Voices of lesbian elders on aging in a rural environment. *Affilia: Journal of Women and Social Work, 19,* 418–436.

Concannon, L. (2009). Developing inclusive health and social care policies for older LGBT citizens. *British Journal of Social Work, 39,* 403–417.

Cook-Daniels, L. (1997). Lesbian, gay male, bisexual and transgendered elders: Elder abuse and neglect issues. *Journal of Elder Abuse & Neglect, 9,* 35–49.

Cook-Daniels, L. (2006) Transaging. In D. Kimmel, T. Rose, & S. David (Eds.), *Lesbian, gay, bisexual and transgender aging: Research and clinical perspectives* (pp. 290–335). New York, NY: Columbia University Press.

Coon, D. (2007). Exploring interventions for LGBT caregivers: Issues and examples. *Journal of Gay & Lesbian Social Services, 18,* 109–128.

Crenshaw, K. (1995). Mapping the margins: Intersectionality, identity politics, and violence against women of color. In K. Crenshaw, N. Gotanda, G. Peller, & K. Thomas (Eds.), *Critical race theory. The key writings that formed the movement* (pp. 357–383). New York, NY: The New Press.

Cronin, A., & King, A. (2010). Power, inequality and identification: Exploring diversity and intersectionality amongst older LGB adults. *Sociology, 44,* 876–892.

Cronin, A., Ward, R., Pugh, S., King, A., & Price, E. (2011). Categories and their consequences: Understanding and supporting the caring relationships of older lesbian, gay and bisexual people. *International Social Work, 54,* 421–435.

Daley, A. (2006). Lesbian and gay health issues: OUTside of Canada's health policy. *Critical Social Policy, 26,* 794–816.

Dannefer, D., & Settersten, R. A. (2010). The study of the life course: Implications for social gerontology. In C. Phililipson & D. Dannefer (Eds.), *The SAGE handbook of social gerontology* (pp. 3–19). London, England: Sage.

D'Augelli, A. R., & Grossman, A. H. (2001). Disclosure of sexual orientation, victimization, and mental health among lesbian, gay and bisexual older adults. *Journal of Interpersonal Violence, 16,* 1008–1027.

Dauvergne, C., & Millbank, J. (2003). Gender, sex and visibility in refugee claims on the basis of sexual orientation. *Georgetown Immigration Law Journal, 18,* 71–110.

de Saxe, M., & Lovett, K. (2004). *You don't have to roll up your banner when you're sixty!: Ageing and gay and lesbian (and transgender) communities*. Presentation for the Rainbow Visions Hunter Ageing Forum. Retrieved from http://www.rainbowvisions.org.au/resources/RV_AgeingForum_Mannie&KenPlenarySession.pdf

Demczuk, I. (1998). Enquête sur la violence vécue par les lesbiennes [Survey on violence experienced by lesbians]. In I. Demczuk (Ed.), *Des droits à reconnaître—Les lesbiennes face à la discrimination* [Understanding rights—Discrimination against lesbian women] (pp. 199–212). Montreal, Quebec, Canada: Les Éditions du Remue-ménage.

Donahue, P., & McDonald, L. (2005). Gay and lesbian aging: Current perspectives and future directions for social work practice and research. *Families in Society, 86*, 359–366.

Dworkin, S. H. (2006). The aging bisexual: The invisible of the invisible minority. In D. Kimmel, T. Rose, & S. David (Eds.), *Lesbian, gay, bisexual, and transgender aging: Research and clinical perspectives* (pp. 37–52). New York, NY: Columbia University Press.

Egale Canada. (2004). *Outlaws & inlaws: Your guide to LBGT rights, same-sex relationships and Canadian law*. Ottawa: Egale Canada.

Egale Canada. (2012). *2013 Universal Periodic Review submission*. Toronto, ON: Egale Canada. Retrieved from http://lib.ohchr.org/HRBodies/UPR/Documents/Session16/CA/EGALE_UPR_CAN_S16_2013_Eagle_E.pdf

Elder, G. H. (1975). Age differentiation and the life course. *Annual Review of Sociology, 1*, 165–190.

Elder, G. H. (1994). Time, human agency, and social change: Perspectives on the life course. *Social Psychology Quarterly, 57*, 4–15.

Fairbairn, B. (2005). Gay rights are human rights: Gay asylum seekers in Canada. In B. Epps, K. Valens, & B. J. Gonzalez (Eds.), *Passing lines: Sexuality and immigration* (pp. 237–254). Cambridge, MA: Harvard University Press.

First Nations Centre. (2007). *OCAP: Ownership, control, access and possession*. Sanctioned by the First Nations Information Governance Committee, Assembly of First Nations. Ottawa, Canada: National Aboriginal Health Organization.

Fone, B. (2000). *Homophobia: A history*. New York, NY: Metropolitan Books/Holt.

Fredriksen-Goldsen, K. I., & Muraco, A. (2010). Aging and sexual orientation: A 25-year review of the literature. *Research on Aging, 32*, 372–413.

George, L. K. (1993). Sociological perspectives on life transitions. *Annual Review of Sociology, 19*, 353–373.

Giwa, S., & Greensmith, C. (2012). Race relations and racism in the LGBTQ community of Toronto: Perceptions of gay and queer social service providers of color. *Journal of Homosexuality, 59*, 149–185.

Greene, B. (2002). Older lesbians' concerns and psychotherapy: Beyond a footnote to the footnote. In F. K. Trotman & C. M. Brody (Eds.), *Psychotherapy and counseling with older women: Cross-cultural, family, and end-of-life issues* (pp. 161–174). New York, NY: Springer.

Grenier, A. (2012). *Transitions and the lifecourse: Challenging the constructions of 'growing old'*. Bristol, England: Policy Press.

Grenier, A., & Ferrer, I. (2010). Age, ageing and growing old: Contested definitions of age. In N. Guberman, M. Charpentier, & A. Grenier (Eds.), *Gerontologies sociale: Problemes sociaux et interventions socials* [Social gerontology: Social problems and interventions] (pp. 35–54). Quebec, Canada: Presses de l'Universite du Quebec.

Grossman, A. H., D'Augelli, A. R., & O'Connell, T. S. (2001). Being lesbian, gay, bisexual and 60 or older in North America. *Journal of Gay & Lesbian Social Services, 13*, 23–40.

Haber, D. (2009). Gay aging. *Gerontology & Geriatrics Education, 30*, 267–280.

Hamburger, L. (1997). The wisdom of non-heterosexually based senior housing and related services. *Journal of Gay and Lesbian Social Services, 6*, 11–25.

Harrison, J. (1999). A lavender pink grey power: Gay and lesbian gerontology in Australia. *Australasian Journal on Ageing, 18*, 32–37.

Harrison, J. (2005) Pink lavender and grey: Gay, lesbian, bisexual, transgender and intersex ageing in Australian gerontology. *Gay and Lesbian Issues and Psychology Review, 1*, 11–16.

Heaphy, B., Yip, A., & Thompson, D. (2003). *Lesbian, gay and bisexual lives over 50: A report on the project "The Social and Policy Implications of Non-heterosexual Ageing."* Nottingham, England: York House. Retrieved from http://ess.ntu.ac.uk/heaphy/LGB50+.doc

Hequembourg, A. L., Bimbi, D., & Parsons, J. T. (2011). Sexual victimization and health-related indicators among sexual minority men. *Journal of LGBT Issues in Counseling, 5*, 2–20.

Hequembourg, A. L., Parks, K. A., & Vetter, C. (2008). Sexual identity and gender differences in substance use and violence: An exploratory study. *Journal of LGBT Issues in Counseling, 2*, 174–198.

Hightow-Weidman, L. B., Phillips, G., Jones, K. C., Outlaw, A. Y., Fields, S. D., Smith, J. C., & YMSM of Color SPNS Initiative Study Group. (2011). Racial and sexual identity-related maltreatment among minority YMSM: Prevalence, perceptions, and the association with emotional distress. *AIDS Patient Care and STDs, 25*(Suppl. 1), S39–S45.

Hockey, J. L., & James, A. (2003). *Social identities across the life course.* Houndmills, England: Palgrave Macmillan.

Hubbard, R., & Rossington, J. (1995). *As we grow older: A study of the housing and support needs of older lesbians and gay men.* London, England: Polari. Retrieved from http://www.casweb.org/polari/file-storage/download/As%20We%20Grow%20Older.pdf?version_id=66608

Hughes, M. (2005). *Sexual identity in health & aged care: Narrative research in the Blue Mountains.* Retrieved from http://www.rainbowvisions.org.au/resources/SexualIdentityInHealthAndAgedCare.pdf

Hughes, T. L., Johnson, T., & Wilsnack, S. C. (2001). Sexual assault and alcohol abuse: A comparison of lesbians and heterosexual women. *Journal of Substance Abuse, 13*, 515–532.

Hulko, W. (2009). The time and context contingent nature of intersectionality and interlocking oppressions. *Affilia: Journal of Women & Social Work, 24*, 44–55.

Jacobs, R. J., Rasmussen, L. A., & Hohman, M. M. (1999). The social support needs of older lesbians, gay men, and bisexuals. *Journal of Gay & Lesbian Social Services, 9*, 1–30.

Jenicek, A., Lee, E., & Wong, A. D. (2009). Dangerous shortcuts: Representations of sexual minority refugees in the post-9/11 Canadian press. *Canadian Journal of Communication, 71*, 4, 635.

Jones, M. A., & Gabriel, M. A. (1999). Utilization of psychotherapy by lesbians, gay men and bisexuals: Findings from a nationwide survey. *American Journal of Orthopsychiatry, 69*, 209–219.

Kauth, M. R., Hartwig, M. J., & Kalichman, S. C. (2000). Health behavior relevant to psychotherapy with lesbian, gay, and bisexual clients. In R. Perez, K. A. DeBord, & K. J. Bieschke (Eds.), *Handbook of counseling and psychotherapy with lesbian, gay, and bisexual clients* (pp. 435–456). Washington, DC: American Psychological Association.

Keppel, B. (2006). Affirmative psychotherapy with older bisexual women and men. In R. C. Fox (Ed.), *Affirmative psychotherapy with bisexual women and bisexual men* (pp. 85–104). New York, NY: Harrington Park Press.

Kingston, T. (2002). The challenges and rewards of life as an outspoken bisexual elder. *Outword, 8*, 6.

Kirby, S. L. (1997). *A report on the needs assessment survey of senior gays and lesbians.* Winnipeg, MB: Sum Quod Sum Foundation.

Koehn, S., Neysmith, S., Kobayashi, K., & Khamisa, H. (2012). Revealing the shape of knowledge using an intersectionality lens: Results of a scoping review on the health and health care of ethnocultural minority older adults. *Ageing and Society, 33*, 437–464.

Langley, J. (2001). Developing anti-oppressive empowering social work practice with older lesbian women and gay men. *British Journal of Social Work, 31*, 917–932.

LaViolette, N. (2007). Gender-related refugee claims: Expanding the scope of the Canadian guidelines. *International Journal of Refugee Law, 19*, 169–214.

Lee, E. O. J., & Brotman, S. (2011). Identity, refugeeness, belonging: Experiences of sexual minority refugees in Canada. *Canadian Review of Sociology/Revue Canadienne De Sociologie, 48*, 241–274.

McFarland, P. L., & Sanders, S. (2003). A pilot study about the needs of older gays and lesbians: What social workers need to know. *Journal of Gerontological Social Work, 40*, 67–80.

McLeod, D. W. (1996). *Lesbian and gay liberation in Canada: A selected annotated chronology, 1964–1975.* Toronto, Ontario, Canada: ECW Press/Homewood Books.

Meezan, W., & Martin, J. I. (2009). *Handbook of research with lesbian, gay, bisexual, and transgender populations.* New York, NY: Routledge.

Miller, A. (2005). Gay enough: Some tensions in seeking the grant of asylum and protecting global sexual diversity. In B. Epps, K. Valens, & B. J. Gonzalez (Eds.), *Passing lines: Sexuality and immigration* (pp. 137–188). Cambridge, MA: Harvard University Press.

Moore, D. (2009). Designing long-term care for lesbian, gay, transsexual and transgender people. In P. Armstrong, M., Soscoe, B. Clow, K. Grant, M., Haworth-Brockman, B. Jacksone, . . . J. Springer (Eds.), *A place to call home. Long-term care in Canada* (pp. 105–110). Halifax, Canada: Fernwood.

Moore, W. R. (2002). Lesbian and gay elders: Connecting care providers through a telephone support group. *Journal of Gay & Lesbian Social Services, 14*, 23–41.

Mullaly, R. P. (2010). *Challenging oppression and confronting privilege: A critical social work approach.* Don Mills, Canada: Oxford University Press.

Namaste, V. (1999). The use and abuse of queer tropes: Metaphor and catachresis in queer theory and politics. *Social Semiotics, 9*, 213-234.

Namaste, V. (2009). Undoing theory: The "transgender question" and the epistemic violence of Anglo-American feminist theory. *Hypatia, 24*, 11–32.

National Gay and Lesbian Task Force. (2005). *Make room for all: Diversity, cultural competency and discrimination in an aging America.* Retrieved from http://www.thetaskforce.org/downloads/MakeRoom%20for%20All.pdf

Nystrom, N. M., & Jones, T. C. (2003). Community building with aging and old lesbians. *American Journal of Community Psychology, 31*, 293–300.

O'Brien, C.-A., Abualsameed, S., Carolo, H., Heung, F., Ridgley, A., & Scanlon, K. (2004). International migration: Newcomer and refugee youth. In *Youth migration project.* Toronto, Ontario, Canada: AIDS Committee of Toronto. Retrieved from http://www.actoronto.org/research.nsf/pages/youthmigration

Opening Doors Thanet. (2003). *Equally different: Report on the situation of older lesbian, gay, bi-sexual and transgendered people in Thanet, Kent.* Ramsgate. Retrieved from http://www.ageofdiversity.org.uk/sites/default/files/EquallyDifferent.pdf

Orel, N. A. (2004). Gay, lesbian, and bisexual elders: Expressed needs and concerns across focus groups. *Journal of Gerontological Social Work, 43*, 57–77.

Orel, N. A., & Fruhauf, C. A. (2013). Lesbian, gay, bisexual, and transgender grand-parents. In A. E. Goldberg & K. R. Allen (Eds.), *LGBT parent families: Innovations in research and implications for practice* (pp. 177–192). New York, NY: Springer.

Peacock, J. R. (2000). Gay male development: Some stage issues of an older cohort. *Journal of Homosexuality, 40*, 13–29.

Persson, D. I. (2009). Unique challenges of transgender aging: Implications from the literature. *Journal of Gerontological Social Work, 52*, 633–646.

Phillips, J., & Marks, G. (2006). Coming out, coming in: How do dominant discourse around aged care facilities take into account the identities and needs of ageing lesbians? *Gay and Lesbian Issues and Psychology Review, 2*, 67–77.

Porter, M., Russell, C., & Sullivan, G. (2003). Gay, old, and poor: Service delivery to aging gay men in inner city Sydney, Australia. *Journal of Gay & Lesbian Social Services, 16*, 43–57.

Rancourt, R., & Limoges, T. (1967). Homosexuality among women. *The Canadian Nurse, 63*, 42–44.

Rawls, T. W. (2004). Disclosure and depression among older gay and homosexual men: Findings from the Urban men's health study. In G. Herdt & B. de Vries (Eds.), *Gay and lesbian aging: Research and future directions* (pp. 117–142). New York, NY: Springer.

Rehaag, S. (2008). Patrolling the borders of sexual orientation: Bisexual refugee claims in Canada. *The McGill Law Journal, 53*, 1, 59.

Riggs, D. (2007a). Queer theory and its future in psychology: Exploring issues of race privilege. *Social and Personality Psychology Compass, 1*, 39–52.

Riggs, D. W. (2007b). Recognizing race in LGBTQ Psychology: Power, privilege and complicity. In V. Clarke & E. Peel (Eds.), *Out in psychology: Lesbian, gay, bisexual, trans and queer perspectives* (pp. 59–76). Chichester, England: Wiley.

River, L. (2006). *A feasibility study of the needs of older lesbians in Camden and surrounding boroughs*. Report to Age Concern Camden. Retrieved from http://www.ageofdiversity.org.uk/sites/default/files/OlderLesbianReport.pdf

Rodriguez-Rust, P. C. (2012). Aging in the bisexual community. In T. M. Witten & A. E. Eyler (Eds.), *Gay, lesbian, bisexual and transgender aging* (pp. 162–186). Baltimore, MD: Johns Hopkins University Press.

Rosenfeld, D. (1999). Identity work among lesbian and gay elderly. *Journal of Aging Studies, 13*, 121–144.

Rosenfeld, D. (2003). *The changing of the guard: Lesbian and gay elders, identity, and social change*. Philadelphia, PA: Temple University Press.

Ryan, B., Brotman, S., & Baradaran, A. (2008) The color of queer health care: Experiences of multiple oppression in the lives of queer people of color in Canada. In S. Brotman, J. Josy Levy, & F. Chatrand (Eds.), *Homosexualités: variations linguistiques et culturelles [Homosexuality: Linguistic and cultural variations]*. Québec: Presses de l'Université du Québec, Coll. Santé et Société.

Ryan, B., & Canadian AIDS Society. (2003). *A new look at homophobia and heterosexism in Canada*. Ottawa, Canada: Canadian AIDS Society.

Seabold, G. (1997). Surviving a partner's death deeply in the closet. *Journal of Gay & Lesbian Social Services, 7*, 7–14.

Stein, G. L., & Beckerman, N. L. (2010). Lesbian and gay elders and long-term care: Identifying the unique psychosocial perspectives and challenges. *Journal of Gerontological Social Work, 53*, 421–435.

Stonewall. (2011). *Lesbian, gay and bisexual people in later life*. London, England: Stonewall. Retrieved from http://www.stonewall.org.uk/documents/lgb_in_later_life_final.pdf

Sussman, T., Brotman, S., Chamberland, L., Daley, A., Dumas, J., MacDonnell, J., . . . Ryan, B. (2012, October). *Developing a program of research to identify and address the health and social service needs of lesbian, gay, bisexual and transgender (LGBT) older adults who reside in long-term care homes.* CIHR Planning Meeting, Montreal, Quebec, Canada.

Tasker, F. (2013). Lesbian and gay parenting post-heterosexual divorce and separation. In A. E. Goldberg & K. R. Allen (Eds.), *LGBT parent families: Innovations in research and implications for practice* (pp. 3–20). New York, NY: Springer.

Tomsen, S. (2006). Homophobic violence, cultural essentialism and shifting sexual identities. *Social & Legal Studies, 15,* 389–407.

Toronto Long Term Care Homes and Services. (2008). *Diversity our strength: LGBT toolkit.* Toronto, Ontario, Canada: City of Toronto.

Turcotte, M., & Schellenberg, G. (2007). *A portrait of seniors in Canada: 2006.* Ottawa: Statistics Canada. Retrieved from http://www.statcan.ca/english/freepub/89-519-XIE/89-519-XIE2006001.pdf

Van de Ven, P., Rodden, P., Crawford, J., & Kippax, S. (1997). A comparative demographic and sexual profile of older homosexually active men. *Journal of Sex Research, 34,* 349–360.

Walker, B., & Ephross, P. (1999). Knowledge and attitudes toward sexuality of a group of elderly. *Journal of Gerontological Social Work, 31,* 85–107.

Wane, N. N., & Massaquoi, N. (2007). *Theorizing empowerment: Canadian perspectives on Black feminist thought.* Toronto, Ontario, Canada: Inanna.

Ward, R., River, L., & Fenge, L.-A. (2008). Neither silent nor invisible: A comparison of two participative projects involving older lesbians and gay men in the United Kingdom. *Journal of Gay & Lesbian Social Services, 20,* 147–165.

Whitford, G. S. (1997). Realities and hopes for older gay males. *Journal of Gay & Lesbian Social Services, 6,* 79–95.

Witten, T. M. (2012). The aging of sexual and gender minority persons: An overview. In T. M. Witten & A. E. Eyler (Eds.), *Gay, lesbian, bisexual and transgender aging: Challenges in research, practice and policy* (pp. 1–58). New York, NY: Johns Hopkins University Press.

Witten, T. M., & Eyler, A. E. (2012). Transgender and aging: Beings and becomings. In T. M. Witten & A. E. Eyler (Eds.), *Gay, lesbian, bisexual and transgender aging: Challenges in research, practice and policy* (pp. 187–269). New York, NY: Johns Hopkins University Press.

Zodikoff, B. D. (2006). Services for lesbian, gay, bisexual and transgender older adults. In B. Berkman (Ed.), *Handbook of social work in health and aging* (pp. 569–576). New York, NY: Oxford University Press.

7

COMMUNITY RESOURCES AND GOVERNMENT SERVICES FOR LGBT OLDER ADULTS AND THEIR FAMILIES

SEAN CAHILL

Lesbian, gay, bisexual, and transgender (LGBT) elders have unique needs and life experiences that necessitate particular kinds of community resources and access to government services. In most instances, these resources and services are identical to the ones that heterosexual older adults need. However, due to widespread anti-LGBT prejudice among older adults and service providers, LGBT elders need protections to guarantee access to such resources and services. Services targeted toward LGBT elders, such as LGBT-specific congregate meal programs and LGBT senior centers, can also provide much-needed social support and reduce social isolation. In this chapter, I examine how coming of age in an intensely antigay society influences the aging process for LGBT elders and their willingness to interact with mainstream senior service providers. I describe LGBT-specific senior services, congregate meal programs, and housing that can meet expressed needs for social support. I also discuss the effects of recent policy changes on LGBT older adults.

DOI: 10.1037/14436-007
The Lives of LGBT Older Adults: Understanding Challenges and Resilience, N. A. Orel and C. A. Fruhauf (Editors)
Copyright © 2015 by the American Psychological Association. All rights reserved.

THE LIFE COURSE PERSPECTIVE, THE CLOSET,
AND EXPERIENCES OF DISCRIMINATION

The *life course perspective* holds that social context, structural factors, and age cohort influence aging processes (Elder, 1994), including the health needs and experiences of older LGBT adults (Institute of Medicine [IOM], 2011). Cancer and cardiovascular disease can become greater threats among middle-aged and older gay men, whereas some issues span the life course, such as body image and eating disorders, substance use, and mental health (Makadon, Mayer, Potter, & Goldhammer, 2008). Different age cohorts of LGBT people have had different experiences with coming out and cultural homophobia. These influence LGBT individuals' willingness to be out to their health care providers and to be out in a variety of social contexts (Mayer et al., 2008).

Within the same age cohort, different life experiences can affect experiences of being out or closeted in various contexts. For example, gay veterans' advocates report that Vietnam veterans often have negative associations with their military service related to homophobia and the stress of hiding their sexuality or a dishonorable discharge based on accusations of homosexuality; this can cause them not to access Veterans Affairs services. The mental health implications of hiding one's sexual orientation provide lucid examples of minority stress. Minority stress is caused by experiences of antigay prejudice, expectations of such events, the internalization of societal attitudes, and concealment of one's sexual orientation. Minority stress can affect mental and physical health across the life trajectory (Meyer, 2003). Although many LGBT elders have concealed their sexuality or gender identity as a survival strategy in a hostile society, many LGBT baby boomers have been out for decades and do not want to go back into the closet to be able to access senior services.

Among gay and bisexual men and transgender women who were ages 25 to 44 at the peak of the AIDS epidemic (1987–1996), AIDS "decimated their social networks" and "shap[ed] their personal and social lives during the epidemic" (Rosenfeld, Bartlam, & Smith, 2012, p. 255). Many of these older gay men are now reaching retirement age. The AIDS epidemic intensified antigay sentiment and homophobia in the United States. The viewing of AIDS as a gay men's issue led the federal government largely to ignore HIV/AIDS during the 1980s and adopt a number of policies that have undermined public health, such as the ban on using federal funds for syringe exchange and the HIV entry ban (Vaid, 1995). The view of AIDS as a gay White man's issue also caused many Black gay and bisexual men to believe they were not at risk (Cohen, 1999).

Being African American is a highly significant contextual variable for older Black gay men (Adams & Kimmel, 1997). Many Black LGBT people report experiences of racial discrimination in predominately White gay bars, clubs, and other social contexts (Adams & Kimmel, 1997; Cahill, Battle,

& Meyer, 2003). A survey of Black lesbians attending the Zuna Institute's National Black Lesbian Conference found "high health-related quality of life, in spite of a high frequency of health impairments" (p. 820) The most common health issue was obesity. Thirteen percent of respondents were morbidly obese; only 15% of the women were in a healthy weight range (Dibble, Eliason, & Crawford, 2012).

Andersen and Fetner (2008) found that older Americans were more likely to hold antigay views than younger age cohort(s). Many older LGBT people experience prejudicial treatment from heterosexual age peers or service providers or fear that they will experience such treatment. These fears are often based on past experiences of discrimination. Antigay discrimination, or discrimination based on real or perceived sexual orientation, was once widespread in both public sector and private sector employment (D'Emilio, 1998). A review of 50 studies of sexual orientation discrimination conducted from the 1980s through 2007 found that between 16% and 68% of gay, lesbian, and bisexual respondents reported experiencing workplace discrimination. Experiences included being fired, denied employment, denied a promotion, and receiving a bad job rating or evaluation (Badgett, Lau, Sears, & Ho, 2007). Many LGBT people have also experienced family and social rejection. Older Americans are also more likely to hold inaccurate beliefs about the casual transmission of HIV (Kaiser Family Foundation, 2010).

Despite the significant changes in American society in recent decades, most LGBT youth report discrimination and harassment in school (Kosciw, Diaz, & Greytak, 2008). Such experiences were even more intense for people growing up in the 1940s and 1950s. These individuals, now LGBT elders in their 60s or older, "came of age in a psychosocial environment in which heterosexism, homophobia, and stigmatization were more powerful and less challenged than they are today" (Grossman, 2006, p. 53). Homosexuality was listed as a mental illness in the *Diagnostic and Statistical Manual of Mental Disorders* until 1973 (Grossman, 2006, p. 53) and continued to be criminalized in 13 states until 2003, when archaic sex laws were struck down by the U.S. Supreme Court in *Lawrence v. Texas* (Cahill, 2004). Many Americans continue to consider homosexuality a sin and morally unacceptable.

The lack of training available for medical and other service providers in meeting the unique needs of LGBT and HIV-positive older adults requires immediate attention. Because AIDS was viewed as gay disease (originally known as *gay-related immune deficiency*) in the early years of the epidemic and still disproportionately burdens gay men in the United States, public opinion about HIV/AIDS in this country is linked to attitudes toward homosexuality (Vaid, 1995). Therefore, even heterosexuals living with HIV can experience antigay stigma due to the association of HIV with homosexuality (Cahill & Valadez, 2013).

Mainstream Senior Services

Institutions that provide services to older adults, such as senior centers, congregate meal programs, housing assistance, food stamps, and other entitlements, may not be meeting the needs of LGBT elders. A federal government survey in 2001 found that LGBT elders were only 20% as likely as heterosexual elders to access such services (U.S. Administration on Aging, 2001). A survey of more than 1,100 LGB elders in Michigan and Ohio found that 53% were dissatisfied with the services offered at their senior centers, even though the kinds of services available to the general older adult population in the United States—physical health, mental health, housing, legal rights, supports for family and social networks, and spirituality- or religion-based groups—should be LGBT affirming (Orel, 2006). One respondent who requested an educational program on LGBT aging was told that this type of program was "not needed at this particular senior center" (Orel, 2006, p. 238).

Many LGBT older adults have expressed a desire for LGBT "exclusive" senior centers. However, one study found that LGBT elders believed that mainstream senior centers that were LGBT accepting "probably would meet more of their needs because of the expansive services currently in place at government-sponsored senior centers" (Orel, 2006, p. 235).

LGBT-Specific Senior Services

Services and Advocacy for GLBT Elders (SAGE) was founded as Senior Action in a Gay Environment in 1977 in New York City. The group began by organizing monthly social events for gay and lesbian seniors. In 1984, it started a senior drop-in center at the New York City Gay and Lesbian Community Center. More recently, its services have expanded to include clinical services, counseling, assistance in accessing government benefits and legal services, visiting homebound elders, and caregiving assistance. It has also expanded its work in training and technical assistance to mainstream senior service providers and policy advocacy (Kling & Kimmel, 2006). In 2012, SAGE opened the country's first LGBT-specific senior center in New York City (Johnston, 2012).

Services and Advocacy for GLBT Elders, in partnership with 14 aging organizations, including the LGBT Aging Project in Boston, also leads the National Resource Center on LGBT Aging. Founded in 2010 with funding from the U.S. Department of Health and Human Services (DHHS), the center provides training, technical assistance, and educational resources to providers of services for the aging, LGBT organizations, and LGBT older adults. The LGBT Aging Project and the Fenway Institute partner with several local universities and aging service providers to lead the Massachusetts LGBT Aging Needs Assessment coalition. This coalition has studied LGBT participants at congregate meal sites to better understand LGBT older adults in Greater Boston (Van Wagenen, Sass, & Bradford, 2012). Such community-based research collaborative efforts are another important community resource for LGBT older adults.

Many medium and large U.S. cities, although not all, have LGBT community centers. Many of these centers offer targeted services for LGBT elders. For example, the Los Angeles Gay and Lesbian Community Services Center, one of the largest LGBT organizations in the world, offers a wide array of social, educational, and support services to LGBT elders, all at low or no cost. These include health and wellness activities, enrichment classes, monthly dinners, social networking opportunities, support groups, and case management support (Los Angeles Gay and Lesbian Community Services Center, 2012).

HEALTH DISPARITIES AFFECTING LGBT ELDERS

Among the most important government and community services for LGBT elders is access to clinically competent health care. Successful aging requires good physical and mental health as well as social functioning (de Vries & Blando, 2004). Good health requires the prevention, or early detection and treatment, of conditions that can complicate life. There are significant documented health disparities affecting LGBT people (Healthy People 2020, 2010; Mayer et al., 2008). The exact causes of these health disparities are still understudied and therefore not well understood (Mayer et al., 2008). Meyer and Northridge (2007) suggested that the social stigma and systematic discrimination based on sexual orientation and gender identity create a stressful social environment that has a significant negative impact on the overall health of LGBT individuals. Fredriksen-Goldsen et al. (2011) reported that LGBT health disparities correlate with minority stress and experiences of anti-LGBT prejudice. Health disparities are exacerbated by not being out to health care providers (Bernstein et al., 2008) and lack of access to health insurance (Badgett, 1994, cited in Committee on LGBT Health Issues, 2011; Cahill, 2007a; Cochran, 2001, cited in Committee on LGBT Health Issues, 2011; Diamant, Wold, Spritzer, & Gelberg, 2000, cited in Committee on LGBT Health Issues, 2011; Ponce, Cochran, Pizer, & Mays, 2010). Lesbians are more likely than heterosexual and bisexual women to be overweight and obese, increasing their risk for cardiovascular disease, lipid abnormalities, glucose intolerance, and morbidity related to inactivity (Boehmer, Bowen, & Bauer, 2007). Gay and bisexual men in the United States are at least

44 times as likely as other men and 40 times as likely as all women to be living with HIV (Centers for Disease Control and Prevention [CDC], 2010). At least half of the people living with HIV in the United States are gay or bisexual men (CDC, 2010). Also, nearly half of the people with HIV in the United States are age 50 or older (Effros et al., 2008). Therefore, of an estimated 1.1 million Americans living with HIV, at least a quarter million are older gay and bisexual men. In addition to HIV, gay and bisexual men have elevated rates of cigarette smoking, alcohol and recreational drug use; sexually transmitted infections, including viral hepatitis; eating disorders; cardiovascular disease; anal cancer and AIDS-related cancers; and violence and trauma stemming from hate crimes, domestic violence, and sexual assault (Fenway Guide to LGBT Health Module 3, 2012). Finally, a study in Massachusetts showed that bisexuals experience poorer health compared with homosexuals and heterosexuals, as well as higher rates of mental health issues and smoking (Conron, Mimiaga, & Landers, 2010). Transgender patients may be at greater risk of cardiovascular disease due to exogenous hormone use (Futterweit, 1998).

Research on racial disparities within the LGBT population is extremely limited. However, HIV inflicts a disproportionate burden on Black gay and bisexual men compared with other gay and bisexual men (Millett, Peterson, Wolitski, & Stall, 2006). Black and Latina transgender women experience higher rates of HIV than White non-Hispanic and Asian transgender women (Herbst et al., 2008; Hwahng & Nuttbrock, 2007). Mays, Yancey, Cochran, Weber, and Fielding (2002) found higher rates of obesity and tobacco and alcohol use and lower rates of health coverage among Black and Latina lesbians compared with Black and Latina heterosexual women.

The IOM (2011) has documented health disparities among LGBT people, and LGBT elders in particular. Health issues affecting older gay and bisexual men include HIV and other sexually transmitted infections, sexual function, cardiovascular disease, prostate and anal health, cancer, eating disorders, and body image. Issues affecting older lesbian and bisexual women include cardiovascular disease, cancer, and osteoporosis. Research has suggested that LGBT older adults are disproportionately at risk for substance use or abuse and mental health issues. Health issues affecting transgender elders include many of the aforementioned, as well as hepatitis C and hormone-related complications such as venous thromboembolism. Also, many female-to-male transgender elders should be screened for ovarian cancer, and many male-to-female older adults should be screened for prostate cancer. For transgender elders to receive the health care they need, open communication with health providers regarding gender history is essential (Appelbaum, 2008).

A provider's knowledge of a patient's sexual orientation and gender identity is essential for appropriate screening and care (Makadon, 2011). Patients who disclose their sexual orientation to health care providers may feel safer discussing their health and risk behaviors as well (Klitzman & Greenberg, 2002). A sample of New York City men who have sex with men (MSM) from the 2004–2005 National HIV Behavioral Surveillance system found that 61% had not disclosed their same-sex orientation or behavior to their medical providers. White and native-born MSM were more likely to have disclosed than Black, Latino, Asian, and immigrant MSM. Disclosure was found to correlate with having been tested for HIV (Bernstein et al., 2008).

Barriers to culturally competent health care for LGBT people include a reluctance on the part of LGBT patients to disclose their sexual and gender identity; a lack of providers trained to address the specific health care needs of LGBT people; structural barriers to health insurance, such as the outlawing of domestic partner health benefits for public sector employees in Michigan, Ohio, Georgia, and other states (Cahill, 2007b); and a lack of culturally appropriate prevention services (Mayer et al., 2008).

Many health care providers are uncomfortable providing care to LGBT people. Although antigay attitudes among providers appear to have declined significantly over the past 2 decades, a 2007 study found that 18% of doctors in California are "sometimes" or "often" uncomfortable caring for gay patients (Smith & Mathews, 2007). A recent survey of deans of medical education at medical schools in the United States and Canada found that the median time dedicated to teaching LGBT-related content in the entire medical school curriculum was 5 hours. One third of medical schools reported that zero hours of LGBT content were taught. Only 24% of the deans considered their school's overall coverage of LGBT material "good" or "very good" on a five-category Likert scale (Obedin-Maliver et al., 2011). A number of studies of transgender people show high levels of dissatisfaction with health care and even widespread experiences of discrimination and harassment in health care settings (Grant et al., 2010; Nemoto, Operario, & Keatley, 2005).

INITIATIVES THAT CAN HELP LGBT ELDERS

Designating LGBT Elders a Population of "Greatest Social Need" Under the Older Americans Act

Mainstream health and social service providers should be trained on the unique needs of LGBT older adults, including those living with HIV. This training should address cultural competency and be accompanied by ongoing technical assistance and capacity-building assistance to support integration of new information critical to improving elder care. The Older Americans Act (OAA) was passed by Congress in 1965 and is considered to be the major vehicle for the organization and delivery of social and nutritional services for people ages 60 and older and their caregivers. Services include a wide range of programs related to elder abuse and neglect, mental health, benefits counseling, civil engagement, nutritional services, healthy aging, evidence-based health promotion and disease prevention, adult day care, transportation, and caregiving (U.S. Administration on Aging, 2012). The OAA also funds workforce training and research. The OAA, currently overdue for reauthorization, should broaden the definition of older adults with "greatest social need" to include older adults living with HIV and LGBT elders. This would allow resources to be targeted to train aging network provider staff and conduct research to better understand the experiences of these populations in elder service settings. A federal nondiscrimination law inclusive of sexual orientation and gender identity that covers housing and public accommodations as well as employment would ensure LGBT elders' access to senior services from private providers as well as those run by government agencies.

State laws can also protect LGBT elders' ability to access mainstream senior services. A law passed in New York State in 2011 mandates an annual needs assessment of older adults from underserved communities, including LGBT elders. The law requires the New York State Office of Aging to report annually on the extent to which services are meeting the needs of LGBT elders and other demographic groups and how services need to be expanded or improved. It also requires the state's aging director to fund training, outreach, and education to improve senior services for LGBT elders, including in senior centers and care facilities (Ford, 2011).

Housing and Assisted Living

Increasingly, "aging in place" (i.e., the ability to live independently and safely in one's own home) is considered the preferred course for older adults in the United States. LGBT elders are no different from their heterosexual peers in seeking to age in place (Orel, 2006). To this end, in 2009 the Los Angeles Gay and Lesbian Community Services Center received U.S. Administration on Aging funding for a 3-year LGBT Aging in Place Initiative. This initiative provides targeted support services and training for service providers who assist Los Angeles LGBT elders as they age in place (Los Angeles Gay and Lesbian Community Services Center, 2009).

As discussed in other chapters in this book, LGBT elders have also expressed a desire for LGBT-only nursing homes and retirement communities (Orel, 2006). In addition to long-term-care facilities and retirement communities, there are several million federally subsidized senior housing units in the United States that provide low-cost housing for seniors living on a fixed income. Most LGBT elders who enter senior housing will access mainstream senior housing. It is essential that nondiscrimination policies be adopted and implemented and that service providers receive extensive training on the particular experiences and needs of older LGBT people.

The Housing Opportunities Made Equal Act, introduced into the 112th Congress, would amend the Fair Housing Act to include nondiscrimination on the basis of sexual orientation, gender identity, or marital status ("Kerry, Nadler Propose Fair Housing Bill for LGBTs," 2011). A U.S. Department of Housing and Urban Development (HUD) rule issued in 2011 and finalized in 2012 guarantees equal access to HUD programs regardless of sexual orientation or gender identity ("Equal Access to Housing in HUD Programs," 2012). This would include senior housing that is funded by HUD or subject to a Federal Housing Administration–insured mortgage. State nondiscrimination laws also protect against discrimination in public housing, including public senior housing (Gay and Lesbian Advocates and Defenders, GLAD Legal InfoLine response, October 17, 2012). Furthermore, 16 states prohibit discrimination on the basis of sexual orientation and gender identity; five additional states prohibit sexual orientation discrimination but not gender identity. Most of these laws cover housing, but owner-occupied multifamily homes are often exempted (National Gay and Lesbian Task Force, 2012).

An increasing number of LGBT elders are seeking housing in LGBT senior housing developments or in mainstream subsidized housing that is LGBT friendly. Examples of these include Triangle Square in Hollywood, California; the for-profit Rainbow Vision in Santa Fe, New Mexico; an open-house retirement village in San Francisco, California; and William Way Senior Residences in Philadelphia, Pennsylvania (Adelman, Gurevitch, de Vries, & Blando, 2006; Gay and Lesbian Elder Housing, 2012; Grant, 2010; Wiggin, 2012). As of 2009, at least eight LGBT-specific or LGBT-friendly housing communities existed across the United States (Koskovich, 2009, cited in Grant, 2010, p. 95).

Older LGBT people may be more likely than their heterosexual peers to move into nursing homes because they often lack immediate family members, such as children, to move in with when they become unable to live on their own (Ritter, 2011). Gay and lesbian elders in nursing homes and assisted living facilities are often presumed to be heterosexual and believe that it is necessary to hide their sexual orientation from staff and other residents (Johnson, Jackson, Arnette, & Koffman, 2005). Long-term relationships with same-sex partners are often devalued, and those who are discovered or assumed to be lesbian or gay often experience discrimination, abuse, and neglect by staff (Fairchild, Carrino, & Ramirez, 1996). Many gay and lesbian elders fear rejection or neglect by health care providers, including personal care aides, as well as other residents of long-term-care facilities and nursing homes (Stein & Bonuck, 2001).

Although research on HIV-positive elders (half of whom are gay and bisexual men in the United States) in congregate living facilities is limited, evidence suggests that stigma persists among other residents, as well as staff charged with the care and well-being of residents (CDC, 2010). For example, a 75-year-old former university provost was ejected from an Arkansas assisted living facility in 2009 because of his HIV status, in violation of the Americans With Disabilities Act, the Fair Housing Act, and analogous state nondiscrimination laws. Management at the facility insisted they could not guarantee the safety of its kitchen and laundry staff if the man stayed (Lambda Legal HIV Project, 2010).

A number of studies have found widespread fear among older lesbians and gay men of being rejected in senior care settings by both residents and staff because of their sexual orientation (Rivera, Wilson, & Jennings, 2011; Stein, Beckerman, & Sherman, 2010). Ritter (2011) called for amending the Nursing Home Reform Act, which "heavily regulated nursing homes receiving federal funds," by "adding a statutory right of nondiscrimination based on sexual orientation and gender identity to the residents' bill of rights" (p. 1001), and requiring nursing aides to receive cultural competency training in LGBT elder issues. Gay seniors were particularly concerned about possible discriminatory treatment from personal care aides (Stein, Beckerman, & Sherman, 2010). It is also critical that personal care aides, especially those who treat LGBT elders in their homes, be trained in clinically competent and nondiscriminatory care by state elder service agencies. One successful training program for assisted living and elder service staff was conducted in Colorado by the Boulder County Aging Services department. The program, Project Visibility, trained senior service staff on LGBT issues. Evaluations showed that 84% of those trained reported "an increased awareness of LGBT aging issues," and 78% "better understood the fears experienced by some LGBT elders" (Grant, 2010, p. 99).

Caregiving

People who self-identify as LGBT are less likely to have children than heterosexuals. Only 17% of same-sex couples who self-identified during the 2010 Census reported raising their own children (Gates & Cooke, 2011). The term *own* is understood to mean children to whom they gave birth or fathered. Hence, most LGBT elders are without children later in life (de Vries, 2006). Generally, LGBT elders are more likely to live alone (Brookdale Center on Aging & Senior Action in a Gay Environment, 1999; Cahill, South, & Spade, 2000; Frazer, 2009; Rosenfeld, 1999) and to be single (de Vries, 2006; MetLife Mature Market Institute and American Society on Aging, 2010). Not having a partner and not having children are particularly common among older gay men. Because most elder caregiving in the United States is provided by children or partners/spouses, LGBT elders may have a greater need for senior services, including formal caregiving assistance (U.S. DHHS, 1998).

As part of the OAA, the federal Family Caregivers Support Program has a broad definition of *family* that includes same-sex partners and spouses (Grant, 2010). States use funding from this program to refer caregivers to services; provide training, counseling, and support groups; and offer respite care. A 2004 study found that LGBT older adults were heavily involved in caregiving both to members of their families of origin and to same-sex partners and close friends (Cantor, Brennan, & Shippy, 2004). Until 2013, a key federal policy that protects people's ability to take unpaid leave from their jobs to care for family members when a health crisis hits did not cover same-sex partners; the Family Medical Leave Act (FMLA) covered opposite-sex spouses but not same-sex partners and spouses. However, in the wake of the U.S. Supreme Court's *United States v. Windsor* ruling striking down federal nonrecognition of same-sex marriages, the Department of Labor took steps to treat same-sex spouses equally under the FMLA and other policies (Cahill & Makadon, 2013).

Hospitals

The recent decision by the Joint Commission to require hospital non-discrimination policies covering sexual orientation and gender identity will go a long way toward improving health care for LGBT people (Joint Commission, 2010). Another positive step would be for the DHHS to designate LGBT people as a medically underserved population (MUP) and to designate providers trained in LGBT health as a health professional shortage area (HPSA). MUPs may include groups of persons who face economic, cultural or linguistic barriers to health care (Health Resources Services Administration, 2011a). LGBT people are a demographic group experiencing a shortage of primary medical care and mental health providers, or at least a shortage of providers trained and willing to serve them (HPSAs) in a culturally competent and nondiscriminatory manner (Health Resources Services Administration, 2011b). The Negotiated Rule Making Committee, a body appointed by the DHHS to examine the issue, voted overwhelmingly in November 2011 to designate LGBT people as an MUP and LGBT competent providers as an HPSA. As of November 2013, the DHHS had not taken action on the recommendation.

Sexual Health Education

For LGBT elders, anti-LGBT stigma is compounded by stereotypes and misconceptions of sexuality in later adulthood. Many people remain sexually active well into old age, despite prevailing assumptions to the contrary (Lindau et al., 2007). Stereotypes that older adults are not sexually active limit sexual health education from reaching older populations. Health care providers tend not to assess older patients for sexual health–related risks, regardless of sexual orientation and gender. In one national study, adults over age 50 at risk for HIV were 80% less likely to be tested for HIV than younger people (Stall & Catania, 1994).

This lack of sexual health knowledge inevitably translates into greater levels of high-risk behaviors and practices within the older adult population. For example, lower rates of condom use among older adults may be linked to lack of knowledge about HIV transmission and the effectiveness of condoms in preventing HIV and sexually transmitted infections. The prevalence of erectile dysfunction, a common issue for older men, may also make the effective use of a condom more difficult. It is essential that sexual health education be targeted toward older LGBT people.

Mental Health Services

LGBT people experience barriers to accessing mental health services. Experiences of discrimination among LGBT people can make them less likely to seek needed mental health services and "experiences of discrimination may engender negative expectations among stigmatized groups about how they will be treated within larger institutional systems, making them wary of entering those situations" (Burgess, Lee, Tran, & van Ryn, 2007, p. 11). Compared with heterosexuals, LGBT people were more likely to report "that they did not receive mental services, or that such services were delayed" (Burgess et al., 2007, p. 11). Researchers examining mental health and substance use services in rural areas found widespread experiences of discrimination among LGBT clients at the hands of both providers and heterosexual clients (Willging, Salvador, & Kano, 2006). Clients who were LGBT were frequently silenced and told not to raise issues of sexuality or gender identity in group settings. Counselors expressed disapproval of homosexuality and sought to convert clients to heterosexuality. Clients who self-identified as being LGBT were often refused entry into programs to "protect" them from discrimination or placed in isolation from other clients. Of the 20 providers interviewed, only one had had formal training in LGBT mental health issues (Willging, Salvador, & Kano, 2006).

One way to improve mental health services for LGBT people would be for the DHHS to mandate this through the "essential health benefit" provision of the Affordable Care Act (ACA). The ACA mandates that all insurers cover certain *essential health benefits*. An insurer's essential health benefits package must cover 10 categories of benefits—including mental health and substance abuse services. The ACA could lead to a dramatic expansion in access to behavioral health services for LGBT people. The DHHS should issue a regulation requiring that mental health and substance use services—statutorily covered as essential health benefits—be clinically competent to serve LGBT people.

Health Insurance Coverage

The ACA of 2010 expands access to health insurance and seeks to improve outcomes and reduce costs. It requires insurance companies to cover all who apply for insurance and offer the same rates without regard to preexisting health conditions (U.S. DHHS, 2010). Thanks to the ACA, LGBT elders in the 35 states that do not recognize same-sex marriage will have more affordable insurance options. Most of these states also ban domestic partner recognition, including health insurance for same-sex partners of municipal or state government workers. Because of the slew of antigay family laws and amendments that stripped thousands of same-sex partners of their employer-provided health insurance, as well as discrimination against LGBT families by private insurance companies, LGBT people are much less likely to have insurance coverage (Badgett, 1994, cited in IOM, 2011; Cahill, 2007a; Cochran, 2001, cited in IOM, 2011; Diamant et al., 2000, cited in IOM, 2011; Ponce et al., 2010). Lesbian and bisexual women are less likely than heterosexual women to access preventive health care, such as Pap smears and mammograms (Fish, 2009; IOM, 1999). This is also true of transgender people (Grant et al., 2010). For all these reasons, the ACA's expansion of health care access is critically important to LGBT Americans.

The ACA also provides support for preventative care and HIV testing, treatment, and prevention services. It prohibits insurance companies from denying coverage for preexisting medical conditions, such as HIV infection. Today only 13% of the estimated 1.2 million Americans living with HIV have private insurance, and 25% have no insurance (Cahill, 2012). Only half of people with HIV in the United States receive regular medical care, and less than a third are being treated effectively, such that they are virally suppressed (CDC, 2011). The preexisting condition provision will enable thousands of people living with HIV to receive health coverage. This in turn will improve treatment outcomes, a key goal of President Barack Obama's National HIV/AIDS Strategy.

Medicare and Medicaid, furthermore, provide critical support to thousands of LGBT elders and elders living with HIV in the United States. Most LGBT elders qualify for Medicare if they have paid into the system sufficiently during their working lives. At least 10% of all people living with HIV in the United States, or 120,000 people, are Medicare beneficiaries (Gilden, Kubisiak, & Gilden, 2007). People living with HIV qualify for Medicare based on age and having paid into the system or because they have received Social Security Disability Insurance for at least 2 years, after which 93%

go on to qualify for Medicare (Kaiser Family Foundation, 2009). With the expansion of Medicare into prescription drug coverage (i.e., Medicare Part D), Medicare spending on people with HIV now surpasses Medicaid spending on people with HIV (Kaiser Family Foundation, 2009).

Many people with HIV receive Medicaid, a means-tested health insurance program for the poor and disabled. However, until the passage of the ACA, childless adults could not qualify for Medicaid unless they were disabled. This meant that they had to have an AIDS diagnosis. The Medicaid expansion to individuals who earn up to 138% of the poverty level, a key component of the ACA, will change this starting in 2014. This would allow many childless low-income LGBT individuals, including older LGBT people, to access Medicaid. However, the June 2012 U.S. Supreme Court ruling struck down the mandatory expansion of Medicaid (*National Federation of Independent Business et al. v. Sebelius, Secretary of Health and Human Services, et al.*, 2012). About half of the 30 million people newly able to access health coverage under the ACA would be covered under Medicaid expansion, including low-income adults who are not disabled and who do not have dependent children (Washington Post Staff, 2010). This expansion would benefit many older LGBT people not yet eligible for Medicare, many older people living with HIV, and millions of other low-income Americans.

Medicaid covers long-term care or home-based care for people without private insurance to cover such services. To qualify, however, individuals must "spend down" their assets. Spousal impoverishment protections protect the healthy spouse from having to become poor for the other spouse to qualify for Medicaid coverage. Unfortunately, under federal law, these protections only apply to an opposite-sex married spouse. As a result, same-sex partners have lost their homes to pay for the partner's health care. In recent years, Vermont and Massachusetts amended their Medicaid regulations to allow same-sex spouses to be protected under the spousal impoverishment protection (SAGE, 2010). In June 2011, the U.S. Center for Medicare and Medicaid Services issued guidance to states explaining what Vermont and Massachusetts had done and letting them know that this was an option for them as well (Mann, 2011). States should follow suit and protect the ability of LGBT elders to age in place and avoid unnecessary impoverishment.

In August 2013, the Centers for Medicare and Medicaid Services announced that same-sex spouses would, like heterosexual spouses, be entitled to care in the same nursing home in which their spouse resides (Cahill & Makadon, 2013). Previously, same-sex spouses in need of contemporaneous nursing home care and on Medicare Advantage either had to go to separate nursing homes or one had to disenroll from Medicare Advantage, which meant paying more out-of-pocket for care.

Community Connectedness

Connectedness to LGBT communities is an important coping resource for LGBT people that provides nonstigmatizing environments and affirms positive self-appraisals (Meyer, 2010). Friend (1990) found that having a social network of family and friends accepting of gay and lesbian elders' homosexuality was essential to successful aging among gay men and lesbians. Grossman, D'Augelli, and Hershberger (2000) found that satisfaction with social support networks was greater among those who were out to the members of their social support networks. Community connectedness—including supportive social relationships—has also proven protective against HIV infection (Lauby et al., 2012). Greater community involvement counters the negative effects of antigay bias on safer sex practices among gay men by providing social support, enhancing feelings of self-efficacy and positive self-identity, and reinforcing peer norms supporting safer sex practices (Ramirez-Valles, 2002). Interventions are needed that support and nurture affirming social networks for older LGBT people.

The Fenway Institute piloted a group intervention in 2008 to reduce HIV sexual risk, depression-related withdrawal, and anxiety-related social avoidance in gay and bisexual men ages 40 years and older; nearly all the participants were 50 or older. The intervention, titled "40 and Forward," was a series of 2-hour weekly sessions that brought together groups of gay men, ranging from 49 to 71 years of age and of multiple races, to socialize and discuss topics such as safer sex. Men who participated in the intervention reported a significant decrease in depressive symptoms as well as a significant increase in condom use self-efficacy (Reisner et al. 2011). Importantly, the intervention also helped socially isolated older gay men develop social support networks, a critical resiliency factor against HIV.

Congregate meal programs can also provide social support and reduce isolation for LGBT elders. Few states offer LGBT-specific congregate meal programs (Porter, 2012). In the Greater Boston area, more than half a dozen sites offer meals on a weekly or monthly basis. These congregate meals not only provide nutritional support but also allow LGBT elders to find others like them and develop social support and friendship networks (Van Wagenen, Sass, & Bradford, 2012).

Veterans Affairs

The Department of Veterans Affairs (VA; 2009) is the largest single provider of medical care to people with HIV in the United States. It has served 64,000 HIV-positive veterans since 1981 and currently serves 23,000 HIV-infected veterans. With more than 8 million individuals enrolled in the

VA health care system, many LGBT elders, especially gay and bisexual men, receive health care there. Little is known about the experiences and needs of LGBT veterans. A few State Behavioral Risk Factor Surveillance Surveys (BRFSS) ask about sexual orientation; all ask about veteran status. An analysis of Massachusetts BRFSS data from 2005 through 2010 found that lesbian, gay, and bisexual veterans reported higher rates of suicidal ideation compared with heterosexual veterans (Blosnich, Bossarte, & Silenzio, 2012b).

Other issues that may disproportionately affect gay veterans are "trauma from childhood adversity interacting with military trauma" (Blosnich, Bossarte, & Silenzio, 2012a, p. e10–11). Because so many gay veterans associate their military service with concealing their sexual orientation, and because some were dishonorably discharged under the previous policies banning homosexuals from serving, it is essential that the VA undertake affirmative outreach to LGBT veterans to ensure that they access the health care services and benefits to which they are entitled. It is also critical that VA staff be trained in LGBT issues so that they can provide clinically competent care. Such trainings have been conducted in New York, Massachusetts, and elsewhere.

The VA also provides support groups, congregate meals, and other opportunities for social support. For example, the Manhattan VA has a gay men's support group, and Fenway Health in Boston runs an LGBT veterans support group. Such groups are critical to reducing social isolation for older LGBT veterans and improving access to services.

A directive mandating nondiscriminatory access to care and services on the basis of gender identity was issued by VA leadership in 2011; it is critical that such a directive covering sexual orientation also be issued (Cray, 2011). In September 2013, U.S. Attorney General Eric Holder sent a letter to Congress stating that, in response to the U.S. Supreme Court ruling in *United States v. Windsor*, the administration will no longer enforce opposite-sex spouse–only language, clearing the way for same-sex spouses to access benefits (Cahill & Makadon, 2013).

Income Support Programs: Social Security, Pensions, and 401(k)s

Until 2013, Social Security regulations denied LGBT older persons with partners or spouses access to funds from systems they paid into throughout their working lives, but could not access due to the unequal treatment of same-sex couples (Cahill & Makadon, 2013; Cahill & South, 2002). Social Security represents 39% of all income received by elders in the United States. Fifty-three percent of married couples and 74% of unmarried individuals receive half or more of their income from Social Security (Social Security Administration, 2012). Social Security survivor benefits allow widows, widowers, and dependent children to put food on the table and fairly compensate them when their spouse pays into the system his or her whole life but dies before being able to enjoy these retirement savings. Until 2013, however, surviving same-sex partners and spouses were not eligible for these benefits, even though they have paid taxes into the system for their entire lives.

The September 11, 2001, terrorist attacks illustrated the unfairness of this policy: Same-sex survivors of victims were denied Social Security and worker's compensation survivor benefits. They also had to struggle to access funds from the victims' compensation fund administered by the U.S. Justice Department. Same-sex partners were also ineligible for spousal benefits, which allow a partner to earn about half his or her life partner's Social Security payment if that rate is higher. As a result of the 2013 *United States v. Windsor* ruling striking down federal nonrecognition of same-sex marriages, the Social Security Administration is now treating same-sex couples residing in a state with marriage equality who were married in such a state equally under spousal and survivor benefits. It is less clear whether same-sex couples married in a marriage equality state (of which there were 17 in January 2014) who move to a state without marriage equality are eligible or whether same-sex couples who are in a civil union or domestic partnership are eligible. The latter may be eligible because individuals in civil unions and domestic partnerships can inherit a partner's personal property without a will. The Social Security Administration urges any couple who believe they are eligible for marriage-related Social Security benefits to apply; if they are found eligible, the benefits will be retroactive to the date of application (Cahill & Makadon, 2013).

Until recently, same-sex partners were also treated unequally under many retirement plans, such as pensions and 401(k)s. When they are able to access their deceased partner's benefits, they often must pay taxes on the income that opposite-sex partners are not required to pay. A surviving same-sex partner can be a beneficiary of a pension upon the participant's death. However, the pension proceeds are not tax favored as they are for a heterosexual widow or widower. Opposite-sex widows and widowers can roll over a 401(k) distribution into an IRA without paying income tax on the disbursement. Until recently, a same-sex surviving partner or spouse had to pay a federal withholding tax of 20% on 401(k) disbursements (Cahill, 2007a). Thankfully, starting in 2010, "nonspousal beneficiaries," including same-sex spouses and domestic partners, were able to roll over a lump sum 401(k) distribution into an IRA and shelter this from income taxes. Nonspousal beneficiaries are still treated differently from opposite-sex married spouses in that they must start taking distributions immediately (unlike federally recognized spouses), but they no longer must pay a 20% tax on a mandatory, lump sum distribution from a 401(k) (Lambda Legal, 2010). This final inequality will likely change as a result of *Windsor*.

Immigration Policy and Same-Sex Couples

Until *Windsor*, same-sex couples in which one partner is not a U.S. citizen or legal resident were often forced to leave the United States to stay together. After *Windsor*, couples married in the 17 states with marriage equality are now treated equally to heterosexual married spouses under U.S. immigration law. The U.S. Citizenship and Immigration Services focuses on where marriage was celebrated, not where the spouse or spouses live. This means that if you were married in one of the 17 states where same-sex marriage is legal, even if you live in a nonmarriage equality state now, you as a U.S. citizen should be able to sponsor your noncitizen spouse for a green card (lawful permanent resident; Cahill& Makadon, 2013).

RESEARCH GAPS

In February 2010, the IOM held the first of five committee meetings to develop a report on *The Health of Lesbian, Gay, Bisexual, and Transgender People: Building a Foundation for Better Understanding* (IOM, 2011). The National Institutes of Health (NIH) commissioned the report and charged the committee to assess current knowledge of the health status of LGBT people, to identify research gaps and opportunities, and to outline a research agenda to help NIH focus its research in this area. The committee's research agenda called attention to pressing areas of need—demographic research, social influences, intervention research, and transgender-specific health needs. The committee recommended collecting data on sexual orientation and gender identity in health surveys administered by the DHHS, and in other relevant federally funded surveys. Sexual orientation and gender identity measures should be included with other demographic information, in the same way as race and ethnicity data. Similarly, data on sexual orientation and gender identity should be collected in electronic health records in clinical settings, along with other demographic measures.

Asking questions about sexual orientation and gender identity is important because there are significant documented health disparities affecting LGBT people (Healthy People 2020, 2010; Mayer et al., 2008), and wide gaps in research on LGBT health remain. Gathering sexual orientation and gender identity data in a standardized way will allow a better understanding of LGBT health disparities and improve efforts at prevention, screening, and early detection of conditions that disproportionately affect LGBT people and older adults (Bradford, Cahill, Grasso, & Makadon, 2012). Every state conducts the Youth Risk Behavior Survey and the Behavioral Risk Factor Surveillance Survey, yet few states gather data on sexual orientation and even fewer on gender identity. The same is true of most national surveys. Thankfully, the DHHS added a sexual orientation question to the National Health Interview Survey in 2012 and is considering adding a gender identity question. Gathering sexual orientation and gender identity data in clinical settings allows providers to better understand and treat their patients and to compare their patients' health outcomes with national samples of LGB or LGBT people from national health surveys (Gates, 2011).

Gerontological research distinguishes among the "young-old," ages 65 to 74; the "old-old," ages 75 to 84; and the "oldest old," ages 85 and above. In general, the frequency of illnesses and chronic conditions increases with age (McMahan & Lutz, 2004). The majority of research on LGBT elders looks at the young-old LGBT cohort. More research is needed on the old-old and oldest-old LGBT people. We also need more research on LGBT elders from racial and ethnic minority backgrounds and LGBT elders living in rural areas. It would be useful to better understand resiliency factors among LGBT elders, as well as their specific experiences in a wide range of senior settings, from assisted living and nursing homes to senior centers and elder housing communities. The OAA and the National Institute on Aging should fund much of this research.

CONCLUSION

LGBT elders need access to mainstream senior services as well as policies that can support them. These include government-run and government-funded programs such as senior centers, senior housing, and congregate meal programs, as well as those of private organizations serving elders. Although many LGBT elders express a desire for LGBT-specific services, most want the option of seeking services through mainstream providers, who may be able to offer the broadest array. Still, LGBT programs at mainstream senior centers, LGBT elder programs at LGBT community centers, and LGBT-specific and LGBT-friendly housing communities are proliferating across the country.

The OAA should be amended to list LGBT elders and HIV-positive elders as populations of "greatest social need." This would facilitate training of service providers in LGBT elder issues and allow for much-needed research into the experiences of LGBT elders in mainstream senior settings, including assisted living and long-term-care facilities. State aging departments can take this step, as the federal Administration on Aging noted in 2012; Massachusetts was the first state to take this step (Cahill & Makadon, 2013). Nondiscrimination laws and policies, such as the regulations recently adopted by HUD, can also protect LGBT elders and provide peace of mind. Full implementation of the ACA will significantly expand access to health care for LGBT elders. The *United States v. Windsor* Supreme Court ruling means that legally married same-sex couples are now eligible to be treated equally to heterosexual spouses for income support programs such as Social Security, protections under Medicaid, and taxation policies regarding retirement plan disbursements to a same-sex beneficiary. These policies provide important income security to LGBT elders. Finally, creative efforts to promote community connectedness and reduce social isolation among LGBT elders can improve health and promote successful aging.

REFERENCES

Adams, C., & Kimmel, D. (1997). Exploring the lives of older African American gay men. In B. Greene (Ed.), *Ethnic and cultural diversity among lesbians and gay men. Psychological perspectives on lesbian and gay issues* (pp. 132–151). Thousand Oaks, CA: Sage.

Adelman, M., Gurevitch, J., de Vries, B., & Blando, J. (2006). openhouse: Community building and research in the LGBT aging population. In D. Kimmel, T. Rose, & S. David (Eds.), *Lesbian, gay, bisexual, and transgender aging: Research and clinical perspectives* (pp. 247–264). New York, NY: Columbia University Press.

Andersen, R., & Fetner, T. (2008). Cohort differences in tolerance of homosexuality: Attitudinal change in Canada and the United States, 1981–2000. *Public Opinion Quarterly, 72,* 311–330. doi:10.1093/poq/nfn017

Appelbaum, J. (2008). Late adulthood and aging: Clinical approaches. In H. Makadon, K. Mayer, J. Potter, & H. Goldhammer (Eds.), *The Fenway guide to lesbian, gay, bisexual and transgender health* (pp. 135–156). Philadelphia, PA: American College of Physicians.

Badgett, M. V. L. (1994, October). *Civil rights, civilized research: Constructing a sexual orientation anti-discrimination policy based on the evidence.* Paper presented at Association for Public Policy Analysis and Management Research Conference, San Francisco.

Badgett, M. V. L., Lau, H., Sears, B., & Ho, D. (2007). *Bias in the workplace: Consistent evidence of sexual orientation and gender identity discrimination.* Los Angeles, CA: UCLA Williams Institute. Retrieved from http://escholarship.org/uc/item/5h3731xr

Bernstein, K. T., Liu, K. L., Begier, E. M., Koblin, B., Karpati, A., & Murrill, C. (2008). Same-sex attraction disclosure to health care providers among New York City men who have sex with men. *Archives of Internal Medicine, 168,* 1458–1464. doi:10.1001/archinte.168.13.1458

Blosnich J. R., Bossarte R. M., & Silenzio, V. M. (2012a). Blosnich et al. respond. *American Journal of Public Health, 102,* e10–11. doi:10.2105/AJPH.2012.300815

Blosnich J. R., Bossarte R. M., & Silenzio V. M. (2012b). Suicidal ideation among sexual minority veterans: Results from the 2005–2010 Massachusetts Behavioral Risk Factor Surveillance Survey. *American Journal of Public Health, 102*(Suppl. 1), S44–S47.

Boehmer, U., Bowen, D. J., & Bauer, G. R. (2007). Overweight and obesity in sexual minority women: Evidence from population-based data. *American Journal of Public Health, 97*, 1134–1140. doi:10.2105/AJPH.2006.088419

Bradford, J. B., Cahill, S., Grasso, C., & Makadon, H. J. (2012). *Policy focus: Why gather data on sexual orientation and gender identity in clinical settings.* Boston, MA: Fenway Institute. Retrieved from http://www.fenwayhealth.org/site/DocServer/Policy_Brief_WhyGather..._v6_01.09.12.pdf?docID=9141

Brookdale Center on Aging at Hunter College & Senior Action in a Gay Environment. (1999). *Assistive housing for elderly gays and lesbians in New York City: Extent of need and the preferences of elderly gays and lesbians.* New York, NY: Author.

Burgess, D., Lee, R., Tran, A., & van Ryn, M. (2007). Effects of perceived discrimination on mental health and mental health services utilization among gay, lesbian, bisexual and transgender persons. *Journal of LGBT Health Research, 3*, 1–14. doi:10.1080/15574090802226626

Cahill, S. (2004). *Same-sex marriage in the United States: Focus on the facts.* New York, NY: Lexington.

Cahill, S. (2007a) The coming GLBT senior boom. *The Gay and Lesbian Review Worldwide*, 19–21.

Cahill, S. (2007b) The role of antigay family amendments in the 2004 election. In M. Strasser (Ed.), *Defending same-sex marriage: Volume 1. "Separate but equal" no more: A guide to the legal status of same-sex marriage, civil unions, and other partnerships* (pp. 119–140). Westport, CT: Praeger.

Cahill, S. (2012, June 28). The Supreme Court's ruling upholding the ACA is especially important for LGBT people and those living with HIV/AIDS. *Huffington Post.* Retrieved from http://www.huffingtonpost.com/sean-cahill/supreme-court-health-care-ruling-lgbt-people_b_1634742.html

Cahill, S., Battle, J., & Meyer, D. (2003). Partnering, parenting, and policy: Family issues affecting black lesbian, gay, bisexual and transgender people. *Race and Society, 6*, 85–98. doi:10.1016/j.racsoc.2004.11.002

Cahill, S., & Makadon, H. (2013, September). *LGBT elder health care and policy issues.* Paper presented at the Gay and Lesbian Medical Association Annual Meeting, Denver, CO.

Cahill, S., & South, K. (2002). Policy issues affecting lesbian, gay, bisexual, and transgender people in retirement. *Generations, 26*(2), 49–54.

Cahill, S., South, K., & Spade, J. (2000). *Outing age: Public policy issues affecting gay, lesbian, bisexual and transgender elders.* New York, NY: National Gay and Lesbian Task Force Policy Institute.

Cahill, S., & Valadez, R. (2013). Growing older with HIV/AIDS: New public health challenges. *American Journal of Public Health, 103*, e7–e15. doi:10.2105/AJPH.2012.301161

Cantor, M., Brennan, M., & Shippy, A. (2004). *Caregiving among lesbian, gay, bisexual and transgender New Yorkers*. New York, NY: National Gay and Lesbian Task Force Policy Institute.

Centers for Disease Control and Prevention. (2010, September). *HIV among gay, bisexual, and other men who have sex with men (MSM): Fact Sheet*. Retrieved from http://www.cdc.gov/hiv/risk/gender/msm

Centers for Disease Control and Prevention. (2011, December 2). Vital signs: HIV prevention through care and treatment—United States. *MMWR. Morbidity and Mortality Weekly Report, 60*, 1618–1623. Retrieved from http://www.cdc.gov/mmwr/preview/mmwrhtml/mm6047a4.htm

Cochran, S. D. (2001). Emerging issues in research on lesbians' and gay men's mental health: Does sexual orientation really matter? *American Psychologist, 56*, 931–947.

Cohen, C. J. (1999). *The boundaries of Blackness: AIDS and the breakdown of Black politics*. Chicago, IL: University of Chicago Press.

Committee on Lesbian, Gay, Bisexual, and Transgender Health Issues and Research Gaps and Opportunities; Board on the Health of Select Populations; Institute of Medicine. (2011). *The health of lesbian, gay, bisexual, and transgender (LGBT) people: Building a foundation for better understanding* (pp. 2–32). Washington, DC: National Academies Press.

Conron, K. J., Mimiaga, M. J., & Landers, S. J. (2010). A population-based study of sexual orientation identity and gender differences in adult health. *American Journal of Public Health, 100*, 1953–1960. doi:10.2105/AJPH.2009.174169

Cray, A. (2011). *Reaching all who served: An analysis of Department of Veterans Affairs LGBT health policies*. Washington, DC: National Coalition for LGBT Health. Retrieved from http://lgbthealth.webolutionary.com/sites/default/files/VA%20Final%20Report%20_0.pdf

D'Emilio, J. (1998). *Sexual politics, sexual communities: The making of a homosexual minority in the United States, 1940–1970*. Chicago, IL: University of Chicago Press. doi:10.7208/chicago/9780226922454.001.0001

de Vries, B. (2006). Home at the end of the rainbow: Supportive housing for LGBT elders. *Generations, 29*, 64–69.

de Vries, B., & Blando, J. (2004). The study of gay and lesbian aging: Lessons for social gerontology. In G. Herdt & B. de Vries (Eds.), *Gay and lesbian aging: Research and future directions* (pp. 3–28). New York, NY: Springer Publishing Company.

Diamant, A. L., Wold, C., Spritzer, K., & Gelberg, L. (2000). Health behaviors, health status, and access to and use of health care: A population-based study of lesbian, bisexual, and heterosexual women. *Archives of Family Medicine, 9*, 1043–1051.

Dibble, S. L., Eliason, M. J., & Crawford, B. (2012). Correlates of wellbeing among African American lesbians. *Journal of Homosexuality*, 59, 820–838. doi:10.1080 /00918369.2012.694763

Effros, R. B., Fletcher, C. V., Gebo, K., Halter, J. B., Hazzard, W. R. . . . High, K. P. (2008). Aging and infectious diseases: Workshop on HIV infection and aging: What is known and future research directions. *Clinical Infectious Diseases*, 47, 542–553. doi:10.1086/590150

Elder, G., Jr. (1994). Time, human agency, and social change: Perspectives on the life course. *Social Psychology Quarterly*, 57, 4–15. doi:10.2307/2786971

Equal Access to Housing in HUD Programs Regardless of Sexual Orientation or Gender Identity. Office of the Secretary, Department of Housing and Urban Development. Final Rule. 77 Fed. Reg. 5662-5676 (24 CFR Parts 5, 200, 203, 236, 400, 570, 574, 882, 891, and 982 [Docket No. FR 5359-F-02] RIN 2501-AD49).

Fairchild, S. K., Carrino, G. E., & Ramirez, M. (1996). Social workers' perceptions of staff attitudes toward resident sexuality in a random sample of New York State nursing homes: A pilot study. *Journal of Gerontological Social Work*, 26, 153–169. doi:10.1300/J083V26N01_10

Fenway Institute. (2012). *Fenway guide to LGBT health, module 3: Health promotion and disease prevention*. Boston, MA: The Fenway Institute. Retrieved from http://www.lgbthealtheducation.org/training/learning-modules

Fish, J. (2009). *Cervical screening in lesbian and bisexual women: A review of the worldwide literature using systematic methods*. Leicester, England: NHS Cervical Screening Programme, de Montfort University.

Ford, Z. (2011, September 26). New York Law to improve services for LGBT seniors. *Think Progress*. Retrieved from http://thinkprogress.org/lgbt/2011/09/26/328545/ new-york-law-to-improve-services-for-lgbt-seniors

Frazer, S. (2009). *LGBT health and human services needs in New York State*. Albany, NY: Empire State Pride Agenda.

Fredriksen-Goldsen, K. I., Kim, H.-J., Emlet, C. A., Muraco, A., Erosheva, E. A., Hoy-Ellis, C. P., . . . Petry, H. (2011). *The aging and health report: Disparities and resilience among LGBT older adults*. Seattle, WA: Institute for Multigenerational Health. doi:10.1037/e561402013-001

Friend, R. A. (1990). Older lesbian and gay people: A theory of successful aging. *Journal of Homosexuality*, 20, 99–118. doi:10.1300/J082v20n03_07

Futterweit, W. (1998). Endocrine therapy of transsexualism and potential complications of long-term treatment. *Archives of Sexual Behavior*, 27, 209–226. doi:10.1023/A:1018638715498

Gates, G. J. (2011). *How many people are lesbian, gay, bisexual, and transgender?* Los Angeles, CA: UCLA Williams Institute.

Gates, G. J., & Cooke, A. M. (2011). *United States Census Snapshot: 2010*. Los Angeles, CA: UCLA Williams Institute. Retrieved from http://williamsinstitute.law.ucla. edu/wp-content/uploads/Census2010Snapshot-US-v2.pdf

Gay and Lesbian Elder Housing. (2012). *What we do: Affordable housing developer.* Retrieved from http://gleh.org/what-we-do

Gilden, D. E., Kubisiak, J. M., & Gilden, D. M. (2007). Managing Medicare's caseload in the era of suppressive therapy. *American Journal of Public Health, 97,* 1053–1059. doi:10.2105/AJPH.2005.063636

Grant, J. M. (2010). *Outing age 2010: Public policy issues affecting lesbian, gay, bisexual and transgender elders.* Washington, DC: National Gay and Lesbian Task Force.

Grant, J. M., Mottet, L. A., Tanis, J., Herman, J. L., Harrison, J., & Keisling, M. (2010). *National transgender discrimination survey report on health and health care.* Washington, DC: National Center for Transgender Equality and National Gay and Lesbian Task Force.

Grossman, A. H. (2006). Physical and mental health of older lesbian, gay and bisexual adults. In D. Kimmel, T. Rose, & S. David (Eds.), *Lesbian, gay, bisexual, and transgender aging: Research and clinical perspectives* (pp. 53–69). New York, NY: Columbia University Press.

Grossman, A. H., D'Augelli, A. R., & Hershberger, S. L. (2000). Social support networks of lesbian, gay, and bisexual adults 60 years of age and older. *The Journals of Gerontology: Series B. Psychological Sciences and Social Sciences, 55,* 171B–179B. doi:10.1093/geronb/55.3.P171

Health Resources Services Administration. (2011a). *Medically underserved areas and populations (MUAs/Ps): Guidelines for MUA and MUP designation.* Retrieved from http://bhpr.hrsa.gov/shortage/muaps

Health Resources Services Administration. (2011b). *Shortage designation: Health professional shortage areas & medically underserved areas/populations.* Retrieved from http://bhpr.hrsa.gov/shortage

Healthy People 2020. (2010). *Lesbian, gay, bisexual, and transgender health.* Retrieved from http://www.healthypeople.gov/2020/topicsobjectives2020/overview.aspx?topicid=25

Herbst, J. H., Jacobs, E. D., Finlayson, T. J., McKelroy, V. S., Neumann, M. S., & Crepaz, N. (2008). Estimating HIV prevalence and risk behaviors of transgender persons in the United States: A systematic review. *AIDS and Behavior, 12,* 1–17. doi:10.1007/s10461-007-9299-3

Hwahng, S. J., & Nuttbrock, L. (2007). Sex workers, fem queens, and cross-dressers: Differential marginalizations and HIV vulnerabilities among three ethno-cultural male-to-female transgender communities in New York City. *Sexuality Research & Social Policy, 4,* 36–59. doi:10.1525/srsp.2007.4.4.36

Institute of Medicine, Board on the Health of Select Populations, Committee on LGBT Health Issues and Research Gaps and Opportunities. (2011). *The health of lesbian, gay, bisexual, and transgender (LGBT) people: Building a foundation for better understanding.* Washington, DC: National Academies Press.

Institute of Medicine, Committee on Lesbian Health Research Priorities. (1999). *Lesbian health: Current assessments and directions for the future.* Washington, DC: National Academies Press.

Johnson, M. J., Jackson, N. C., Arnette, J. K., & Koffman, S. D. (2005). Gay and lesbian perceptions of discrimination in retirement care facilities. *Journal of Homosexuality, 49*, 83–102. doi:10.1300/J082v49n02_05

Johnston, G. (2012, March 22). NYC (and America's) first gay senior center has opened. *The Gothamist*. Retrieved from http://gothamist.com/2012/03/02/nyc_and_americas_first_gay_senior_c.php

Joint Commission. (2010, January). Official publication of new and revised requirements: New and revised hospital requirements. *Joint Commission Perspectives, 30*, 5–6. Retrieved from http://www.hrc.org/files/assets/resources/health_joint commissionperspectives_2010.pdf

Kaiser Family Foundation. (2009). *HIV/AIDS policy fact sheet: Medicare and HIV/AIDS*. Retrieved from http://www.kff.org/hivaids/7171.cfm

Kaiser Family Foundation. (2010). *2009 survey of Americans on HIV/AIDS*. Retrieved from http://www.kff.org/kaiserpolls/7890.cfm

Kerry, Nadler Propose Fair Housing Bill for LGBTs. (2011). Retrieved from http://www.advocate.com/news/daily-news/2011/09/22/kerry-nadler-introduce-fair-housing-bill-lgbts

Kling, E., & Kimmel, D. C. (2006). SAGE: New York City's pioneer organization for LGBT elders. In D. C. Kimmel, T. Rose, & S. David (Eds.), *Lesbian, gay, bisexual, and transgender aging: Research and clinical perspectives* (pp. 265–276). New York, NY: Columbia University Press.

Klitzman, R. L., & Greenberg, J. D. (2002). Patterns of communication between gay and lesbian patients and their health care providers. *Journal of Homosexuality, 42*, 65–75. doi:10.1300/J082v42n04_04

Kosciw, J., Diaz, E., & Greytak, E. (2008). *2007 national school climate survey: The experiences of lesbian, gay, bisexual and transgender youth in our nation's schools*. New York, NY: Gay, Lesbian and Straight Education Network. Retrieved from http://www.glsen.org/binary-data/GLSEN_ATTACHMENTS/file/000/001/1290-1.pdf

Koskovich G. (2009, February 23). *LGBT retirement housing*. Unpublished table prepared for the LGBT Aging Issues Network (LAIN) of the American Society on Aging. Available in the LAIN subject files at the GLBT Historical Society in San Francisco (collection no. 2008-02; file: "Housing—Clippings: ASA Publications and Backgrounders").

Lambda Legal. (2010). *Tax considerations for same-sex couples*. Updated January 18, 2012. Retrieved from http://www.lambdalegal.org/publications/tax-considerations

Lambda Legal HIV Project. (2010, November). *HIV stigma and discrimination in the U.S.: An evidence-based report*. Retrieved from http://data.lambdalegal.org/publications/downloads/fs_hiv-stigma-and-discrimination-in-the-us.pdf

Lauby, J. L., Marks, G., Bingham, T., Liu, K., Liau, A., Stueve, A., & Millett, G. A. (2012). Having supportive social relationships is associated with reduced risk of unrecognized HIV infection among Black and Latino men who have sex with men. *AIDS and Behavior, 16*, 508–515. doi:10.1007/s10461-011-0002-3

Lindau, S. T., Schumm, L. P., Laummann, E. O., Levinson, W., Muicheartaigh, C., & Waite, L. J. (2007). A study of sexuality and health among older adults in the United States. *The New England Journal of Medicine, 357,* 762–774. doi:10.1056/NEJMoa067423

Los Angeles Gay and Lesbian Community Services Center. (2009). Community Innovations for Aging in Place, project summary. http://www.aoa.gov/AoA_programs/HCLTC/CIAIP/docs/The_LA_LGBT_Center_CA_Summary.pdf

Los Angeles Gay and Lesbian Community Social Services Center. (2012). *Senior services.* Retrieved from http://laglc.convio.net/site/PageServer?pagename=YW_Seniors_Program

Makadon, H. J. (2011). Ending LGBT invisibility in health care: The first step in ensuring equitable care. *Cleveland Clinic Journal of Medicine, 78,* 220–224. doi:10.3949/ccjm.78gr.10006

Makadon, H. J., Mayer, K. H., Potter, J., & Goldhammer, H. (Eds.). (2008). *The Fenway guide to lesbian, gay, bisexual, and transgender health.* Philadelphia, PA: American College of Physicians.

Mann, C. (2011). *Letter to state Medicaid directors: Same sex partners and Medicaid liens, transfers of assets, and estate recovery.* Retrieved from http://downloads.cms.gov/cmsgov/archived-downloads/SMDL/downloads/SMD11-006.pdf

Mayer, K. H., Bradford, J. B., Makadon, H. J., Stall, R., Goldhammer, H., & Landers, S. (2008). Sexual and gender minority health: What we know and what needs to be done. *American Journal of Public Health, 98,* 989–995. doi:10.2105/AJPH.2007.127811

Mays, V. M., Yancey, A. K., Cochran, S. E., Weber, M., & Fielding, J. E. (2002). Heterogeneity of health disparities among African American, Hispanic, and Asian American women: Unrecognized influences of sexual orientation. *American Journal of Public Health, 92,* 632–639. doi:10.2105/AJPH.92.4.632

McMahan, S., & Lutz, R. (2004). Alternative therapy use among the young-old (ages 65 to 74): An evaluation of the MIDUS database. *Journal of Applied Gerontology, 23,* 91–103. doi:10.1177/0733464804265604

MetLife Mature Market Institute and American Society on Aging. (2010). *Still out, still aging: The MetLife study of lesbian, gay, bisexual and transgender baby boomers.* Westport, CT: MetLife.

Meyer, I. H. (2003). Prejudice, social stress, and mental health in lesbian, gay, and bisexual populations: Conceptual issues and research evidence. *Psychological Bulletin, 129,* 674–697. doi:10.1037/0033-2909.129.5.674

Meyer, I. H. (2010). Identity, stress, and resilience in lesbians, gay men, and bisexuals of color. *The Counseling Psychologist, 38,* 442–454. doi:10.1177/0011000009351601

Meyer, I. H., & Northridge, M. (Eds.). (2007). *The health of sexual minorities: Public health perspectives on lesbian, gay, bisexual and transgender populations.* New York, NY: Springer Science and Business Media. doi:10.1007/978-0-387-31334-4

Millett, G. A., Peterson, J., L., Wolitski, R. J., & Stall, R. (2006). Greater risk for HIV infection of black men who have sex with men: A critical literature review. *American Journal of Public Health*, 96, 1007–1019. doi:10.2105/AJPH.2005.066720

National Federation of Independent Business et al. v. Sebelius, Secretary of Health and Human Services, et al., No. 11–393 (U.S. June 28, 2012).

National Gay and Lesbian Task Force. (2012, January). *State nondiscrimination laws in the U.S.* Retrieved from http://www.thetaskforce.org/reports_and_research/nondiscrimination_laws

Nemoto, T., Operario, D., & Keatley, J. (2005). Health and social services for male-to-female transgender persons of color in San Francisco. *International Journal of Transgenderism*, 8, 5–19. doi:10.1300/J485v08n02_02

Obedin-Maliver, J., Goldsmith, E. S., Stewart, L., White, W., Tran, E., Brenman, S., . . . Lunn, M. R. (2011). Lesbian, gay, bisexual and transgender-related content in undergraduate medical education. *JAMA*, 306, 971–977. doi:10.1001/jama.2011.1255

Orel, N. (2006). Community needs assessment: Documenting the need for affirmative services for LGB older adults. In D. C. Kimmel, T. Rose, & S. David (Eds.), *Lesbian, gay, bisexual, and transgender aging: Research and clinical perspectives* (pp. 227–246). New York, NY: Columbia University Press.

Ponce, N. A., Cochran, S. D., Pizer, J. C., & Mays, V. M. (2010). The effects of unequal access to health insurance for same-sex couples in California. *Health Affairs*, 29, 1539–1548. doi:10.1377/hlthaff.2009.0583

Porter, K. (2012, October 10). *Congregate meal programs: A national perspective*. Presentation at "Still rarin' to go": A community forum on recent research findings about LGBT older adults in Greater Boston, Massachusetts LGBT Aging Needs Assessment Coalition. Boston, MA: Fenway Institute.

Ramirez-Valles, J. (2002). The protective effects of community involvement for HIV risk behavior: A conceptual framework. *Health Education Research*, 17, 389–403. doi:10.1093/her/17.4.389

Reisner, S. L., O'Cleirigh, C., Hendriksen, E. S., McLain, J., Ebin, J., Lew, K., . . . Mimiaga, M. J. (2011). "40 & Forward": Preliminary evaluation of a group intervention to improve mental health outcomes and address HIV sexual risk behaviors among older gay and bisexual men. *Journal of Gay & Lesbian Social Services*, 23, 523–545. doi:10.1080/10538720.2011.611113

Ritter, M. J. (2011). Quality care for queer nursing home residents: The prospect of reforming the Nursing Home Reform Act. *Texas Law Review*, 89, 999–1018.

Rivera, E., Wilson, S. R., & Jennings, L. K. (2011). Long-term care and life planning preferences for older gays and lesbians. *Journal of Ethnographic and Qualitative Research*, 5, 157–170.

Rosenfeld, D. (1999). Identity work among the homosexual elderly. *Journal of Aging Studies*, 13, 121–144. doi:10.1016/S0890-4065(99)80047-4

Rosenfeld, D., Bartlam, B., & Smith, R. D. (2012). Out of the closet and into the trenches: Gay male baby boomers, aging, and HIV/AIDS. *The Gerontologist, 52,* 255–264. doi:10.1093/geront/gnr138

Services and Advocacy for GLBT Elders, Movement Advancement Project, and the Center for American Progress. (2010, September). *LGBT older adults and long-term care under Medicaid.* Retrieved from http://www.lgbtagingcenter.org/resources/pdfs/LGBTOlderAdultsandMedicaid.pdf

Smith, D. M., & Mathews, W. C. (2007). Physicians' attitudes toward homosexuality and HIV: Survey of a California medical society-revisited (PATHH-II). *Journal of Homosexuality, 52,* 1–9. doi:10.1300/J082v52n03_01

Social Security Administration. (2012). *Fact sheet.* Retrieved from http://www.ssa.gov/pressoffice/factsheets/basicfact-alt.pdf

Stall, R., & Catania, J. (1994). AIDS risk behaviors among late middle-aged and elderly Americans. The National AIDS Behavioral Surveys. *Archives of Internal Medicine, 154,* 57–63. doi:10.1001/archinte.1994.00420010085010

Stein, G. L., Beckerman, N. L., & Sherman, P. A. (2010). Lesbian and gay elders and long-term care: Identifying the unique psychosocial perspectives and challenges. *Journal of Gerontological Social Work, 53,* 421–435. doi:10.1080/01634372.2010.496478

Stein, G. L., & Bonuck, K. A. (2001). Physician-patient relationships among the lesbian and gay community. *Journal of the Gay and Lesbian Medical Association, 5,* 87–93. doi:10.1023/A:1011648707507

U.S. Administration on Aging. (2001). *Fact sheet: The many faces of aging.* Washington, DC: Author.

U.S. Administration on Aging. (2012). *Older Americans Act.* Retrieved from http://www.aoa.gov/AoA_programs/OAA/index.aspx

U.S. Department of Health and Human Services. (1998, June). *Informal caregiving: Compassion in action.* Retrieved from http://aspe.hhs.gov/daltcp/reports/carebro2.pdf

U.S. Department of Health and Human Services. (2010). *How does the health care law protect me?* Retrieved from http://www.healthcare.gov/law/features/index.html

U.S. Department of Veterans Affairs. (2009). *The state of care for veterans with HIV/AIDS.* Retrieved from http://www.hiv.va.gov/provider/state-of-care/summary.asp

Vaid, U. (1995). *Virtual equality: The mainstreaming of gay and lesbian liberation.* New York, NY: Anchor Books.

Van Wagenen, A., Sass, S., & Bradford, J. (2012, September 20). *Care and service needs of older adult men & women: A comparative study of sexual minorities and heterosexuals.* Poster presentation at the Gay and Lesbian Medical Association, San Francisco, CA.

Washington Post Staff. (2010). *Landmark: The inside story of America's new health-care law and what it means for us all*. New York, NY: Public Affairs/Perseus.

Wiggin, T. (2012, April 19). *1st gay-friendly public housing to rise in Philadelphia*. http://realestate.aol.com/blog/2012/04/19/1st-gay-friendly-public-housing-project-planned-in-philadelphia

Willging, C. E., Salvador, M., & Kano, M. (2006). Unequal treatment: Mental health care for sexual and gender minorities in a rural state. *Psychiatric Services, 57*, 867–870. doi:10.1176/appi.ps.57.6.867

8

FAMILY ISSUES FOR
LGBT OLDER ADULTS

KRISTIN S. SCHERRER AND JAMES P. FEDOR

For many people, families are a foundational and lifelong source of economic, education, social, and emotional support (Demo, Allen, & Fine, 2000). Family members often provide for each other in times of need, and positive family relationships are important for one's overall health and happiness. The importance of family relationships is particularly salient for older adults, who may rely on family members for care (Fredriksen-Goldsen et al., 2011) or find relationships with kin to be particularly meaningful (Carstensen, 1991). Yet although recent research has made advances in understanding the diversity that characterizes later life families, less is known about the family lives of older lesbian, gay, bisexual, and transgender (LGBT) adults in contemporary society. This chapter provides an overview of the existing scholarship on contemporary LGBT older adults and their families, with a focus on identifying and understanding the issues confronting them.

DOI: 10.1037/14436-008
The Lives of LGBT Older Adults: Understanding Challenges and Resilience, N. A. Orel and C. A. Fruhauf (Editors)
Copyright © 2015 by the American Psychological Association. All rights reserved.

Life course theoretical insights contextualize older LGBT adults' family lives, offering a dynamic framework for analyzing social and historical context, understanding changes over time, and examining the ways that family members' lives are linked (Bengtson & Allen, 1993; Cohler, 2005; Elder, 1998; Rosenfeld, 1999). A central component of life course approaches is the role that social and historical contexts play in both early and later life experiences (Bengtson & Allen, 1993; Elder, 1998). For instance, many older LGBT adults have lived much of their lives in a social context in which it was expected that they hide their sexual orientation and romantic relationships from family and friends, essentially living a double life "in the closet" (Seidman, 2002). Life course theory suggests that an early life experience such as this would likely shape older adults' interest in talking about their sexual orientation or romantic relationships with their family members. For more details about historically relevant LGBT issues, see Cook-Daniels's (2008) comprehensive review of events that inform older LGBT adults' contemporary experiences, including, among others, the U.S. State Department hearings and subsequent dismissal of its employees based on allegations of homosexuality (1950), the inclusion of homosexuality as a psychiatric diagnosis in the *Diagnostic and Statistical Manual of Mental Disorders* (*DSM*; 1952), the Stonewall riots (1969), the removal of homosexuality as a psychiatric illness from the *DSM* (1973), and the debut of the rainbow flag as a symbol of LGBT people (1978).

Scholarship on these issues has often focused on older adults with lesbian or gay identities, as these are the most historically relevant identity categories for contemporary older LGBT adults (Reid, 1995; Rosenfeld, 1999). As such, when referencing this literature, we refer to lesbian and gay older adults and include transgender or bisexual identities only as appropriate. Researchers often define *older adults* as people over age 50 years, and existing scholarship about older LGBT adults often includes multiple cohorts of older adults (American Association of Retired Persons, 2004; Fredriksen-Goldsen & Muraco, 2010). Although this approach is widely acknowledged to be problematic for its lack of analytic specificity, this is a common limitation. In this chapter, we specify these issues of age, cohort, and generational context as the existing theoretical and empirical literatures allow.

We categorize this review into four major areas of family life: coming out in later life, relationships with significant others, relationships with family members of origin, and families of choice. For analytic clarity, we discuss these issues separately, although we also recognize that these categories are not discreet and that there is a great deal of overlap between them. We conclude this chapter with a discussion about gaps in this scholarship and suggestions for future research.

COMING OUT IN LATER LIFE

Throughout their lives, LGBT people face countless situations in which the decision to come out or not has to be made; thus, coming out may be best conceptualized as a lifelong process (Hunter, 2005; Morrow, 2006). This means that LGBT people are constantly managing information about who knows about their sexual orientation or gender identity with many groups of people, including friends, family, coworkers, neighbors, and medical professionals. As such, LGBT people may be known as LGBT in some contexts but not others.

Services and Advocacy for Gay, Lesbian, Bisexual, and Transgender Elders (SAGE; 2011) estimated that more than 2 million adults over age 50 self-identify as lesbian, gay, or bisexual. Many LGBT elders who were secretive or discreet about their sexuality or gender identity in their younger years will remain so as they age; conversely, this generation also contains the pioneers of the gay rights movement who may continue to strongly identify with this aspect of their life (Morrow, 2006). In general, older adults are less likely than their younger counterparts to be open about their sexual orientation or gender identity in all social contexts (Morrow, 2006; Seidman, 2002), but perhaps particularly with their families of origin (Heaphy, 2009; Seidman, 2002; Weston, 1991; Witten, 2009).

Some older LGBT people came out to themselves early in their lives, but, faced with homophobic social conditions, decided not to tell others about their sexual orientation or gender identity. Even though social conditions have changed somewhat, some older LGBT people are still uncomfortable being out about their sexual orientation (Morrow, 2006). There are also differences between the experiences of those who come out as lesbian, gay, bisexual, or transgender; in other words, this process is not something that is experienced in the same way among all sexual minority identities. For example, Witten and Eyler (2012) wrote that transgender older adults are "less likely to be 'out' regarding the transgender history than their younger peers" (p. 188).

Some LGBT people do not come out until later life. This can happen for a variety of reasons, including not realizing one was lesbian or gay earlier in his/her life, already being in an opposite-sex marriage, fear of the loss of heterosexual privilege, or a combination of such factors (Hunter, 2005). There is a dearth of literature specifically addressing coming out in mid- and older adulthood (Johnston & Jenkins, 2003). Some older LGBT individuals who have lived for much of their life as an out person may feel the need to "go back in the closet" by hiding their sexual orientation or gender identity from others (Cronin, Ward, Pugh, King, & Price, 2011). The reasons for this are many: fear of being discriminated against by a health care system that is heteronormative; fear of family rejection; or the desire to assimilate into a new living environment, such as an assisted living or retirement community (Cahill, South, & Spade, 2000; Fullmer, 2006). These fears about going back into the closet may be particularly salient for older transgender adults, who may feel concerned about "being mistreated in case settings on the basis of transgender presentation (including 'anatomical mismatch'), some to the point of considering 'de-transition' (resuming presentation in the birth-assigned gender)" (Witten & Eyler, 2012, p. 188). Little is known about how often older LGBT people elect to conceal their sexual or gender identity from other people in their lives.

LGBT ELDERS' RELATIONSHIPS WITH SIGNIFICANT OTHERS

Although LGBT people have always formed romantic partnerships, gaps exist in what is known about the demographics of couplehood among older LGBT adults. The Williams Institute estimated that lesbian, gay, and bisexual (LGB) people age 65 or older number 1.5 million today and may grow to nearly 3 million by 2030 (SAGE, 2010); the 2010 U.S. Census documented 365,823 unmarried same-sex partner households over age 65 (U.S. Census Bureau, 2012). Other research finds that around 60% of older lesbian and bisexual women and 40% of older gay and bisexual men report being in a coupled relationship, with younger participants more likely to be currently coupled (Heaphy, Yip, & Thompson, 2004).

Differences From Heterosexual Marriages

Historically, same-sex relationships differed from heterosexual married relationships because they may have been more temporary, been geographically distant, or involved maintaining separate households or keeping financial resources separate (Barker, Herdt, & de Vries, 2006). For these reasons, LGBT people in same-sex relationships were able to remain closeted to family, coworkers, and the community at large, but they could still selectively disclose (Barker et al., 2006). Financial planning is of particular concern among older LGBT couples; same-sex couples are significantly more likely to be poor than are heterosexual married couples (Albelda, Badgett, Schneebaum, & Gates, 2009). Lesbian couples are particularly vulnerable: Women in same-sex relationships who are 65 or older are twice as likely to be poor as heterosexual, married couples (Albelda et al., 2009). As a federal benefit of marriage, heterosexual married couples are entitled to their deceased spouse's Social Security benefits and presumed 50% mutual property ownership; same-sex couples are denied such benefits, and in situations where the deceased partner earned significantly more than the surviving partner, the financial impact of widowhood can be devastating (Cahill & South, 2002). Although financial stability is a significant concern for many aging LGBT people, one study of 1,000 older LGBT adults found that 85% had not purchased long-term care insurance, only 12% expected assistance from their families, and 31% reported unspecified or uncertain plans in financing their long-term-care needs (MetLife Mature Market Institute, 2006). In light of these important differences, the same-sex relationships of older adults should not be assumed to be the same as those of older heterosexual married couples, but rather examined for their unique traits.

Previous Opposite-Sex Marriage

Many older LGBT people came to their sexual or gender identity later in life (Fullmer, 2006; Hunter, 2005). For some, this meant that they were previously married to someone of the opposite sex, as was particularly common among older cohorts (Barker et al., 2006; Cahill et al., 2000; Reid, 1995). Coming out in later life may be additionally complicated by ageist attitudes (Cahill et al., 2000; Heaphy, 2009; Higgins et al., 2011) because "an older person who comes out late in life may find it difficult to meet people of the same age and develop relationships because of a youth-oriented culture both within and outside the GLBT communities" (Fullmer, 2006, p. 294).

HIV/AIDS

Yet another important factor in older gay and bisexual men's relationships is HIV/AIDS (Blank, Asencio, Descartes, & Griggs, 2009; Fredriksen-Goldsen et al., 2011; Grossman, 1995). Today's older gay, bisexual, and transgender men may have experienced significant losses of community support, friends, lovers, or partners during the AIDS epidemic of the 1980s and 1990s and as a result could display elements of "survivor guilt" that have an impact on intimate attachments in later life (Barker et al., 2006; Shernoff, 1998). Older gay men may continue to pose a special problem in the HIV/AIDS epidemic because they may be less likely to take safer sex precautions, less willing to disclose their HIV/AIDS status to sexual partners, and less comfortable discussing their sexual orientation with health practitioners (Blank et al., 2009; Cahill et al., 2000; Grossman, 1995).

Same-Sex Relationships and Long-Term Care

Older LGBT couples consistently describe housing and long-term-care placement as an issue wrought with fear and uncertainty (Fullmer, 2006;

Higgins et al., 2011; Reid, 1995). Although the possibility of institutionalization remains a source of anxiety for many people, regardless of sexual orientation or gender identity, older LGBT couples cope with additional concerns as they contemplate living in an environment where their sexual orientation is rendered invisible or where LGBT discrimination occurs (Higgins et al., 2011; Jenkins, Walker, Cohen, & Curry, 2010; MetLife Mature Market Institute, 2010). Although long-term-care facilities typically provide accommodation for married couples in the same room, same-sex couples may have their partnership reduced to that of "roommates" so that they can live together. Furthermore, because same-sex couples are less likely to have a legally recognized relationship, medical decision making will often fall to a next of kin who may not be aware of the patient's health care wishes or relationship (Hash & Netting, 2007; Powell & Neustifter, 2012).

Disenfranchised Grief

The grief and loss reactions experienced by LGBT people after the death of a same-sex partner have been described as *disenfranchised grief* (Doka, 2002) in which the loss is not, or cannot, be openly acknowledged, socially sanctioned, or publicly mourned. This loss might not be validated by society, family, or friends, ultimately having a significant impact on the mental health of the LGBT elder (Higgins et al., 2011). Furthermore, for the grief to be acknowledged, the survivor must have some degree of "outness" to supportive others (Hornjatkevyc & Alderson, 2011). The grieving process might be additionally complicated by external issues, for instance, as same-sex partners are denied the protections that a heterosexual spouse receives at the death of his or her spouse, such as inheritance benefits or a Social Security pension (Blank et al., 2009; Cahill et al., 2000).

Transgender Relationships

The relationships of transgender people deserve attention in their own right, particularly considering how stigmatized and pathologized gender transitions are in contemporary society (Erich, Tittsworth, Dykes, & Cabuses, 2008; Istar Lev, 2006). One key aspect of older transgender people's relationships is the timing of their gender transition relative to the relationship (Bischof, Warnaar, Barajas, & Dhaliwal, 2011). For instance, a social or medical gender transition early in life might yield challenges, for example, if and when to disclose this history to a new romantic interest in later adulthood. This disclosure could be emotionally challenging because the significant other might experience difficulty coping with his or her feelings, be forced to decide whom to trust to speak with about this sensitive topic, and confront his or her own stereotypes about what it means to be transgender (Bischof et al., 2011; Istar Lev, 2006; Zamboni, 2006). In contrast, if an older person undergoes a gender transition later in life, not only would a significant other face many of these same emotional issues, but both members of the couple would also confront the changing dynamics of their relationship. For instance, a transgender person may require his or her partner's support with medical procedures or the renegotiation of the partner's own sexual identity (Pfeffer, 2010, 2012; Zamboni, 2006). These issues of timing are central to life course analyses because they examine not only the presence of a given life event, such as a gender transition, but also when the event happens (Elder, 1998). As this example illustrates, the timing of an event within a person's life could lead to profoundly different life experiences.

RESILIENCE FROM ADVERSITY

Interestingly, some research shows that the adversity older LGBT adults have faced over their lives often results in a resilience that many LGBT elders are able to use in creating meaningful lives for themselves and their families (Fredriksen-Goldsen, 2009). These lifelong experiences of discrimination and self-sufficiency may enable older LGBT people to adjust to the challenges of aging more successfully than their heterosexual peers (Fullmer, 2006; Powell & Neustifter, 2012; Reid, 1995). Recent gerontological research shows that older LGBT people belong to many types of families (Fredriksen-Goldsen, 2009) and are aging with "significant strength of spirit, fortitude, forgiveness and compassion" (Higgins et al., 2011, p. 100). One example drawn from the second author's hospice experience is that of Anne, a 65-year-old lesbian who was diagnosed with inoperable lung cancer and given 6 months to live. During life review sessions, Anne stated that being a lesbian did not fit in with her conservative Irish Catholic family environment, so as a young woman, she moved to the city where she felt as though she could pursue a more authentic life. Anne's contact with her family remained "superficial," their reaction to learning about her sexual orientation having led to varying degrees of estrangement. Coming out did, however, allow her to meet people and make friends "from all walks of life, other people who also did not fit in with the mainstream. And we formed a bond where our race, sex, religion or education did not matter." As her conditioned worsened, these friends and relationships (including an ex-partner) assumed constant caregiving for Anne, enabling her to live independently. Anne reflected that as a young woman, she had felt as though she had a choice to either suppress her sexual attractions and retain her family relationships or take a risk and establish relationships that felt more authentic. Although Anne was sad regarding her terminal illness, she found much comfort in knowing that she had truly "lived" her life. She jokingly stated that, compared with her coming-out experience, dying would be "a piece of cake."

RELATIONSHIPS WITH FAMILIES OF ORIGIN

Contemporary older gay men and lesbian women have lived much of their lives in a social context in which gay or lesbian lives were seen as incompatible with positive relationships with families of origin (Seidman, 2002; Weston, 1991). As a result, many older gay men and lesbian women felt as though they had to choose between living an authentic life as an LGBT person and maintaining ties with their families of origin. Consequently, some older LGBT people do experience strained relationships with their families of origin because of their sexuality (Heaphy, 2009; Witten, 2009). This may particularly be the case for older bisexual people, who report less accepting families than their lesbian or gay counterparts (MetLife Mature Market Institute, 2010).

Many gay and lesbian people have found ways both to maintain ties with family members and to live satisfying lives as an out gay or lesbian person (Connidis, 2010; Fullmer, 2006; Heaphy, 2009). Indeed, Heaphy's (2009) research with 266 gay men and lesbians over age 50 indicates that for almost two thirds of participants, "relationships with family members were important," they "were open about their sexuality and same-sex relationships to at least some relatives," and that "relationships with families of origin were, therefore, more important than is suggested by much of the existing literature" (p. 128). Considerably less is known about the family relationships of older transgender people; however, formative scholarship indicates that their family relationships may be particularly complex (Witten & Eyler, 2012).

Relationships With Adult Children and Grandchildren

In contrast to their heterosexual peers, little is known about older LGBT people's relationships with their adult children. This gap may be partially attributed to a "reluctance to acknowledge the families of gay and lesbian individuals" (Connidis, 2010, p. 143) and partially to barriers many older gay and lesbian adults faced regarding parenting (Claassen, 2005; Connidis, 2010; de Vries, 2006; Espinoza, 2011; Heaphy, 2009). Historical analyses indicate that parenting has been a challenge for gay and lesbian people because they may have faced hostility from their heterosexual coparent, worried about being emotionally rejected by their child because of her or his negative stereotypes about homosexuality, and faced significant barriers to obtaining legal custody of their children.

That said, some older gay and lesbian people do have biological or adoptive children, often through previous heterosexual relationships (Cronin et al., 2011; Hunter, 2005; Tasker, 2013). One study of older gay men and lesbians found that "42% of women and 24% of men were parents" (Heaphy, 2009, p. 128). Other research found that among 341 older LGBT persons in New York, 20% had children, and 7% had grandchildren (Cantor, Brennan, & Shippy, 2004), and younger cohorts of older adults may be even more likely to be parents (Claassen, 2005). These studies indicate that children may be important, and potentially overlooked, family members of older LGBT people.

Because of the challenges associated with parenting, some gay men and lesbians have elected not to disclose their sexual orientation to ex-spouses, children, or other kin (Higgins et al., 2011; Quam & Whitford, 1992). Others waited until much later in life to come out to family members (Connidis, 2010; Hunter, 2005). Coming out to children often happens indirectly and is an emotionally challenging milestone for many LGBT persons, although children often suspected their parent's sexual orientation (Higgins et al., 2011; Hunter, 2005; Orel & Fruhauf, 2006).

Little is known about how adult children respond to the news of having an LGBT parent; how their responses may be shaped by other factors, such as race, gender, or age; and how these relationships may change over time. Scholarship suggests that coming out as transgender to children may be particularly difficult because children must adjust to new pronouns, pre-ferred names, and even family names (e.g., mom or dad; Downing, 2013; Witten & Eyler, 2012). The relationships between older LGBT persons and their adult children hold promise as an increasingly important area for social research.

A small but growing body of literature has examined older lesbian and gay individuals' relationships with their grandchildren (Fruhauf, Orel, & Jenkins, 2009; Orel & Fruhauf, 2006; S. Patterson, 2005a, 2005b; Whalen, Bigner, & Barber, 2000), with the majority of studies focusing on lesbian grandmothers. In one early study (Whalen et al., 2000), findings on lesbian grandmothers' grandparenting practices were similar to those of previous research with (presumably) heterosexual grandmothers. Orel and Fruhauf (2006) found that not all lesbian and bisexual grandmothers decide to come out to their grandchildren, sometimes to protect a grandchild from discrimination or because an adult child asked them not to. When grandmothers did come out to their grandchild, the disclosure often happened indirectly and depended on the grandchild's age or developmental stage. Research also indicates that lesbian grandmothers' own experiences of discrimination and marginalization shape their interests in wanting their grandchildren to grow up with fewer negative conceptions about same-sex relationships (Orel & Fruhauf, 2006; S. Patterson 2005a, 2005b).

To date, only one study has examined gay grandfathers' relationships with their grandchildren (Fruhauf et al., 2009), and these researchers found that adult children played a significant, and largely positive, mediating role in grandfathers' coming-out process with grandchildren, which was true for lesbian and bisexual grandmothers as well (Orel, 2006). The grandfathers interviewed by Fruhauf et al. (2009) reported adopting a variety of roles in their grandchildren's lives, reflecting the diversity of grandparenting experiences more generally. Furthermore, coming out to grandchildren was described as an easier process than coming out to children for gay grandfathers, potentially because of parents' mediating roles. In this way, adult children acted as a mediator for both grandmothers and grandfathers as they sometimes facilitated more authentic relationships between grandparents and grandchildren—for instance, as they talked with their child about their grandparent's sexual orientation. However, adult children were also complicit in cultivating more distant relationships between grandparents and grandchildren—for instance, when their own disapproving views about sexual orientation facilitated more distant grandparent–grandchild relationships. To date, there is no empirical research on older transgender people's relationships with their grandchildren.

Caregiving

Relationships with families of origin become particularly salient for older adults who are faced with declining cognitive or physical abilities. In the general population, older adults often rely on adult children, spouses, parents, or other family members for care and support in their activities of daily living (National Alliance for Caregiving & American Association of Retired Persons, 2009). These caregiving relationships may be additionally complicated for older LGBT adults, given that some older LGBT individuals have strained relationships with their families of origin because of their sexual orientation or gender identity. Despite these challenges, research indicates that older LGBT adults are often significant sources of care and support for their families of origin as well as recipients of care from their own families (Brotman et al., 2007; Cantor et al., 2004; Coon, 2003; Cronin et al., 2011; Fredriksen, 1999; Price, 2011; Shippy, 2007).

Older LGBT adults provide a great deal of care for their families of origin, particularly for their own aging parents (Cantor et al., 2004; Cronin et al., 2011; Fredriksen, 1999; Fredriksen-Goldsen et al., 2011; Price, 2011), parent-in-law, another relative, or adult child (Fredriksen-Goldsen et al., 2011). Price (2011) noted that some older gay and lesbian people experience pressure to provide care to their families, potentially because "their personal relationships and responsibilities were perceived as being of limited importance when contrasted with those of their heterosexual/married siblings" (p. 1293). This privileging of heterosexual families contributes to inequalities where LGBT individuals may be expected to do more care work than their heterosexual family members (Cahill, Ellen, & Tobias, 2002; Price, 2011).

Older LGBT persons also receive care from their families of origin. The majority of older LGBT individuals who are in need of care are cared for by a significant other (Fredriksen-Goldsen et al., 2011). However, if the LGBT person is single, or if his or her partner is unable to provide the level of care needed, biological family members may step in (Fredriksen-Goldsen et al., 2011; Heaphy, 2009). Fredriksen-Goldsen and colleagues (2011) find that of LGBT older adults who were receiving care, only 11% were receiving care from biological family members, a much lower proportion than in the general population. LGBT persons are often reluctant to accept care from biological family members, possibly as a result of distant or strained relationships over the life course. Furthermore, older LGBT persons may be concerned that biological family members might not be knowledgeable about their caregiving needs or might not honor their decisions around living preferences.

Medical Decision Making

In the United States, our system of health care decision making largely follows legal kinship definitions, a reality that becomes keenly important for older LGBT people. Although it is assumed that in heterosexual marriages the spouse would be the one making such decisions, the same cannot be presumed for LGBT couples. For instance, older LGBT couples must consider the legal recognition of same-sex relationships in their resident state. Even couples who do reside in a state that recognizes their relationship must take additional steps to document their relationship according to the state's procedures. Thus, many same-sex couples are not afforded legal protections regarding making end-of-life decisions for a partner or spouse (de Vries, Mason, Quam, & Acquaviva, 2009; MetLife Mature Market Institute, 2006; Stein & Bonuck, 2001). When LGBT older adults become ill, medical decision making will likely fall to a next of kin who may not be aware of the patient's health care wishes or may not acknowledge the importance of the patient's significant other. The LGBT couple can complete an advance directive or medical power of attorney, with the option to designate the other as their health care decision maker. Yet despite being aware of the importance of advance care planning, relatively few LGBT elders have completed such documentation (MetLife Mature Market Institute, 2006).

FAMILIES OF CHOICE

Families of choice is a term that emerged to describe the kin networks that gay and lesbian people form, particularly when families of origin are not the source of support and care one might expect of familial relationships (Weston, 1991). Chosen families developed initially when relationships with families of origin were strained. "In the absence of tradition, biological, support systems, gay men and lesbian women have embraced the need to develop and maintain diverse and, arguably, unique networks of support" (Price, 2011, p. 1297). These family members often provide many of the same supportive functions as families of origin, including emotional and instrumental support (Barker et al., 2006; de Vries & Megathlin, 2009). Indeed, "lesbians and gay men consider friendships equally—or sometimes even more—important than relationships with partners or relatives" (Heaphy, 2009, p. 129). Furthermore, although friendships are important for older adults more generally (Adams, Blieszner, & de Vries, 2000; Blieszner, 1995), they are particularly important for older LGBT individuals given their unique social and historical experiences (Barker et al., 2006).

Engagement with a gay or lesbian community or social network has been conceptualized as a critical aspect of successful aging for LGBT older adults (Quam & Whitford, 1992). Indeed, "for gay men and lesbians, the enlarged role of friends is likely to be complex and broadly based, as kinship is for blended families" (Barker et al., 2006, p.13). Having supportive social networks that know about the older adult's sexual orientation is associated with positive outcomes such as decreased feelings of loneliness and more positive mental and emotional health statuses (Grossman, D'Augelli, & Hershberger, 2000). Friendship networks vary among lesbians, gay men, transgender and bisexual people. For example, lesbians tend to have close friendships with other lesbians and heterosexual women (Claassen, 2005; Grossman et al., 2000; Quam & Whitford, 1992), whereas gay men tend to have more gay or bisexual men in their networks (Grossman et al., 2000). In contrast, bisexual people tend to have more heterosexual people in their social networks than lesbian women or gay men (Grossman et al., 2001). The social support systems for older transgender people will vary depending on the level of their desire to completely blend into society in their corrected gender, with many seeking kinship and support from Internet communities (Persson, 2009).

Research indicates that older lesbian women and gay men prefer to rely on partners, friends, or members of their chosen family for care and support instead of members of their biological family (Heaphy, 2009; Price, 2011) and are more likely to seek assistance or care from families of choice (Fredriksen-Goldsen et al., 2011; Hash, 2006). Receiving care from other LGBT persons may offer particular benefits to older LGBT adults, for instance, because they may feel that they don't have to "de-sexualize" or otherwise erase aspects of their sexual orientation from their home or their stories for the comfort of a heterosexual caregiver (Cronin et al., 2011).

Some scholars have suggested that housing transitions may be difficult for LGBT older adults (Cahill et al., 2000; Higgins et al., 2011), particularly when coupled with anticipated or actual experiences of marginalization within assisted living facilities (de Vries, 2006; Hash, 2006). Yet, some recent research suggests that "older lesbian and gay individuals do not need to be involved in their lesbian and gay community to experience life satisfaction" (Jenkins et al., 2010, p. 415). Rather, the identity management skills and ability to seek out community support that many older LGBT people have needed at different points in their lives emerge as potential strengths, as they may be able to find community and adapt to new relationships more easily than others.

AREAS FOR FUTURE RESEARCH

Perhaps one of the most obvious gaps in the scholarship on older LGBT adults' family lives is that of inequalities in knowledge about certain identity groups, including older LGBT people of color, older bisexual and transgender people, as well as differences between different age cohorts of older LGBT persons. The gap in knowledge about older LGBT persons of color is consistent with research about the intersections of racial and ethnic identities among LGBT people more generally (Croom, 2000; DeBlaere, Brewster, Sarkees, & Moradi, 2010), as well as with older adults of diverse racial backgrounds (Curry & Jackson, 2003; Feldman, Radermacher, Bird, Browning, & Thomas, 2008). Given the extensive empirical and theoretical scholarship on how family structures, roles, and support vary depending on racial background and ethnic identities (Demo, Allen, & Fine, 2000), scholars may reasonably expect that older LGBT people of color would also have unique experiences in forming and maintaining intimate partnerships as well as with their families of origin and chosen family members. The drawbacks to racially homogenous empirical samples are considerable for scholars interested in using this research to inform policy and practice interventions that are relevant to a diverse group of LGBT older adults and their families. As a result, future research should incorporate issues that are relevant to a racially diverse group of older LGBT people and their families.

Comparatively less is known about the family lives of older bisexual and transgender people. In particular, "there has been very little study of men and women who self-define as bisexual in a continuing preference across the course of life" (Cohler, 2005, p. 87). Although older bisexual people's family lives are often examined alongside those of gay men and lesbian women, they are rarely studied on their own or in comparison with lesbian and gay identities. For exceptions, see Dworkin (2006), Rodriguez-Rust (2012), and Keppel and Firestein (2007). Future research may examine older bisexual people's coming-out experiences in families of origin, experiences in forming intimate relationships or constructing chosen families, and what unique strengths or particular challenges bisexual older adults demonstrate in their family lives.

Older transgender people's family lives also deserve more attention in scholarly research. Little is known about how the timing of gender transitions within one's life course shapes aspects of family and relational life. For example, how gender transitions are discussed within family systems is currently underexplored. It may be that adult children (or other family members) are uncomfortable talking about their parent's gender transition with other family members, potentially straining the older transgender adult's relationships with other family members. At the same time, as transgender identities become increasingly visible, older transgender adults may find supportive allies in younger family members, who may be more accepting or understanding of the transition process. Empirical research on older transgender people's family lives would be of value, given that existing scholarship is largely theoretical or conducted with small samples.

In empirical research, participants' ages range greatly but often start at age 50, so differences between younger and older cohorts of older LGBT people are expected. Future research on LGBT older adults' family relationships should include cohort-specific analyses of the issues facing LGBT older adults, because their experiences are sometimes overshadowed by those of younger cohorts. Furthermore, purposefully using a life course approach in these analyses would provide useful insight into how social and historical experiences have shaped the family lives of different age cohorts of older LGBT adults. For example, a younger cohort of baby boomer LGBT older adults may be more likely to have friends and family members with more accepting beliefs about same-sex relationships and policies that are affirming of same-sex relationships by virtue of their cohort's involvement in the civil rights, feminist, and antiwar movements of the 1960s and 1970s (Barker et al., 2006).

"There is a dearth of research about the ties of adult children with their gay fathers or lesbian mothers or about the ties of older parents with their adult gay and lesbian children" (Connidis, 2010, p. 144). Subjects for study include adult children's advocacy work on behalf of their parent(s), their potentially unique caregiving experiences, and how their degree of acceptance of their parent(s)' sexual orientation (or gender identity) might motivate how they enact that parent's end-of-life wishes.

Initial findings about older lesbians' and gay men's relationships with their grandchildren have provided important insights into these older adults' relationships with their families of origin. Future research should build on these initial findings to examine the experiences of the partner of a grand-mother or grandfather and how these "step-grandparents" may experience inclusion in family events or develop relationships with grandchildren. Furthermore, little is known about how these relationships have changed over time, how changing social norms or policies may have influenced these relationships, or how coming out as transgender may shape grandparent–grandchild relationships. Although grandchildren and adult children may be particularly salient relationships for older LGBT people, little is known about the roles that other family members of origin play in their lives; it may be that families of origin are more involved than has been previously assumed (Connidis, 2010).

Given the changing social conditions for LGBT people, continuing to use a life course approach for examining how policy changes or changing attitudes about LGBT people will be particularly important for contextu-alizing older adults' family lives within a sociocultural context. Although many older LGBT persons have had children in the context of a previous heterosexual relationship, in contemporary society, LGBT individuals of all ages are experiencing greater opportunities for parenting through biological technologies and improved opportunities for adoption. Future research may usefully use a life course framework to examine how changes in reproductive technology and state policies on adoption have altered the family lives of older LGBT people.

Given the many concerns LGBT older adults have about making a housing transition, future research should continue to examine the long-term viability of LGBT-specific housing options as well as the efficacy of cultural competency trainings with existing long-term-care facilities. Scholars may also wish to examine the changing roles of families of choice in the lives of older LGBT adults in long-term-care facilities, including how LGBT older adults are able to maintain ties with families of choice or how they may form new communities of support.

IMPLICATIONS FOR PRACTICE

The findings conveyed in this chapter indicate that families of choice and families of origin shape psychosocial functioning and quality of life for older LGBT adults. Therefore, practitioners should empower clients to pro-vide their own definition(s) of *family* in assessing the social support of older LGBT individuals. For this effort to be successful, practitioners must explore their own definitions of family and be willing to expand them to include nontraditional familial systems. It is likely that each member of the client's family of choice has their own unique role and identity within this system. Attending to the meanings that older LGBT adults make of these relationships, rather than only family structure, will provide opportunities for practitioners to better support this population (C. Patterson, 2000).

A general familiarity with the coming-out process, including intra-personal and sociohistorical influences, will be helpful as practitioners assess their older LGBT clients' coping strategies and resilience. Likewise, familiarity with the legal concerns facing LGBT clients and same-sex couples must be understood, particularly in the areas of health care and financial decision making. Practitioners also need to be conscious of how they present themselves to the older adult LGBT client, being sensitive to gendered pronouns and how the client describes his or her significant relationship (e.g., husband or wife, partner, significant other). And because older LGBT clients have likely endured discrimination, rejection, and disparate treatment throughout their lives, establishing positive rapport is of critical importance. At the same time, practitioners should also recognize that this history may have cultivated unique strengths, such as enhanced coping skills or a wide network of supportive relationships. Like other older adults, each LGBT person is shaped by his or her own history, and it could be important for practitioners to explore the meaning their clients have given to their sexuality or gender identity, including how it has shaped their life experiences.

CONCLUSION

Older LGBT adults have faced numerous challenges in their lives. Experiences of homophobia and heterosexism have shaped many aspects of older LBGT adults' lives, including their coming-out experiences and their relationships with significant others and their families. Because of these experiences, older LGBT adults may be reluctant or unwilling to share their authentic selves with others; may experience strained family relationships; and may have limited health, legal, financial, and housing resources. Yet practitioners should also attend to client strengths, as older LGBT adults demonstrate impressive resiliency in the face of considerable challenges. As this field moves forward, we encourage researchers and practitioners to focus on advancements for the most vulnerable among this population, particularly regarding race, ethnicity, gender identity, socioeconomic sta-tus, and geographic location. Examining the family relationships of older LGBT adults encourages us to attend to the diversity of older adults' family relationships more generally, as researchers and practitioners alike seek to improve the health and well-being of older adults in contemporary U.S. society.

REFERENCES

Adams, R., Blieszner, R., & de Vries, B. (2000). Definitions of friendship in the third age: Age, gender, and study location effects. *Journal of Aging Studies, 14,* 117–133. doi:10.1016/S0890-4065(00)80019-5

Albelda, R., Badgett, M. V. L., Schneebaum, A., & Gates, G. J. (2009). *Poverty in the Lesbian, Gay and Bisexual Community.* Los Angeles, CA: The Williams Institute, UCLA School of Law.

American Association of Retired Persons. (2004). *Designing websites for older adults: A review of the literature.* Washington, DC: Author.

Barker, J. C., Herdt, G., & de Vries, B. (2006). Social support in the lives of lesbians and gay men midlife and later. *Sexuality Research & Social Policy, 3,* 1–23. doi:10.1525/srsp.2006.3.2.1

Bengtson, V., & Allen, K. (1993). The life course perspective applied to families over time. In P. Boss, W. Doherty, R. LaRossa, W. Schumm, & S. Steinmetz (Eds.), *Sourcebook of family theories and methods: A contextual approach* (pp. 469–504). New York, NY: Plenum Press. doi:10.1007/978-0-387-85764-0_19

Bischof, G. H., Warnaar, B. L., Barajas, M. S., & Dhaliwal, H. K. (2011). Thematic analysis of the experiences of wives who stay with husbands who transition male-to-female. *Michigan Family Review, 15,* 16–34.

Blank, T. O., Asencio, M., Descartes, L., & Griggs, J. (2009). Aging, health and GLBTQ family and community life. *Journal of GLBT Family Studies, 5*(1–2), 9–34. doi:10.1080/15504280802595238

Blieszner, R. (1995). Friendship processes and well-being in the later years of life: Implications for interventions. *Journal of Geriatric Psychiatry, 28,* 165–182.

Brotman, S., Ryan, B., Collins, S., Chamberland, L., Cormier, R., Julien, D., Peterkin, A., & Richard, B. (2007). Coming out to caregivers of gay and lesbian seniors in Canada. *The Journals of Gerontology: Social Sciences, 47,* 490–503.

Cahill, S., Ellen, M., & Tobias, S. (2002). *Family policy: Issues affecting gay, lesbian, bisexual and transgender families.* New York, NY: The Policy Institute of the National Gay and Lesbian Task Force.

Cahill, S., & South, K. (2002). Policy issues affecting lesbian, gay, Bisexual, and transgender people in retirement. *Generations (San Francisco, CA), 26,* 49–54.

Cahill, S., South, K., & Spade, J. (2000). *Outing age: Public policy issues affecting gay, lesbian, bisexual and transgender elders.* New York, NY: The Policy Institute of the National Gay and Lesbian Task Force Foundation.

Cantor, M. H., Brennan, M., & Shippy, R. A. (2004). *Caregiving among older lesbian, gay, bisexual, and transgender New Yorkers.* New York, NY: National Gay and Lesbian Task Force Policy Institute.

Carstensen, L. (1991). Socioemotional selectivity theory: Social activity in life-span context. *Annual Review of Gerontology & Geriatrics, 17,* 195–217.

Claassen, C. (2005). *Whistling women: A Study of the lives of older lesbians.* New York, NY: The Haworth Press.

Cohler, B. J. (2005). Life course social science perspectives on the GLBT family. *Journal of GLBT Family Studies, 1*, 69–95. doi:10.1300/J461v01n01_06

Connidis, I. A. (2010). *Family ties and aging.* Thousand Oaks, CA: Sage.

Cook-Daniels, L. (2008). Living memory GLBT history timeline: Current elders would have been this old when these events happened . . . . *Journal of GLBT Family Studies, 4*, 485–497. doi:10.1080/15504280802191731

Coon, D. W. (2003). *Lesbian, gay, bisexual and transgender (LGBT) issues and family caregiving.* San Francisco, CA: Family Caregiving Alliance.

Cronin, A., Ward, R., Pugh, S., King, A., & Price, E. (2011). Categories and their consequences: Understanding and supporting the caring relationships of older lesbian, gay and bisexual people. *International Social Work, 54*, 421–435. doi:10.1177/0020872810396261

Croom, G. L. (2000) Lesbian, gay, and bisexual people of color: A challenge to representative sampling in empirical research. In B. Greene & G. L. Croom (Eds.), *Education, research, and practice in lesbian, gay, bisexual, and transgendered psychology: A resource manual* (Vol. 5, pp. 263–281). Thousand Oaks, CA: Sage.

Curry, L., & Jackson, J. (2003). *The science of inclusion: Recruiting and retaining racial and ethnic elders in health research.* Washington, DC: The Gerontological Society of America. doi:10.1093/geront/43.1.15

DeBlaere, C., Brewster, M. E., Sarkees, A., & Moradi, B. (2010). Conducting research with LGB people of color: Methodological challenges and strategies. *The Counseling Psychologist, 38*, 331–362. doi:10.1177/0011000009335257

Demo, D., Allen, K., & Fine, M. (2000). *Handbook of family diversity.* New York, NY: Oxford University Press.

de Vries, B. (2006). Home at the end of the rainbow. *Generations, 29*, 64–69.

de Vries, B., Mason, A., Quam, J., & Acquaviva, K. D. (2009). State recognition of same-sex relationships and preparations for end of life among lesbian and gay boomers. *Sexuality Research & Social Policy, 6*, 90–101.

de Vries, B., & Megathlin, D. (2009). The meaning of friendship for gay men and lesbians in the second half of life. *Journal of GLBT Family Studies, 5*, 82–98. doi:10.1080/15504280802595394

Doka, K. J. (2002). *Disenfranchised grief: New directions, challenges, and strategies for practice* (pp. 5–22). Champaign, IL: Research Press.

Downing, J. (2013). Transgender-parent families. In A. Goldberg & K. Allen (Eds.), *LGBT-parent families: Innovations in research and implications for practice* (pp. 105–115). New York, NY: Springer. doi:10.1007/978-1-4614-4556-2_7

Dworkin, S. (2006). The aging bisexual: The invisible of the invisible minority. In D. Kimmel, T. Rose, & S. David (Eds.), *Lesbian, gay, bisexual and transgender aging: Research and clinical perspectives* (pp. 36–52). New York, NY: Columbia University Press.

Elder, G. H. (1998). The life course as developmental theory. *Child Development, 69*, 1–12.

Erich, S., Tittsworth, J., Dykes, J., & Cabuses, C. (2008). Family relationships and their correlations with transsexual well-being. *Journal of GLBT Family Studies, 4,* 419–432. doi:10.1080/15504280802126141

Espinoza, R. (2011). The diverse elder coalition and LGBT aging: Connecting communities, issues, and resources in a historic moment. *Public Policy and Aging Report, 21,* 8–12.

Feldman, S., Radermacher, H., Bird, S., Browning, C., & Thomas, S. (2008). Challenges of recruitment and retention of older people from culturally diverse backgrounds in research. *Ageing & Society, 28,* 473–493. doi:10.1017/S0144686X07006976

Fredriksen, K. I. (1999). Family caregiving responsibilities among lesbians and gay men. *Social Work, 44,* 142–155. doi:10.1093/sw/44.2.142

Fredriksen-Goldsen, K. I. (2009). Older GLBT family and community life: Contemporary experiences, realities, and future directions (foreword for special edition). *Journal of GLBT Family Studies, 5(1–2),* 2–4.

Fredriksen-Goldsen, K. I., Kim, H.-J., Emlet, C. A., Muraco, A., Erosheva, E. A., Hoy-Ellis, C. P., . . . Petry, H. (2011). *The aging and health report: Disparities and resilience among lesbian, gay, bisexual, and transgender older adults.* Seattle, WA: Institute for Multigenerational Health.

Fredriksen-Goldsen, K. I., & Muraco, A. (2010). Aging and sexual orientation: A 25-year review of the literature. *Research on Aging, 32,* 372–413. doi:10.1177/0164027509360355

Fruhauf, C. A., Orel, N. A. & Jenkins, D. A. (2009). The coming-out process of gay grandfathers: Perceptions of their adult children's influence. *Journal of GLBT Family Studies, 5,* 99–118.

Fullmer, E. M. (2006). Lesbian, gay, bisexual, and transgender aging. In D. M. Morrow & L. Messinger (Eds.), *Sexual orientation & gender expression in social work practice: Working with gay, lesbian, bisexual & transgender people* (pp. 284–303). New York, NY: Columbia University Press.

Grossman, A. H. (1995). At risk, infected, and invisible: Older gay men and HIV/AIDS. *The Journal of the Association of Nurses in AIDS Care, 6,* 13–19. doi:10.1016/S1055-3290(05)80010-X

Grossman, A. H., D'Augelli, A. R., & Hershberger, S. L. (2000). Social support networks of lesbian, gay, and bisexual adults 60 years of age and older. *The Journal of Gerontology: Series B. Psychological Sciences and Social Sciences, 55B,* 171–179. doi:10.1093/geronb/55.3.P171

Grossman, A. H., D'Augelli, A. R., & O'Connell, T. S. (2001). Being lesbian, gay, bisexual, and 60 or older in North America. *Journal of Gay & Lesbian Social Services, 13,* 23–40. doi:10.1300/J041v13n04_05

Hash, K. (2006). Caregiving and post-caregiving experiences of midlife and older gay men and lesbians. *Journal of Gerontological Social Work, 47,* 121–138. doi:10.1300/J083v47n03_08

Hash, K. M., & Netting, F. E. (2007). Long-term planning and decision-making among midlife and older gay men and lesbians. *Journal of Social Work in End-of-Life & Palliative Care, 3,* 59–77. doi:10.1300/J457v03n02_05

Heaphy, B. (2009). Choice and its limits in older lesbian and gay narratives of relational life. *Journal of GLBT Family Studies, 5,* 119–138. doi:10.1080/15504280802595451

Heaphy, B., Yip, A., & Thompson, D. (2004). Ageing in a non-heterosexual context. *Ageing & Society, 24,* 881–902. doi:10.1017/S0144686X03001600

Higgins, A., Sharek, D., McCann, E., Sheerin, F., Glacken, M., Breen, M., & McCarron, M. (2011). Visible lives: Identifying the experiences and needs of older lesbian, gay, bisexual and transgender (LGBT) people in Ireland. *Dublin: Gay and Lesbian Equality Network.* Dublin, Ireland: GLEN.

Hornjatkevyc, N. L., & Alderson, K. G. (2011). With and without: The bereavement experiences of gay men who have lost a partner to non-AIDS-related causes. *Death Studies, 35,* 801–823. doi:10.1080/07481187.2011.553502

Hunter, S. (2005). *Midlife and older LGBT adults: Knowledge and affirmative practice for the social services.* Binghamton, NY: Haworth Press.

Istar Lev, A. (2006). Transgender emergence within families. In D. M. Morrow & L. Messinger (Eds.), *Sexual orientation & gender expression in social work practice: Working with gay, lesbian, bisexual & transgender people* (pp. 263–283). New York, NY: Columbia University Press.

Jenkins, D., Walker, C., Cohen, H., & Curry, L. (2010). A lesbian older adult managing identity disclosure: A case study. *Journal of Gerontological Social Work, 53,* 402–420. doi:10.1080/01634372.2010.488280

Johnston, L. B., & Jenkins, D. (2003). Coming out in mid-adulthood. *Journal of Gay & Lesbian Social Services, 16,* 19–42. doi:10.1300/J041v16n02_02

Keppel, B., & Firestein, B. (2007). Bisexual inclusion in issues of LGBT aging: Therapy with older bisexuals. In B. Firestein (Ed.), *Becoming visible: Counseling bisexuals across the lifespan* (pp. 164–185). New York, NY: Columbia University Press.

MetLife Mature Market Institute. (2006). *Out and aging: The MetLife study of lesbian and gay baby boomers.* Westport, CT: Author.

MetLife Mature Market Institute. (2010). *Still out, still aging: The MetLife study of lesbian, gay, bisexual, and transgender baby boomers.* New York, NY: Author.

Morrow, D. F. (2006). Coming out as gay, lesbian, bisexual, and transgender. In D. F. Morrow & L. Messinger (Eds.), *Sexual orientation & gender expression in social work practice: Working with gay, lesbian, bisexual & transgender people* (pp. 129–149). New York, NY: Columbia University Press.

National Alliance for Caregiving (NAC) & American Association of Retired Persons. (2009). *Caregiving in the U.S.* Bethesda, MD; Washington, DC: Authors.

Orel, N. (2006). Lesbian and bisexual women as grandparents: The centrality of sexual orientation in the grandparent–grandchild relationship. In D. Kimmel, T. Rose,

& S. David (Eds.), *Lesbian, gay, bisexual and transgender aging: Research and clinical perspectives* (pp. 173–194). New York, NY: Columbia University Press.

Orel, N., & Fruhauf, C. (2006). Lesbian and bisexual grandmothers' perceptions of the grandparent-grandchild relationship. *Journal of Gay, Lesbian, Bisexual, and Transgender Family Studies, 21,* 43–70.

Patterson, C. (2000). Family relationships of lesbians and gay men. *Journal of Marriage and the Family, 62,* 1052–1069. doi:10.1111/j.1741-3737.2000.01052.x

Patterson, S. (2005a). Better one's own path: The experience of lesbian grandmothers in Canada. *Canadian Women's Studies, 24,* 118–122.

Patterson, S. (2005b). This is so you know you have options: Lesbian grandmothers and the mixed legacies of nonconformity. *Journal of the Association for Research on Mothering, 7,* 38–48.

Persson, D. I. (2009). Unique challenges of transgender aging: Implications from the literature. *Journal of Gerontological Social Work, 52,* 633–646. doi:10.1080/01634370802609056

Pfeffer, C. A. (2010). "Women's work"? Women partners of transgender men doing housework and emotion work. *Journal of Marriage and Family, 72,* 165–183. doi:10.1111/j.1741-3737.2009.00690.x

Pfeffer, C. A. (2012). Normative resistance and inventive pragmatism: Negotiating structure and agency in transgender families. *Gender & Society, 26,* 574–602. doi:10.1177/0891243212445467

Powell, L. A., & Neustifter, R. (2012). An updated social context for therapy with elder lesbian couples. *Journal of Feminist Family Therapy, 24,* 213–229. doi:10.1080/08952833.2012.648140

Price, E. (2011). Caring for Mum and Dad: Lesbian women negotiating family and navigating care. *British Journal of Social Work, 41,* 1288–1303. doi:10.1093/bjsw/bcr015

Quam, J. K., & Whitford, G. S. (1992). Adaptation, and age-related expectations of older gay and lesbian adults. *The Gerontologist, 32,* 367–374. doi:10.1093/geront/32.3.367

Reid, J. D. (1995). Development in late life: Older lesbian and gay lives. In A. R. D'Augelli & C. J. Patterson (Eds.), *Lesbian, gay, and bisexual identities over the lifespan: Psychological perspectives* (pp. 215–240). New York, NY: Oxford University Press. doi:10.1093/acprof:oso/9780195082319.003.0009

Rodriguez Rust, P. (2012). Aging in the bisexual community. In T. Witten & A. E. Eyler (Eds.), *Gay, lesbian, bisexual and transgender aging: Challenges in research, practice and policy* (pp. 162–186). Baltimore, MD: Johns Hopkins University Press.

Rosenfeld, D. (1999). Identity work among lesbian and gay elderly. *Journal of Aging Studies, 13,* 121–144. doi:10.1016/S0890-4065(99)80047-4

Seidman, S. (2002). *Beyond the closet: The transformation of gay and lesbian life*. New York, NY; London, England: Routledge.

Services and Advocacy for Gay, Lesbian, Bisexual, and Transgender Elders. (2010). *Improving the lives of LGBT older adults*. Denver, CO: Movement Advancement Project.

Services and Advocacy for Gay, Lesbian, Bisexual, and Transgender Elders. (2011). Integrating lesbian, gay, bisexual, and transgender older adults into aging policy and practice. *Public Policy & Aging Report, 21*, 1–36. Washington, DC: Gerontological Society of America.

Shernoff, M. (1998). Gay widowers: Grieving in relation to trauma and social supports. *Journal of the Gay and Lesbian Medical Association, 2*, 27–33.

Shippy, R. A. (2007). We cannot go it alone: The impact of informal support and stressors in older gay, lesbian and bisexual caregivers. *Journal of Gay & Lesbian Social Services, 18*(3–4), 39–51. doi:10.1300/J041v18n03_03

Stein, G. L., & Bonuck, K. A. (2001). Attitudes on end-of-life care and advanced care planning in the lesbian and gay community. *Journal of Palliative Medicine, 4*, 173–190. doi:10.1089/109662101750290218

Tasker, F. (2013). Lesbian and gay parenting post-heterosexual divorce and separation. In A. Goldberg & K. Allen (Eds.), *LGBT-parent families: Innovations in research and implications for practice* (pp. 3–20). New York, NY: Springer. doi:10.1007/978-1-4614-4556-2_1

U.S. Census Bureau. (2012). *Households and families: 2010*. Retrieved from http://www.census.gov/prod/cen2010/briefs/c2010br-14.pdf

Weston, K. (1991). *Families we choose: Lesbians, gays, kinship*. New York, NY: Columbia University Press.

Whalen, D. M., Bigner, J. J., & Barber, C. E. (2000). The grandmother role as experienced by lesbian women. *Journal of Women & Aging, 12*, 39–58. doi:10.1300/J074v12n03_04

Witten, T. M. (2009). Graceful exits: Intersection of aging, transgender identities, and the family/community. *Journal of GLBT Family Studies, 5*(1–2), 35–61. doi:10.1080/15504280802595378

Witten, T. M., & Eyler, A. E. (2012). Transgender and aging: Beings and becomings. In T. Witten & A. E. Eyler (Eds.), *Gay, lesbian, bisexual and transgender aging: Challenges in research, practice and policy* (pp. 187–269). Baltimore, MD: Johns Hopkins University Press.

Zamboni, B. D. (2006). Therapeutic considerations in working with the family, friends, and partners of transgendered individuals. *The Family Journal, 14*, 174–179. doi:10.1177/1066480705285251

9

TRANSGENDER AGING: WHAT PRACTITIONERS SHOULD KNOW

LOREE COOK-DANIELS

Although *LGBT* (lesbian, gay, bisexual, and transgender) is often used as if it refers to one group, it actually refers to at least four distinct populations, all of which have their own characteristics. Of these populations, transgender individuals have unique needs compared with nontransgender lesbians, gay men, and bisexuals. This chapter first explains how and why so much of the older transgender population is hidden and has not been researched, and then reports some of what we do know about the more visible population. These data focus on some of the primary ways trans elders differ from nontrans elders: the rates at which they experience violence and discrimination; their employment and income disparities; their experiences with health care discrimination; how these social disparities in turn affect their physical health, health risk behaviors, mental health, and willingness to access services; and how relationships with family and friends may be affected when it becomes known that the transgender person is not conforming to social expectations of sex and gender assignment.

DOI: 10.1037/14436-009
The Lives of LGBT Older Adults: Understanding Challenges and Resilience, N. A. Orel and C. A. Fruhauf (Editors)
Copyright © 2015 by the American Psychological Association. All rights reserved.

The second part of the chapter focuses on the practical implications of what we know and do not know about how transgender elders differ from nontransgender elders. First, I review some of the primary issues facing transgender people that do not face their nontransgender lesbian, gay, bisexual (LGB) cohorts: sexual orientation diversity among transgender couples and the transgender community as a whole, the higher risk transgender elders run of being nonconsensually outed, and bathrooms as battlegrounds. I then review some of the major underresearched areas, including the life courses of transgender people, resilience strategies, and the experiences of SOFFAs (significant others, friends, family, and allies). The chapter concludes with three policy and practice implications: discrimination is iterative and requires advocacy; service design must accommodate complexity; and resilience must be identified and strengthened.

THE MISSING COHORT

Not long after Christine Jorgensen went public in 1952, a small number of gender identity clinics opened throughout the country. In the 1960s and 1970s, these clinics worked with thousands of transgender people, putting them through extensive evaluations and granting sex reassignment surgery to only a precious few sex (see, e.g., Califia, 1997, and Meyerowitz, 2002). If they were in their 20s and 30s when they went through these clinics, the majority of these transgender men and women would now be in their 60s and beyond, responding to those few researchers and activists who are now trying to figure out what it means to be both transgender and aging. This cohort remains mostly invisible—not only to researchers and practitioners but also largely to other transgender people and the transgender community.

Over the years, hundreds of people have subscribed, for varied periods of time, to ElderTG, a FORGE-hosted peer support listserv founded in 1998 and open only to transgender people age 50 and older (or to their close SOFFAs). Of these, the moderators can count on one hand the number who went through one of those early clinics; everyone else has come out later in life, a mid- or late-life transitioner. Another telling statistic comes from the groundbreaking *Injustice at Every Turn* study cosponsored by the National Center for Transgender Equality and the National Gay and Lesbian Task Force. Published in 2011, this is the largest survey of transgender people in U.S. history, with more than 6,400 respondents. Six hundred forty-seven respondents were ages 55 to 64 (10.1%), and 114 were ages 65 and older (1.8%). Uniquely, this survey asked respondents when they began living full time in their gender of choice, and so we know that of those 761 transgender respondents ages 55 and older, exactly one transitioned between ages 25 and

44. Of those currently ages 55 to 64, 53% said they had transitioned between the ages of 45 and 54 (between 1 and 10 years before), and 46% had transitioned at age 55 or older. Of those currently ages 65 and older, only one had transitioned between ages 45 and 54; 97% had transitioned at age 55 or later. In other words, virtually all of the older respondents had been living in their gender of choice for only a few years.

The reasons transgender pioneers are invisible as they age are many and may well include the possibility that being transgender is no longer a salient part of their lives. Although there are transgender people who wish to "forget" their years in a gender they were not comfortable in, others are simply like the rest of us: What was important to us decades ago (e.g., playing football, being a member of Girl Scouts, a college fellowship, the European tour we took in our 20s) has simply faded into the background, yielding ground to far more urgent interests and concerns. Having negotiated their public shift from one gender to the other, they now simply view themselves as men or women and have gone on with their lives like everyone else.

However, there may be another reason that segments of this cohort remain largely unattached to other transgender people and the organized transgender community: Those guarding the doors to hormones and surgery often recommended that applicants cut their ties to friends, family, jobs, and other transgender people. However, not everyone agrees with this statement. Some transgender people report strong and enduring relationships among transgender people who went through the clinics, whereas another activist said

> I have met people who were friends with transgender people prior to transition, who were told by their transgender friend that all contact had to cease as part of their treatment plan. These people supported their friend's transition, and were deeply affected by the loss of contact and are still grieving today. (Personal communication, October 20, 2012)

Harry Benjamin, the early psychiatrist credited with doing the most to make it possible for transgender people to access hormones and surgery, wrote that in his opinion, the "ideal adjustment" would be that of a young woman who, postsurgery, married a slightly older man who

> knows only that Joanna as a child had to undergo an operation which prevented her from ever menstruating or having children. They have had a distinctly happy marriage now for seven years. Joanna no longer works but keeps house and they lead the lives of normal, middle-class people. (Benjamin, 1966, p. 126)

Indeed, there are scattered accounts of this being precisely what some people have done. In one case, a woman whose husband did not know she was transgender got prostate cancer. Her physician and other health care providers successfully treated her without ever discussing with her husband exactly what type of cancer she had (Hopwood, 2012). In another case that was brought to the author's attention by a man's widow, a transman facing terminal cancer was urged to consult with a lawyer to protect his family. Unfortunately, the only lawyer he could find that had the requisite expertise in transgender family law was herself widely known as being transgender. Desperately afraid someone would see him entering her office and guess his transgender history (which even his son, let alone his employer—the Boy Scouts—did not know), he made no arrangements for his family. After his death, the Social Security Administration decided that because his birth certificate said he was female, his son's birth certificate, which listed him as the father, was not legal, and denied both his widow and his son survivor benefits. Another fascinating theory about what may have happened to the early transitioners came from a woman who went through one of the largest clinics at age 19. Responding to a question about why her peers might "no longer [be] participating in the trans community," she answered,

> That implies that they ever did participate. Are you referring to the girls I went through the . . . program with? Most of the girls I transitioned with were raised in the '40s and had little or no sense of responsibility towards future transgendered people. (Personal communication, October 2012)

THE VISIBLE COHORT

As previously noted, a large but unmeasurable portion of the transgender elder population is invisible. Those who are visible tend to have transitioned genders or publicly claimed their gender identity (or both) relatively recently. However, one study reported that its older respondents were the cohort that was "most likely to be completely closeted to friends, colleagues, and family members," indicating that either they had not yet disclosed their identity publicly or had transitioned sometime before and established new relationships with people who did not know their gender history (Beemyn & Rankin, 2011, pp. 94–95). The remainder of this chapter reviews selected findings from six studies (three published in 2011 and three in 2010) that broke data out by transgender status and age. The studies reviewed here include the following:

- *Injustice at Every Turn: A Report of the National Transgender Discrimination Study* was published by the National Center for Transgender Equality and the National Gay and Lesbian Task Force (Grant et al., 2011a). This is the largest survey of transgender people in U.S. history, with more than 6,400 respondents. Six hundred forty-seven respondents were ages 55 to 64, and 114 were 65 or older; data analyses of the older cohorts were made available to the author but have not been previously published.

- *The Aging and Health Report* (Fredriksen-Goldsen et al., 2011) was the first federally funded national study of LGBT older adults and attracted more than 2,500 respondents age 50 and older. One hundred seventy-four identified themselves as transgender (either directly or by means of answers to questions about their birth gender or the age at which they first realized they were transgender). Some of the data reported here have not yet been published.

- *The Lives of Transgender People* (Beemyn & Rankin, 2011) studied 3,474 transgender people, 173 of whom were 53 years of age or older.

- FORGE conducted three national surveys between 2004 and 2008. Cook-Daniels and munson's (2010) analysis of respondents over age 50 appeared in a *Journal of GLBT Family Studies* article titled "Sexual Violence, Elder Abuse, and Sexuality of Transgender Adults Age 50+: The Results of Three Surveys." The sexual violence survey had 53 respondents aged 50 or older, and 272 of the respondents to the sexuality study were in that age group. The elder abuse study had only 56 respondents in total, and only 25 gave an age of 50 and older.

At best, these six studies cumulatively accessed fewer than 1,500 transgender people ages 50 and older. Even this number is likely inflated because many individuals undoubtedly participated in more than one survey, given that most recruited through similar online and in-person channels. What we know from the studies is also, obviously, limited to what each research team chose to ask about.

Violence and Discrimination

One of the most salient findings that has emerged so far from research on the transgender population is the ubiquity of experiences of violence and discrimination. At least one "consensus" report named violence and murder prevention as the top health issue affecting transgender people, ranked above HIV, substance abuse, depression, and suicide (Xavier et al., 2004). The National Coalition of Anti-Violence Programs (2009, 2010) reported that transgender women of color made up the largest category of LGBT people murdered in the United States because of their sexual orientation or gender identity for at least the previous 2 years (2008 and 2009). FORGE and other researchers have repeatedly documented sexual assault rates of 50% and higher among transgender people (Cook-Daniels & munson, 2010; Kenagy, 2005; Kenagy & Bostwick, 2005). The *Aging and Health Report* (Fredriksen-Goldsen et al., 2011) discussed that transgender elders were more than twice as likely to have experienced domestic violence in the past year (i.e., 16% compared with 7% of the LGB respondents) and reported an average of 11 lifetime "negative events" (e.g., job loss, housing or health care discrimination, police misconduct, verbal or physical violence) compared with the six reported by their LGB age peers.

It is important to note that contrary to the prevailing belief in the United States that sexual assault is primarily a crime perpetrated by men against women, FORGE's surveys have repeatedly found that transgender sexual assault survivors are roughly evenly divided between those who were perceived as male at the time of the attack(s) and those who were perceived as female (munson & Cook-Daniels, 2004, 2011). Roughly one fifth (22%) of the perpetrators were women (munson & Cook-Daniels, 2004). The majority (55%) of FORGE's older sexual assault respondents said that they believed "the abuser's perception of your gender/gender presentation/gender expression was a contributing factor in the abuse/assault(s)" (Cook-Daniels & munson, 2010, p. 147), meaning that nearly half thought they were targeted for reasons completely unrelated to their transgender status or history.

In a pattern that will be repeated throughout this review, "how bad" older transgender people have it varies tremendously based on whether the comparison is with nontransgender LGB older adults or with younger transgender people. When it comes to violence, transgender elders, compared with their younger peers, were less likely to have experienced domestic violence (13%–14% vs. 19%), physical assault in school (10%–20% vs. 23%), sexual assault in the workplace (2%–3% vs. 6%), and physical assault in any public location (3%–6% vs. 8%; Grant et al., 2011). *The Lives of Transgender People* reported that older transgender people were less afraid for their safety than were younger trans people: "18 percent of those who were nineteen to twenty-two years old reported that they often feared for their physical safety, as compared with just 6 percent of respondents who were at least fifty-three years old" (Beemyn & Rankin, 2011, p. 98). At the other extreme, nearly 30 of the 53 and older participants never felt unsafe, a rate twice that of the younger cohort (Beemyn & Rankin, 2011). Beemyn and Rankin (2011) suggested two reasons their older cohort experienced fewer problems:

> Participants who were at least fifty-three years old experienced the least amount of harassment (11 percent) because, in part, they were the age group most likely to be completely closeted to friends, colleagues, and family members. Ageism may also play a part, since older people are often ignored in modern society or seen as non-threatening. (pp. 94–95)

Interestingly, the older group also had a larger proportion of people who *never* concealed their gender identity: 23% of the 53+ group fell into this category, compared with 11% to 15% of the younger groups. Beemyn and Rankin (2011) suggested that because some of their older respondents had been trans for so long, they felt secure and were no longer concerned if others found out. Another finding illustrates how intersectionality works: Beemyn and Rankin also found that "transgender people who identified as heterosexual were less likely to report harassment than transgender people of other sexual orientations" (p. xiii).

Employment and Income

Employment and income disparities likewise vary in magnitude depending on whether the comparison group is LGB age peers or younger transgender people. In the *Health and Aging Report*, Fredriksen-Goldsen et al. (2011) found that nearly half (48%) of its transgender elder respondents reported household income levels less than 200% of the poverty level, compared with 31% of LGB elders. *Injustice at Every Turn* (Grant et al., 2011a) reported that 56% to 50% of its older respondents had an income of $50,000 or more, compared with just 41% of its overall sample. These disparities clearly demonstrate the existence of rampant antitransgender employment discrimination. Because many of the transgender elders who have participated in surveys did not disclose their gender identity until later in life, many of them were able to establish stable and even lucrative careers free from discrimination, whereas those who are visibly transgender earlier in life may face early employment discrimination from which they may never recover. Yet employment discrimination against older transgender people clearly exists and takes a toll: 29% of both those ages 55 to 64 and those 65 and older had lost a job because they were transgender, and 17% to 22% had been removed from direct contact with clients, customers, or patients—rates that are similar to the overall sample.

More evidence of the impact of early discrimination comes from the data on sex work and other underground economic activity (e.g., drug sales). Only 2% or 3% of the transgender elders in the *Injustice at Every Turn* study reported having done sex work, compared with 11% of the total sample. Yet sex work is not unknown among older transgender people. One of FORGE's respondents reported:

> I prostitute myself at age 55 because even though I'm a [postoperative transsexual] and passable [as a woman], no one passes 100% of the time. NO ONE. Job discrimination is bad because you're stuck with fellow employees 8 hours a day, 40 hours a week. That much harassment is bad for one's mental health. (Cook-Daniels & munson, 2010, p. 159)

One of the most salient findings emerging from the studies reported in the *Injustice at Every Turn* and *Health and Aging Report* is just how many transgender elders are military veterans. Twenty percent of the 6,400 transgender people *Injustice at Every Turn* studied were military veterans, but those rates at least doubled for the older cohorts: 40% of those ages 55 to 64 were veterans, as were 54% of those 65 and older. The *Health and Aging Report* found that whereas 24% of non-LGB older adults were veterans, 41% of the transgender respondents had been in the military.

Health Care Discrimination

In older cohorts, access to health care insurance is influenced by the United States' current safety net of Medicare and Medicaid. Clear evidence of this comes from the *Injustice at Every Turn* study, which documented that only 4% of transgender respondents ages 65 and older were uninsured, compared with 13% of respondents ages 55 to 64 and 19% of the overall respondent pool. The *Aging and Health Report* found that whereas 98% of nontransgender LGB older adults had insurance, the figure dropped to 91% of the transgender respondents. Perhaps more telling is the number who postponed medical care when they were sick or injured because they could not afford it: 21% of those 65 and older and 35% of those 55 to 64 answered affirmatively in the *Injustice at Every Turn* study, whereas the figures were 6% for nontransgender LGB elders and 22% for transgender older adults in the *Aging and Health Report*.

Blatant discrimination by health care providers is also a problem for transgender older adults. Eight percent of those 65 and older and 20% of transgender people ages 55 to 64 had been refused care by a health care provider because of their gender identity or history, and 11% to 12% reported having experienced verbal harassment or disrespect in a doctor's office or hospital (Grant et al., 2011b). One transgender elder shared her discrimination story in a FORGE survey:

> One Navy doctor refused me care when a suture site related to my sex reassignment surgery became infected. (Cook-Daniels & munson, 2010, p. 156)

Physical Health Problems

The *Adverse Childhood Experiences* study (Centers for Disease Control and Prevention, 2006) established that early experiences of trauma and discrimination can have lifelong negative health effects not just for mental and emotional well-being but also when it comes to physical illness. Combine the high rates of violence and discrimination transgender people face throughout their life span with lower access to health care due to being uninsured, inability to afford deductibles or fees, and outright discrimination by health care professionals, and it is not surprising that the *Aging and Health Report* found higher rates of congestive heart disease (20% vs. 12%), diabetes (33% vs. 14%), obesity (40% vs. 25%), and asthma (33% vs. 15%) among its transgender respondents compared with its nontransgender LGB respondents, despite the fact that the transgender cohort in this study was on average younger than the nontransgender sample. However, the cohorts had roughly the same rates of high blood pressure and arthritis, whereas the transgender cohort had lower rates of HIV/AIDS (4% vs. 9%) and cancer (16% vs. 19%).

Transgender older adults were more likely to rate their health as poor than were nontransgender LGB peers in the *Aging and Health Report* study, at a rate of 33% versus 22%. Disability rates also appear to be higher: 62% of the transgender respondents said they had a disability, compared with 46% of the nontransgender LGB sample. Interestingly, whereas disability rates rise with age for the overall population, the pattern was reversed in the *Injustice at Every Turn* study. Asked if they had a disability that "substantially affects a major life activity," 31% of all the respondents said yes, compared with 28% of those 55 to 64 and 18% of those 65 and older.[1]

Health Risk Behaviors

Transgender older adults in the *Aging and Health Report* study were more likely to smoke (15% vs. 9%), drink to excess (12% vs. 8%), use drugs ("other than those required for medical reasons"; 14% vs. 11.5%), and engage in HIV risk behavior (20% vs. 18%). They were also less likely to regularly engage in moderate physical exercise (74% vs. 82%). Again, the *Injustice at Every Turn* comparisons with younger transgender people paint a more nuanced picture: 4% of those 65 and older and 5% of those ages 55 to 64 drink or use drugs "to cope with mistreatment," compared with 8% of the whole sample, and 11% of those 65 and older and 15% of those ages 55 to 64 currently smoke, compared with 19% of all the respondents. In its sexuality survey, FORGE found that 33% of the older respondents said they practiced safer sex in all sexual interactions, whereas 25% said they were celibate or not currently in a relationship, and 19% said they were "fluid bonded" with one or more of their partners. Thirteen percent said they practiced safer sex with some but not all partners, and 10% noted they never practiced safer sex (Cook-Daniels & munson, 2010, p. 164).

---

[1]This finding does not appear to be skewed by the possibility that respondents were considering "gender identity disorder" (a mental health condition as defined by the current *Diagnostic and Statistical Manual*) as their disability because 53% of those with a disability said they had a physical condition (the comparable figures for those ages 55–64 were 27%, and 25% for those 65 and older).

Mental Health

Study after study has found that bias and discrimination, violence, institutional inequality, minority stress, and microaggressions all contribute to higher rates of mental health problems for stigmatized minorities (Institute of Medicine, 2011). Evidence that transgender people face even higher rates of stigma than do nontransgender LGB people comes from several mental health measures. The *Aging and Health Report* found that transgender older adults were roughly twice as likely to experience suicidal ideation as the non-transgender LGB respondents (71% vs. 36%), and were more than twice as likely to experience depression (48% vs. 29%). Again the *Injustice at Every Turn* study provides subtle shading to this picture: Whereas 41% of its overall sample had attempted suicide at some point, the numbers dropped to 33% for those ages 55 to 64 and 16% for those 65 and older.

Resistance to Accessing Services

Given how many transgender people have directly experienced or heard about service providers treating transgender people violently or disrespectfully or refusing to serve them altogether, it is of little surprise that many transgender people sometimes forgo needed care. In addition to documenting those who put off accessing health care due to financial reasons, *Injustice at Every Turn* found that 14% of the respondents ages 55 to 64 and 9% of those 65 and older reported deciding not to seek health care when they were sick or injured because they feared being treated with disrespect or being discriminated against. FORGE has documented hundreds of reasons why transgender people have chosen not to access care; here are a few:

- For rape . . . I was considered a male at the time; no one would have believed I was raped by a female. (Cook-Daniels & munson, 2010, p. 149)
- My [abusive] ex[-wife] had me convinced [that if I reported her abuse] she could turn everyone against me and take my kids and eventually grandkids away from me and that no one would want to deal with a queer (of whatever stripe I was) like me. (Cook-Daniels & munson, 2010, p. 149)
- I have decided not to have any life-extending surgery because of past mistreatment by nurses at [the Veterans Administration hospital]. (Cook-Daniels & munson, 2010, p. 153)
- As a trans 35-year-old, who is a service provider who has borne witness to incidents of violence and abuse for elders, I'm scared to death about my own future. There is Alzheimer's in my family, and I know there's a good chance it's going to claim me as

well. What will happen to me once I can no longer advocate for myself? Will they call me "she"? Will they make fun of my body right in front of me, knowing I won't really understand? Without a significant other, and without children, I fear I'll be left in a nursing home somewhere where no one actually cares about me as a human being. At 35 I've already written a "living will." In Ontario it's called a Power of Attorney for Personal Care. And honestly? I have more or less decided that I just won't let myself get to that point where I can't take care of myself. I'd rather take matters into my own hands and self-euthanize (that's a nice way to say it, don't you think?) while I am mentally cognizant and physically capable of it. Should the time come when I need to take my own life in order to avoid these horrific experiences, I will. (Cook-Daniels & munson, 2010, p. 154)

Family and Friend Relationships

Spouses and partners of people who transition later in life seem to have a somewhat harder time coping with a gender change. For example, 56% to 59% of the older respondents to the *Injustice at Every Turn* survey had lost their partnership because of their transgender identity, compared with 45% of the whole sample. The older group was slightly less likely to agree that their family was as "strong today as before I came out" but slightly more likely to say their family relationships were improving over time. They were also slightly less likely to have their relationship with their children blocked by their ex-partner, although that happened to 22% of those ages 55 to 64 and 27% of those 65 and older (compared with 29% of the full sample). Their children, however, were far more likely to choose not to speak to or spend time with them; 40% to 41% of the older cohort said they had experienced this, compared with 30% of the whole sample. The issue of family rejection played an interesting role in the "elder abuse" study FORGE conducted. The 40 stories of abuse collected by these researchers included a number that do not fit traditional definitions of abuse but were defined as that by those who experienced them:

- I am [a male-to-female postoperative transsexual] and aged 52. I have a 14-year-old daughter who just said to me one day, "My father died." I have had no contact in years. (Cook-Daniels & munson, 2010, p. 156)
- My son and daughter-in-law will not let me see my grandson. They think I will do something to him. I don't even know him now. It breaks my heart not to see him. (Cook-Daniels & munson, 2010, p. 156)

- My ex-wife was very supportive in the beginning but when phys-ical changes started taking place there was anger. She moved away when I went for surgery. Never seen her or my daughter again. (Cook-Daniels & munson, 2010, p. 156)
- My wife cannot accept the fact that I'm trans. I got attacked for lying about who I was, told I'm a sinner, asked what others would think, got the silent treatment. This went on for months. Right now if I don't present myself as female at home things are better between us. (Cook-Daniels & munson, 2010, p. 156)

Older transgender people also reported a great deal of friend loss, with 64% of those ages 55 to 64 and 60% of those 65 and older (compared with 58% of the overall sample) reporting in the *Injustice at Every Turn* study that they had lost close friends because of their transgender status or history. In the FORGE "elder abuse" study, one respondent said:

- My closest friend of over 30 years finally said, "I just can't han-dle this." No contact in years. (Cook-Daniels & munson, 2010, p. 156)

WHAT SETS TRANSGENDER ELDERS APART FROM OTHER ELDERS

The practice of categorizing transgender people under the LGBT umbrella is ubiquitous and makes sense in many contexts. At the same time, as the previous discussion should have made clear, the amounts of discrimina-tion, stigma, violence, and health disparities faced by transgender older adults are often much higher than those faced by nontransgender LGB people. More critical, perhaps, are the ways in which transgender older adults are uniquely different from nontransgender LGB and non-LGB older adults.

Sexual Orientation

Because transgender people are often thought of as part of the "LGBT community," the fact that many transgender people are heterosexual is often overlooked. Even that is too simplistic of a picture. If we described sexual orientation by saying "I'm attracted to women," "I'm attracted to men," or "I'm attracted to people of all genders," transgender people would have little problem answering. Instead, because the very definition of *sexual orienta-tion* inherently assumes a gender identity, transgender people may be unsure which label to claim. A gender transition can easily convert a "heterosexual" into a "lesbian," even if the male-to-female person remains partnered (and sexually attracted) to the same woman. Partners of people who transition genders have an even more difficult time because *their* perceived sexual orientation change happens through no action on their part at all: simply by not leaving their relationship, others may perceive that because they have gone from being partnered with someone of one gender to being partnered with someone of another gender, their sexual orientation has changed. This dynamic also makes "mixed orientation" partnerships—in which one partners identifies as LGB queer and the other identifies as heterosexual—far more common among transgender people than among either nontrans LGB or non-LGBT populations.

The percentage of transgender older adults who identify as one sexual orientation or another varies tremendously from one survey to another. This happens not only because there are different options on each survey and questions may be worded differently but also because the transgender community is segmented by various interests and demographics. It is common, for example, for online (and some in-person) transgender groups to be formed on the basis of gender, race, age, marital status, geography, occupation, or interests, for example. It can be hard to gather a truly representative sample, so each survey result should be viewed as only one part of the proverbial elephant. Table 9.1 lists the available sexual orientation breakdowns for the six studies reviewed here.

These sexual orientation differences have service implications whenever services are segregated by sexual orientation. Will a couple that looks heterosexual (i.e., one looks male and the other female) be (or feel) welcome in LGBT space? Will other attendees treat them as "allies" or even make antiheterosexual comments in their presence? Will a woman who has been heterosexually identified for decades feel comfortable in an LGBT group even though her male-to-female spouse and the rest of those present feel like she belongs there? Obviously, these sorts of questions can only be answered by the individuals involved, but those who are designing services and programs need to be considering the dilemmas that may be created when it is not made explicitly clear who is welcome and who is not.

Nonconsensual Outing

LGB older adults do not always have control over who knows their sexual orientation. Gossip, blackmail, inadvertent innocent statements by friends, the improper release of medical or other records, and the like can all result in people knowing someone is LGB even when that individual would have rather kept that information private. Transgender people are also

TABLE 9.1
Sexual Orientations of Participants

	Study					
	Injustice at Every Turn		Aging and Health Report	FORGE		
Orientation	55–64 (n = 647)	65+ (n = 114)	(n = 174)	Sexuality (n = 272)	Elder abuse (n = 56)[a]	Sexual violence (n = 53)
Gay	29%	36%	32%	8%	2%	0%
Lesbian	"	"		15%	28%	20%
Same gender	"	"	N/A	N/A	N/A	N/A
Bisexual	28%	21%	27%	23%	14%	19%
Queer	3%	3%	N/A	12%	0%	6%
Pansexual	"	"	N/A	9%	7%	7%
Heterosexual	27%	25%	19%	17%	31%	24%
Asexual/ celibate	9%	11%	N/A	9%	24%	9%
Other	4%	4%	22%	N/A	7%	16%
Questioning	N/A	N/A	N/A	7%	N/A	N/A

Note. N/A = not applicable.
[a]Multiple answers allowed.

subject to these nonconsensual outings, but they have two additional risk factors as well.[2]

One risk factor is the body itself. Whether a transgender person "passes" as (is routinely perceived as) their preferred gender is only partially under their control. Some physical features may be unchangeable, or at least financially out of reach if surgery is even possible. The rest retain visible body parts that reflect why they were once believed to be another gender. We have only recently, with the *Injustice at Every Turn* study, been able to begin quantifying what percentage of the transgender population passes. The first relevant question this study asked was whether "people can tell I'm transgender or gender nonconforming even if I don't tell them." Table 9.2 lists what the older respondents answered.

The study also asked whether respondents wanted or had various types of surgery. Because the questions were asked and reported separately, it is not

---

[2]This discussion pertains to transgender people who are living in a gender other than the one they were assigned at birth. Transgender people who have an internal identity different from what they present to the world or who live as another gender only part-time or in limited situations (e.g., cross-dressers) may not be as susceptible to the risks described here. *Injustice at Every Turn* found that 59% to 61% of the older respondents were currently living full time in a gender different from what they were assigned at birth. Of the remainder, 30% to 33% said they wanted to live full time in another gender, and 8% to 9% said they did not want to live full-time as another gender.

TABLE 9.2
Responses to Survey Question in Injustice at Every Turn Study

Response	55–64 (*n* = 647)	65+ (*n* = 114)
Always	4%	5%
Most of the time	14%	18%
Sometimes	30%	21%
Occasionally	36%	35%
Never	16%	20%

Note. The question asked whether "people can tell I'm transgender or gender nonconforming even if I don't tell them."

possible to determine who may have had chest or breast surgery and genital surgery, so this analysis will focus only on those who had genital surgery. Of male-to-female (MTF) respondents, only 19% of the 55- to 64-year-olds and 21% of those 65 and older had genital surgery (although 56%–58% said they "want it someday"). On the female-to-male (FTM) side, exactly zero had genital surgery, although 43% to 67% wanted it. The bottom line is that on the medical examination table or where assistance is needed with such intimate tasks as bathing, toileting, and dressing (e.g., in a nursing home), about 80% of older transwomen and nearly all transmen risk being "outed" as transgender whether they say anything or not. Given how much discrimination and violence transgender people have experienced, it cannot surprise anyone when transgender elders who would not pass when naked decide to forgo needed medical or assistive services to lessen their chances of facing transphobia.

The other risk for inadvertent outing is identification documents. Individuals have many more documents that reveal name or gender than most people realize, ranging from the obvious driver's license to the mostly forgotten high school transcript, birth certificate, or even childhood trophy. Here, too, the *Injustice at Every Turn* study has given us our first measure of the extent of the problem. More than 50% of their older respondents had either not tried to update the name or gender marker on their driver's license or state identification card or had the requested changes denied. More than 60% had not updated (or were denied the right to update) their Social Security records. Although the survey did not specifically ask about health insurance records—which can result in transgender people being nonconsensually outed in health care settings—it did ask, "Of all your IDs and records, which of the following is most true?" Only 21% of those ages 55 to 64 and 28% of those ages 65 plus answered "all identifications list [the] gender I prefer." That means nearly 80% of transgender elders are at risk of being outed, depending on which forms of identification are demanded by a service provider, police officer, or even a retail clerk.

Bathroom Battlegrounds

Another transgender-specific site of problems is public, workplace, and health care facility bathrooms. Bathrooms remain the issue most commonly raised whenever someone transitions genders at work, seeks legislation outlawing antitransgender discrimination, or simply needs to heed the call of nature when away from home. One of the stories told in FORGE's "elder abuse" survey even involved a single-occupancy bathroom:

> A very conservatively dressed trans-woman was eating, with two friends, a man and a woman, at a local pizza place. When she wanted to use the bathroom (a single use bathroom), she was approached by one of the staff, who loudly told her that she could not use either the women's or the men's room. When her friends asked to see the manager, they were told to leave, which they did. There was no follow-up to the incident. (Cook-Daniels & munson, 2010, p. 156)

WHAT WE DO NOT KNOW

Life Course

One of the primary things we do not know about the aging transgender cohort is the extent to which life course events influenced when they decided to transition genders or identify themselves more or less publicly as transgender. Certainly, life course events are salient in the stories some transgender elders tell. For example, Julie waited until both of her parents died, to spare them the necessity of trying to understand a loved son turning into an unwanted daughter. Cindy waited until she retired and no longer spent her days with rugged but narrow-minded male machinists. George waited until his children left the nest, and DJ was jolted into a "now-or-never" decision by a nearly life-ending heart attack. Sam simply says ze was done with spending a lifetime sacrificing self for loved ones: It was time Sam got to be zirself.[3]

This is also the first generation to be able to sit at their desks, securely alone behind closed doors and curtains, and access not only the life-changing information that there were others like them but that they had choices they had not dreamed of. Middle-aged trans person after middle-aged trans person tell stories of sitting wide-eyed, hearts pounding, teary, or ecstatic as they

---

[3]*Ze* and *zirself* are gender-neutral pronouns, often used by transgender people who do not wish to identify as either female or male. A chart of some gender-neutral pronoun systems is available at http://forge-forward.org/wp-content/docs/gender-neutral-pronouns1.pdf.

discovered websites describing others like them. One transgender person told researchers:

- Transgender, genderqueer . . . these terms didn't exist—at least not as we know them now. There were no resources—like the Internet—which I could consult to help me cope with how I felt. I was very much alone with my "dark secrets," and it was not until I went online in 1997 that I realized how un-alone I was. (Beemyn & Rankin, 2011, p. 23)

To be transgender in the early 21st century is to rely on other transgender people to educate you, socialize you, and refer you to required professionals who have been previously vetted by other transgender people, and this has largely happened through the Internet. It no longer matters if you live in an urban area large enough and sophisticated enough to have a well-developed and publicized transgender infrastructure; no matter how isolated your living situation, if you have access to a computer and online services, you can reach other transgender people.

The Internet has also made actual gender transition easier. Many transgender people access their hormones that way, bypassing the need to navigate local pharmacies and sometimes even local physicians. It is also far easier to locate surgeons. Early histories tell of transgender people simply getting on a plane to foreign countries armed only with vague leads that somewhere there was a surgeon who allegedly operated on transgender people (Califia, 1997). Now many surgeons sponsor online photo albums displaying beautiful surgical outcomes. Given just how critical the Internet has been to transgender people, it is not possible to know who might have transitioned earlier in life had they been born after the world had access to online information.

A third possibility why so many transgender people have waited until midlife or later to transition is that there was not the necessary support earlier on. Christine Jorgensen is an icon not just because she was beautiful, gracious, and public but also because she was strong enough to be public when she was all there was. Virtually alone, she withstood the cameras and reporters, inviting the public to examine her womanhood when it was not even clear she had people in her private life who could salve the inevitable wounds. Contrast her example with Chaz Bono, who had more public of a gender transition than anyone else has had so far but who knew of—and utilized—an organized network of transgender supporters and advisors to help keep him afloat while the waters roiled. Less public figures have admitted that although they wanted to transition years or decades earlier than they did, they were daunted by the social price they would have to pay. Only recently, when one can occasionally see a transgender person on television who is not defending his or her dignity on a talk show and when every large city has at least one transgender support group to provide a reassuring backup, have they felt they could dare to be who they are.

A related, unresolved life course question is how transgender identities evolve over the lifetime. *The Lives of Transgender People* study reported that "among the individuals surveyed who grew up in the 1940s through the 1980s, many of the heterosexual FTM participants identified as butch lesbians and many of the MTF participants identified as cross-dressers before gaining a better understanding of themselves" (Beemyn & Rankin, 2011, p. 75). The authors noted that this identity progression was likely related to the (non)existence of the Internet because the transgender people of these generations may not have been able to "fully comprehend the nature of their feelings" given how few identity options seemed to exist before the creation of the Internet (p. 75).

Graphic illustrations of how these factors may interact also come from Beemyn and Rankin (2011). They found that more than two thirds of their 18- to 22-year-old respondents had met other transgender people by the time they came out as transgender. By contrast, only a third of the respondents in their 40s and a quarter of those ages 50 and older already knew another transgender person when they identified themselves as transgender. In addition, this study found that 28% of those ages 43 to 52 and 35% of those 53 and older "did not consider that they might be transgender until at least age forty" (p. 54).

The Internet has certainly played an important part in supporting SOFFAs as well. Numerous websites, chat rooms, listservs, and other platforms have offered partners and sometimes other SOFFAs support and information that had previously been difficult to find or even, depending on location and time, nonexistent. In summary, it will be many years before the Internet's creation can be filtered out of questions of how transgender people develop their identities over the life course.

Resilience

Unfortunately, there have been no studies of the resilience of older transgender adults, although the *Aging and Health Report* touches on some possible resilience strategies. This dearth of research has many explanations, not least of which is our social and scientific tendency to focus on problems or what is not working rather than what is working. The field of psychology itself has only recently begun focusing on what keeps people sane and functioning as opposed to what causes mental illness and dysfunction. LGBT researchers and advocates have also contributed to the bias, focusing on developing data that can justify health and social programs (e.g., HIV education and prevention programs, antibullying efforts) and antidiscrimination legislation (e.g., documenting rates of employment discrimination, hate crimes). There is also the transgender community itself in which a widespread "victim mentality" tends to focus people on losses, setbacks, disrespect, and the like rather than on celebrating and magnifying the skills and outlooks that obviously are there, given the very existence of older transgender people.

Those resilience factors must exist in spades. Although heteronormativity is pervasive and difficult to counteract, it is a weak foe compared with what confronts individuals who hold onto their core belief that they are not the gender that everyone—the law, health professionals, parents and family members, bureaucrats, the media, and even the random stranger on the street—insists they are. An individual's sexual orientation is not announced at birth, but his or her gender is. Toy store aisles are not divided by sexual orientation, but by gender. A lesbian does not have to state her sexual orientation to use a public restroom, but transgender persons often have to make a public declaration of their gender—and perhaps defend that decision—simply by needing to urinate. Nor do others imply a sexual orientation every single time they speak of you the way they speak of your gender ("he," "she," "my daughter," "my uncle," "the mailman"). Being able to retain an invisible internal identity and then assert it in the face of massive opposition over an extended period of time while you convince multiple professionals, institutions, and even strangers to change or at least temporarily disregard their own beliefs about gender is an enormous feat that points to remarkable strengths. Exactly what those strengths are, and what they can teach others who face more typical challenges (e.g., those involved in aging itself), have yet to be articulated.

A small start was made by the *Health and Aging Report*. This research examined a range of physical, mental, and social health issues, including questions that looked at measures of respondents' social support, community belonging, religious activity, and the size and diversity of social networks. Although the transgender respondents reported somewhat lower levels of social support and were a little less likely to feel positive about belonging to the LGBT community than were the nontransgender lesbian, gay, and bisexual respondents, they were far more likely to be involved in religious activities (48% vs. 37%) and had social networks that were much more diverse and larger in size (Fredriksen-Goldsen et al., 2011).

SOFFAs

A third area that desperately needs research is the needs of SOFFAs of transgender older adults. As previously noted, adjusting to having a transgender loved one is neither a simple nor automatic process, and many SOFFAs do not make the adjustment, resulting in lost relationships and much pain on both sides. These losses also compound. For instance, the *Injustice at Every Turn* study found that 48% of those transgender people who had experienced domestic violence as a result of their transgender status or history had also experienced homelessness, a rate nearly 4 times as high as those who had not experienced that level of family distress (Grant et al., 2011a). *Injustice at Every Turn* also provided the first (and so far, only) figures of how much direct employment discrimination SOFFAs face as a result of having a transgender loved one: 14% of spouses or partners and 11% of children of transgender workers were subject to job discrimination "due to associational bias." These rates jumped to 28% and 25%, respectively, if the transgender person experienced job loss due to discrimination. Despite the importance of supportive partners and family members, the difficulty many SOFFAs face in coming to terms with their loved ones' gender identity, and the direct as well as indirect antitransgender discrimination SOFFAs face, extremely little research and few programs and resources exist to support SOFFAs and help them cope with the challenges of an undereducated and prejudiced society.

Other Research Areas

As this chapter demonstrates, some of the data that exist on transgender elders and SOFFAs are contradictory or puzzling. Are disability rates among transgender elders truly higher or lower than among either their age or gender-identity peers? If they are different, what might be the causes? Although we speculated in this chapter why some transgender elders seem to be far less susceptible to various disparities than their younger peers, much more research needs to be done to validate these differences and begin to pin down their causes. We also, of course, need to find some way to reach and study those transgender elders who transitioned decades ago and now seem invisible, both so that we can serve them better and so that we can better understand the cohort, life course, institutional, and peer influences on transgender people of all ages.

POLICY AND PRACTICE IMPLICATIONS

Discrimination Is Iterative and Requires Advocacy

Transgender elders make a good case study of how widespread social prejudice causes problems that are iterative, building on each other in complex and cumulative ways that result in an old age that far too often is impoverished, unhealthy, and unhappy. Clearly, every effort must be made to address prejudice and discrimination throughout the lifespan and at all levels of society. In the meantime, service providers must be aware of and prepared to help compensate for the pile of disparities, risk factors, and barriers that have accumulated for transgender elders. Culturally competent advocacy and accompaniment services may provide enough reassurance to enable some transgender elders to access services they may otherwise shun. Practices must be developed and communicated that assure transgender elders that their privacy and confidentiality needs will be protected and that those who learn of their transgender status or history know how to handle that information respectfully. Wherever possible, the issue of bathrooms must be made moot, preferably by offering single-user facilities that are not labeled by gender.

Service Design Must Accommodate Complexity

Currently, one of the most common ways we accommodate stereotyping, prejudice, and fear is by dividing people by demographic category. Thus, we have gendered public bathrooms, separate programs for LGBT people, domestic violence and sexual assault programs that serve only women, and separate rooms for men and women in many health care or aging facilities. These divisions often do not serve transgender people and their families. Those who wish to serve transgender people and SOFFAs must not only be creative in how they design services, they must also engage other clients and staff in an ongoing effort to create space that is truly safe from bias and disrespect, rather than simply segregated on the basis on stereotypes.

This awareness of complexity is particularly important when supporting the people around transgender elders, many of whom may not identify as either lesbian, gay, bisexual, or transgender. Supportive SOFFAs are critical to transgender individuals' quality of life and yet are routinely addressed only when someone wants to tell them "the proper way to be an ally." Programs and services must be designed to listen to SOFFAs, help them identify their needs for support and information, and then provide those resources.

Resilience Must Be Identified and Strengthened

As previously noted, given the task of asserting a different gender identity from the gender assigned at birth in a highly prejudiced and binary society, the very fact that they have survived into elderhood means transgender older adults must have extensive and effective resilience strategies. Yet a felt sense of resiliency is not as common among transgender elders as is a sense of being beleaguered and victimized. Service providers and researchers can and should help us begin to identify, own, and build on our strengths. Although this effort is imperative for transgender elders' health, it may also have much wider implications: Who is better experienced to teach others how to adapt to a world (and old age) that is seemingly engaged in ever-accelerating change than people who have weathered a change of gender or asserted a gender that no one had imagined before? We need to encourage these pioneers to step forward and take their rightful places as guides to the ever-evolving landscape of aging.

REFERENCES

Beemyn, G., & Rankin, S. (2011). *The lives of transgender people*. New York, NY: Columbia University Press.

Benjamin, H. (1966). *The transsexual phenomenon*. New York, NY: Julian Press.

Califia, P. (1997). *Sex changes: The politics of transgenderism*. San Francisco, CA: Cleis Press.

Centers for Disease Control and Prevention. (2013). *Adverse childhood experiences (ACE) study*. Retrieved from http://www.cdc.gov/ace

Cook-Daniels, L., & munson, m. (2010). Sexual violence, elder abuse, and sexuality of transgender adults, age 50+: Results of three surveys. *Journal of GLBT Family Studies, 6*, 142–177. doi:10.1080/15504281003705238

Fredriksen-Goldsen, K. I., Kim, H.-J., Emlet, C. A., Muraco, A., Erosheva, E. A., Hoy-Ellis, C. P., . . . Petry, H. (2011). *The aging and health report: Disparities and resilience among lesbian, gay, bisexual and transgender older adults*. Retrieved from the National LGBT Health and Aging Center website: http://caringandagingorg/word.press/wp-content/uploads/2011/05/Full-Report-FINAL-11-16-11pdf

Grant, J. M., Mottet, L. A., Tanis, J., Harrison, J., Herman, J. L., & Keisling, M. (2011a). *Injustice at every turn: A report of the national transgender discrimination survey*. Retrieved from National Center for Transgender Equality and National Gay and Lesbian Task Force website: http://www.thetaskforce.org/downloads/reports/reports/ntds_full.pdf

Grant, J. M., Mottet, L. A., Tanis, J., Harrison, J., Herman, J. L., & Keisling, M. (2011b). [National transgender discrimination survey]. Unpublished raw data on older respondents.

Hopwood, R. (2012, August). *Creating a multidisciplinary approach to trans care*. Presented at the Southeastern Trans Health Conference, Asheville, NC.

Institute of Medicine. (2011). *The health of lesbian, gay, bisexual, and transgender people: Building a foundation for better understanding*. Washington, DC: Author.

Kenagy, G. (2005). The health and social service needs of transgender people in Philadelphia. *International Journal of Transgenderism, 8*, 49–56. doi:10.1300/J485v08n02_05

Kenagy, G., & Bostwick, W. (2005). Health and social service needs of transgendered people in Chicago. *International Journal of Transgenderism, 8*(2–3), 57–66. doi:10.1300/J485v08n02_06

Meyerowitz, J. (2002). *How sex changed: A history of transsexuality in the United States*. Cambridge, MA: Harvard University Press.

munson, m., & Cook-Daniels, L. (2004). [Transgender experiences of sexual violence]. Unpublished raw data.

munson, m., & Cook-Daniels, L. (2011). [Transgender individuals' knowledge of and willingness to use sexual assault programs]. Unpublished raw data.

National Coalition of Anti-Violence Programs. (2009). *Hate violence against Lesbian, Gay, Bisexual, Transgender and Queer communities in the United States in 2009*. Retrieved from http://avp.org/storage/documents/Reports/2009_NCAVP_HV_Report.pdf

National Coalition of Anti-Violence Programs. (2010). *Hate violence against lesbian, gay, bisexual, transgender, Queer and HIV-affected communities in the United States in 2010*. Retrieved from http://avp.org/storage/documents/Reports/2011_NCAVP_HV_Reports.pdf

Xavier, J., Hitchcock, D., Hollinshead, S., Keisling, M., Lewis, Y., Lombardi, E., . . . Williams, B. (2004). *An overview of U.S. trans health priorities: A report by the eliminating disparities working group*. National Coalition for LGBT Health. Retrieved from National Center for Transgender Equality website: http://transequality.org/PDFs/HealthPriorities.pdf

10

CONCLUSION: FOSTERING RESILIENCE IN LGBT AGING INDIVIDUALS AND FAMILIES

CHRISTINE A. FRUHAUF AND NANCY A. OREL

Over the past several years, tremendous efforts have been made to advance knowledge and awareness of the lives of older lesbian, gay, bisexual, and transgender (LGBT) adults and their families among researchers, practitioners, students, and other interested individuals. Despite the virtually "invisible" population of sexual and gender minorities in the greater body of gerontological research, several recent noteworthy contributions to the field (e.g., Berger, 1996; Clunis, Fredriksen-Goldsen, Freeman, & Nystrom, 2005; Herdt & de Vries, 2004; Kimmel, Rose, & David, 2006) have brought progress in our understanding of the diversity of the LGBT aging population. The advocacy of individuals active in interest groups within the Gerontological Society of America (i.e., Rainbow Research Group) and the American Society on Aging (i.e., LGBT Aging Issues Network) has further advanced research, practice, and policy in this area. Although these efforts are important, closer attention to the intersection of culture, family, and individuals among LGBT

DOI: 10.1037/14436-010
The Lives of LGBT Older Adults: Understanding Challenges and Resilience, N. A. Orel and
C. A. Fruhauf (Editors)
Copyright © 2015 by the American Psychological Association. All rights reserved.

elders is still needed because these topics are important to advancing the field of gerontology. In the context of the ADDRESSING framework (Hays, 1996, 2008; see also Chapter 1, this volume) over the life course, the chapters in this book further contribute to our knowledge of LGBT older adults and families while providing policy and practice suggestions to support and enrich the lives of LGBT older individuals.

RESILIENCE AND LGBT ELDERS AND THEIR FAMILIES

As indicated throughout this book, LGBT older adults and their families have unique strengths that lead to positive coping strategies and support resilience. The multidimensional nature of resilience includes protective factors and adaptive processes of individuals (Bergeman & Wallace, 1999) who were often thought of as at risk for developing psychopathology (Wright & Masten, 2006), an all too common experience for many LGBT older adults today (see Chapters 2 and 3, this volume). The chapter authors herein who used the life course perspective support previous research (see Lipsitt & Demick, 2011; Smith & Hayslip, 2012) proposing that to fully understand resilience among adults in later life, it is necessary to explore the antecedents of resilience during childhood and adolescence. As outlined in this book, the diversity of LGBT elders and their families supports the need for continuous effort toward research in this population; scholars are only beginning to scratch the surface of resilience and strengths in the often complex lives of LGBT elders. Furthermore, the shift from studying negative outcomes to examining positive factors has the potential to create new, innovative approaches to policy and practice, including prevention and intervention programs (Smith & Hayslip, 2012; see also Chapter 7, this volume) to advance support services for LGBT older adults and their families.

Despite the increased interest in the study of resilience in gerontology (Fry & Keyes, 2010; Hayslip & Smith, 2012; Reich, Zautra, & Hall, 2010; Resnick, Gwyther, & Roberto, 2010), knowledge related to resilience among LGBT older adults and their families is limited. It was our goal for this edited book to shift the paradigm away from negative factors associated with LGBT aging issues and collectively showcase the strengths of LGBT elders. Although this book is the first to focus on positive aspects associated with LGBT aging, it is still unknown whether the processes of resilience among LGBT older adults and their families fluctuate in ways unique to these populations. Furthermore, as scholars continue the dialogue on resilience and strengths related to LGBT older adults and their families, emerging perspectives may lead to innovative theoretical and practice-related approaches to minority resilience, along with discoveries that may prove useful to the well-being of LGBT individuals and their families over the life course.

QUESTIONS FOR FUTURE RESEARCH

In this book, researchers interested in LGBT aging issues have explored various topics important to the lives of individuals and families, emphasizing the importance of studying resilience, strengths, and positive outcomes among LGBT elders. As a result, we express our recommendations for future research, theory, and practice in this light, while revisiting the experiences of the four older LGBT individuals introduced in Chapter 1.

Why Do LGBT Elders Go Back Into the Closet?

One research topic that cuts across many of the chapters for this book (see the chapters by de Vries, Swartz et al., Cahill, and Cook-Daniels) is that of LGBT elders going back into the closet when they age or receive community-based services (e.g., home care, long-term care). There is great potential on the part of researchers and service providers to change the likelihood that older LGBT adults will experience the necessity of nondisclosure, and therefore we explore this further.

Several of the reviewed studies point out the stress, strain, and fear often associated with receiving services from professionals who all too often are not knowledgeable or sensitive to LGBT aging adults and their families. In thinking more about this experience for LGBT elders (in the context of resilience), another question remains to be fully explored. That is, if we suggest that older LGBT adults emerge stronger after a lifetime experiencing such concerns as sexism, racism, chronic stress, and physical and mental health challenges linked with their sexual identity, and therefore may develop protective factors leading to resilience, why do many older LGBT persons find it necessary to go back into the closet when they begin receiving community-based services or enter long-term care?

Following the ADDRESSING framework, additional, subsidiary questions should be asked: (a) How likely is it for older gay men or lesbian women to go back into the closet? What about bisexual or transgender older adults? (b) Does nondisclosure vary based on the race and ethnicity of the LGBT aging adult? (c) How do the cognitive and physical abilities of an LGBT older adult contribute to this experience? (d) How do other factors such as religion, spirituality, and nationality affect the life course experience of coming out, especially as it relates to disclosing this to professionals and thus receiving services later in life?

As Cahill outlined in Chapter 7, there are few services available today for LGBT older adults. As de Vries discusses in Chapter 3, few aging-related services employ practitioners who are welcoming or friendly to older LGBT adults, and even fewer practitioners possess the attitudinal, knowledge, and skill competencies needed to work effectively with LGBT older adults. Therefore, another question needs to be asked: Is going back into the closet when aging services and support are needed a function or a dysfunction of the system? In other words, is it not directly related to the traits, characteristics, and diversity of the LGBT person or his or her family? This final question reaches beyond the ADDRESSING framework to the intersection of environmental, systemic, and community factors that have an influence on LGBT older adults' experiences. Although Alderson (2000, 2003) proposed an ecological model of gay male identity that included the intersection of these factors, the applicability of this model for LGBT older adults has not been systematically explored. However, practitioners can use the ADDRESSING framework and the ecological model as a guide to assist LGBT older adults who are questioning their sexual identities as well as to probe the influences of personal attributes and the environment in their decisions to disclose their sexual identity. The ecological model emphasizes that environmental factors (e.g., family, culture, religion and spirituality, peers) can be both a hindrance and catalyst for the coming-out process. We will use two of the LGBT older adults introduced in Chapter 1 as examples. Edna may be encouraged to publically acknowledge her long-term relationship with her partner, Sue, when she is in the welcoming and affirming senior center. Conversely, Cheryl, who is the older lesbian grandmother, may be hindered in coming out to her grandchildren if her adult children request that she remain closeted.

Are Some People More Resilient?

Several questions need to be answered in the study of resilience in LGBT aging adults. If an LGBT person does not go back into the closet, is she or he more resilient by nature? Or did this person develop coping mechanisms over time to counteract negative factors in the environment as he or she aged? Or do practitioners and service providers who are better educated and knowledgeable about the lives of LGBT older adults and offer affirming support and services ultimately enhance the lives of their older LGBT clients and promote resilience? All of these possibilities might be true, yet these questions have not been fully answered through empirical research. Scholars should consider making resilience a key focus of their work in the future when examining LGBT older adults and their families.

What Are Some Unanswered Questions About Sexual Identity?

Aside from focusing on specific questions related to the issue of coming out (disclosing) or moving back into the closet (nondisclosure), further investigation related to sexual orientation is needed. The bulk of attention in the LGBT aging research has been given to sampling lesbians and gay men, with fewer samples including transgender adults; little, if any, attention has focused on the life course of bisexual older adults who may experience a lifetime of transitions between homosexual and heterosexual relationships and affectional interest and attractions. Although *gay* and *lesbian* are sexual identity labels, *bisexual* may refer to identity, behavior or affectional orientation. Further investigation in this area has the potential to uncover unique aspects of resilience because bisexual adults may develop protective factors unique to their sexual identity and affectional orientation. Qualitative research on sensitive and largely unexplored topics such as bisexuality is significant for the development of effective services and programs to support bisexual older adults. Although this type of data is critical, such data are, unfortunately, not generally obtainable in large-scale designs because in-depth information about and insight into the experiences of resilience might be unique based on sexual orientation over the life course.

How Useful Are Community and Advocacy Groups?

As more community and advocacy groups begin to address the needs of LGBT older adults and their families, and as services for LGBT individuals are further developed, it would be beneficial to evaluate the usefulness of these organizations and the impact they have on individual lives, professional practice, and community awareness (Fruhauf, Bundy-Fazioli, & Miller, 2012). In both Fredriksen-Goldsen et al.'s and Brotman et al.'s chapters in this volume (Chapters 2 and 6, respectively), the use of community-based participatory research (CBPR; Israel, Eng, Schultz, & Parker, 2005) with LGBT older adult populations and organizations is introduced. CBPR is built on partnerships, and because LGBT older adults often include assistance (or estrangement) from multiple parties (e.g., partner, grandchild, other family members, friends, practitioners), the key principles of CBPR can help to guide future research.

The CBPR research approach has been successful in a number of communities (O'Fallon, Tyson, & Dearry, 2000), and success is based primarily on community change that improves the health and well-being of community members (Israel, 2000). CBPR is widely used when examining ways to improve individuals' health (Israel et al., 2005), and the methods and approach to CBPR could also be used to evaluate important health topics related to LGBT seniors. For example, senior centers could establish an advisory group or council, and LGBT seniors could be invited to attend these meetings as council members working to improve the health and well-being of all LGBT elders in the community who attend (and do not attend) the senior center. Annually the senior center director and her or his staff, with input and direction from the LGBT elders and the advisory council, could evaluate the usefulness of the center and its connection with other community agencies that share the mission of assisting older adults with health matters (including physical and mental health). This feedback would help drive projects and foci and could also provide the impetus for other LGBT elders to become more involved with their senior center. It may even lead to better connections with other health-related agencies in the community and could assist in educating providers outside of the LGBT community about LGBT aging strengths and challenges.

IMPLICATIONS FOR THEORY

Future studies should also be theory rich. In line with the suggested theoretical perspectives Kimmel outlined in his chapter and the use of the life course perspective (Bengtson & Allen, 1993), we believe that using the social convoy model (Antonucci & Akiyama, 1987; Kahn & Antonucci, 1980) as a guiding framework for understanding LGBT elders would benefit future research. Highlighted as an important theory in examining aging families (Connidis, 2010), the social convoy is a collection of family and friends who support adults as they age. As discussed by Scherrer and Fedor in Chapter 8 and by Cook-Daniels in Chapter 9 of this book, family and friends play important roles in the lives of LGBT older adults. Furthermore, Swartz et al., Chapter 5, emphasize that the role of the chosen family in the lives of LGBT older adults must be recognized and valued. When examining the social convoy of an LGBT older adult, he or she is placed in the middle, and concentric circles are drawn around this person. The inner circle includes family and friends whom the older adult believes are her or his closest confidants. The outer circles are individuals who are supportive but not at the same level as the individuals in the inner circle (Antonucci & Akiyama, 1987). This model can be used to conceptualize new research related to LGBT individuals and families as well as to identify important individuals in the lives of LGBT older adults for research related to services. Social support and connections with families are important to health and well-being as people age. For example, the social convoy can help an elderly lesbian understand who is in her inner circle, where she might place her children and grandchildren, and where there might be room for more people to support her.

IMPLICATIONS FOR DIRECT PRACTICE

Let us return to the LGBT older adults introduced in Chapter 1. It is well known that social environmental factors can support individuals' strengths or worsen their vulnerabilities (McQuaide & Ehrenreich, 1997).

Thus, coming from both a strengths-based approach (Saleebey, 2011) and the resiliency literature, if Cheryl does come out to her children and grandchildren and they reject her, this loss could potentially contribute to her sense of isolation, loneliness, increased stress, and decreased health because her social convoy might be diminished. However, it could also make her stronger and empower her to advocate on behalf of other older adults who are not out to their family or allow her freedom to include chosen family in her social convoy. Or, if Edna by nature is determined and solid in her decision to find the best care possible for herself and her partner, this passion and drive could propel her to seek out new supportive relationships with other family and friends and may even lead her to no longer worry if Sue shows affection in front of other people.

How LGBT older adults make sense of their internal thoughts and feelings in relation to their external environment is individualistic. This is important; McQuaide and Ehrenreich (1997) stated that "being able to access one's strengths effectively contributes not only to solving an immediate problem, but may also augment the [LGBT older adult's] ability to deal with future problems" (p. 202). Therefore, as practitioners, it is important to actively engage older LGBT adults using the strengths-based approach (Saleebey, 2011).

Often, in practice, assessing for strengths is easier said than done (McQuaide & Ehrenreich, 1997; Saleebey, 2011). The strengths-based approach, in this case, refers to the relationship between the practitioner's philosophical stance and his or her depth of understanding of how each individual perseveres in the face of adversity (Fruhauf & Bundy-Fazioli, 2013). To fully practice from a strengths perspective, the practitioner must embrace the philosophy of working with older LGBT adults as partners in the process while truly fostering mutual collaboration. For example, Saleebey (2011) stated, "the strengths approach obligates us to understand—to believe—that everybody (no exceptions here) has external and internal assets, competencies, and resources" (p. 127). Thus, it would be counterproductive for any practitioner at the senior center to tell Tanna (or any LGBT elder who enters seeking assistance) exactly how she can better take care of herself. Instead, it behooves the practitioner to recognize that individuals learn from the challenges they face and therefore have intrinsic knowledge about themselves and skills that arise from this knowledge (Saleebey, 2011).

As a result, practitioners need to be cognizant of how they interact with LGBT older adults. For example, if a practitioner finds that Jack is resistant or difficult to engage, then it is the practitioner's responsibility to evaluate his or her own beliefs, approach, and demeanor when working with him. It is important, therefore, for practitioners to ask colleagues and supervisors for feedback (Fruhauf & Bundy-Fazioli, 2013) and to ask themselves,

"Do I believe Jack is worthy of receiving services?" and "Do I believe in Jack's strengths and abilities?" The answers to these questions will help pinpoint what the LGBT elder is sensing in his or her interaction with the practitioner and drive the interaction between practitioner and adult as they develop a plan of care.

CONCLUSION

In Chapter 1, we introduced the reader to Edna, Jack, Cheryl, and Tanna, who were visiting the senior center with the assumption that it would be welcoming and responsive to their unique needs and concerns as LGBT older adults. Because they possess multiple identities, and because many of these identities are nondominant (non-Caucasian, physically challenged, cognitively challenged, non-European American), they may also face obstacles in accessing services and programs that address these multiple identities. There are a host of services and programs within the aging network of providers that should be specifically welcoming and accessible to LGBT individuals, but they must also employ practitioners who are capable of recognizing the importance and relevance of LGBT older adults' multiple minority identities.

Historically, the emphasis in the development of culturally competent programs and services for older adults has primarily been on issues specific to ethnic and racial minority populations (Bidell, Turner, & Casas, 2002; Min, 2005; Naito-Chan, Damron-Rodriguez, & Simmons, 2005). Despite this emphasis, "no commonly accepted, gerontological knowledge-based skills or competencies have been identified for social workers to possess to effectively serve older clients" (Naito-Chan et al., 2005, p. 59).

Most important, there remains a tremendous need for gerontological practitioners to be trained to work with older adults who self-identify as LGBT. Because sexual orientation and gender identity are separate issues (Bidell, 2013), it is especially important that practitioners also develop distinctive competencies regarding transgender elders (see Chapter 9 in this book). Sexual orientation and gender identity competency would include attitudinal knowledge and skill competencies needed to effectively work with LGBT older adults (and their families). The attitudinal component would include the practitioners' personal beliefs about LGBT individuals in general, and LGBT older adults specifically. This would include heterosexist and ageist stereotypic assumptions regarding older adults who self-identify as LGBT. Knowledge competencies would include the social, political, physical/mental health, cognitive, religious, financial, and legal issues facing LGBT older adults. Skills competencies include experience with assessment, case management, intervention development, and program and policy advocacy.

All practitioners working with LGBT older adults and their families must develop the specific attitudes, knowledge, and skills for age-competent and LGBT-affirmative practice. As illustrated throughout this book (and especially in Chapter 7), affirmative practice must be available, appropriate, and affirming on multiple levels (e.g., individual, organizational, community, overarching policies) and through services for LGBT older adults and their families. A few guidelines and models have been developed that would assist practitioners in understanding the unique experiences and issues for LGBT older adults. These include the *Guidelines for Psychological Practice With Lesbian, Gay, and Bisexual Clients* (American Psychological Association, 2012) and Crisp, Wayland, and Gordon's (2008) competency-based model of "age competent and gay affirmative practice" (p. 6). Furthermore, Keppel's (2006) model stresses the importance of viewing clients "through several lenses at once" (p. 88). We believe that the ADDRESSING framework would facilitate this process as well as illuminate our observations of the strengths and resiliency of the LGBT older adult population over time. The recognition of the resiliency and strengths of the LGBT older adult population will enable these elders to age with dignity and receive collective respect.

REFERENCES

Alderson, K. G. (2000). *Beyond coming out: Experiences of positive gay identity.* Toronto, Canada: Insomniac Press.

Alderson, K. G. (2003). The ecological model of gay male identity. *Canadian Journal of Human Sexuality, 12,* 75–85.

American Psychological Association. (2012). Guidelines for psychological practice with lesbian, gay, and bisexual clients. *American Psychologist, 67,* 10–42. doi:10.1037/a0024659

Antonucci, T. C., & Akiyama, H. (1987). Social networks in adult life and a preliminary examination of the convoy model. *Journal of Gerontology, 42,* 519–527.

Bengtson, V. L., & Allen, K. R. (1993). The life course perspective applied to families over time. In P. G. Boss, W. J. Doherty, R. Larossa, W. R. Schumm, & S. K. Steinmentz (Eds.), *Sourcebook of family theories and methods: A contextual approach* (pp. 469–504). New York, NY: Plenum Press. doi:10.1007/978-0-387-85764-0_19

Bergeman, C. S., & Wallace, K. A. (1999). Resiliency in later life. In T. L. Whitman, T. V. Merluzzi, & R. D. White (Eds.), *Life-span perspectives on health and illness* (pp. 207–225). Hillsdale, NJ: Erlbaum.

Berger, R. M. (1996). *Gay and gray: The older homosexual man* (2nd ed.). Binghamton, NY: The Haworth Press.

Bidell, M. P. (2013). The sexual orientation counselor competency scale. In K. Alderson (Ed.), *Counseling LGBTI clients* (pp. 253–258). Los Angeles, CA: Sage.

Bidell, M. P., Turner, J. A., & Casas, M. (2002). First impressions count: Ethnic/racial and lesbian/gay/bisexual content of professional psychology application materials. *Professional Psychology: Research and Practice, 33,* 97–103. doi:10.1037/0735-7028.33.1.97

Clunis, D. M., Fredriksen-Goldsen, K. I., Freeman, P. A., & Nystrom, N. M. (2005). *Lives of lesbian elders: Looking back, looking forward.* Binghamton, NY: The Haworth Press.

Connidis, I. A. (2010). *Family ties and aging.* Thousand Oaks, CA: Pine Forge Press.

Crisp, C., Wayland, S., & Gordon, T. (2008). Older gay, lesbian, and bisexual adults: Tools for age-competent and gay affirmative practice. *Journal of Gay & Lesbian Social Services, 20,* 5–29. doi:10.1080/10538720802178890

Fruhauf, C. A., & Bundy-Fazioli, K. (2013). Grandparent caregivers' self-care practice: Moving toward a strengths-based approach. In B. Hayslip, Jr., & G. C. Smith (Eds.), *Resilient grandparent caregivers: A strengths based perspective* (pp. 88–102). New York, NY: Routledge.

Fruhauf, C. A., Bundy-Fazioli, K., & Miller, J. (2012). The Larimer County Alliance for Grandfamilies: An innovative approach to meeting a community need. *Journal of Applied Gerontology, 31,* 193–214. doi:10.1177/0733464810385094

Fry, P. S., & Keyes, C. L. M. (Eds.). (2010). *New frontiers in resilient aging: Life-strengths and well-being in later life.* New York, NY: Cambridge University Press. doi:10.1017/CBO9780511763151

Hays, P. (1996). Culturally responsive assessment with diverse older adults. *Professional Psychology: Research and Practice, 27,* 188–193. doi:10.1037/0735-7028.27.2.188

Hays, P. (2008). *Addressing cultural complexities in practice: Assessment, diagnosis, and therapy* (2nd ed.). Washington, DC: American Psychological Association.

Hayslip, B., Jr., & Smith, G. C. (Eds.). (2012). *Annual review of gerontology and geriatrics: Vol. 32. Emerging perspectives on resilience in adulthood and later life.* New York, NY: Springer.

Herdt, G., & de Vries, B. (Eds.). (2004). *Gay and lesbian aging: Research and future directions.* New York, NY: Springer.

Israel, B. (2000). *Community-based participatory research: Principles, rationale and policy recommendations.* Keynote Address for the National Institute of Environmental Sciences Conference, Washington, DC.

Israel, B., Eng, E., Schultz, A. J., & Parker, E. A. (Eds.). (2005). *Methods in community-based participatory research for health.* San Francisco, CA: Jossey-Bass.

Kahn, R. L., & Antonucci, T. C. (1980). Convoys over the life course: Attachment, roles, and social support. *Life-span development and behavior, 3,* 253-286.

Keppel, B. (2006). Affirmative psychotherapy with older bisexual women and men. *Journal of Bisexuality, 6,* 85–104. doi:10.1300/J159v06n01_06

Kimmel, D., Rose, T., & David, S. (Eds.). (2006). *Lesbian, gay, bisexual, and transgender aging: Research and clinical perspectives.* New York, NY: Columbia Press.

Lipsitt, L. P., & Demick, J. (2011). Resilience science comes of age: Old age that is. *PsycCRITIQUES, 36*(26).

McQuaide, S., & Ehrenreich, J. (1997). Assessing client strengths. *Families in Society: The Journal of Contemporary Human Services, 78,* 201–212. doi:10.1606/1044-3894.759

Min, J. W. (2005). Cultural competency: A key to effective social work with racially and ethnically diverse elders. *Families in Society, 86,* 347–358. doi:10.1606/1044-3894.3432

Naito-Chan, E., Damron-Rodriquez, J., & Simmons, J. (2005). Identifying competencies for geriatric social work practice. *Journal of Gerontological Social Work, 43,* 59–78. doi:10.1300/J083v43n04_05

O'Fallon, L., Tyson, F., & Dearry, A. (Eds.). (2000, March). *Successful models of community-based participatory research.* National Institute of Environmental Sciences Conference, Washington, DC.

Reich, J. W., Zautra, A. J., & Hall, J. S. (2010). *Handbook of adult resilience.* New York, NY: Guilford Press.

Resnick, B., Gwyther, L. P., & Roberto, K. A. (2010). *Resilience in aging: Concepts, research, and outcomes.* New York, NY: Springer.

Saleebey, D. (2011). *The strengths perspective in social work practice* (6th ed.). New York, NY: Allyn & Bacon.

Smith, G. C., & Hayslip, B., Jr. (2012). Resilience in adulthood and later life: What does it mean and where are we heading? In B. Hayslip, Jr., & G. C. Smith (Vol. Eds.), *Annual review of gerontology and geriatrics: Vol. 32. Emerging perspectives on resilience in adulthood and later life* (pp. 3–28). New York, NY: Springer Publishing Company.

Wright, M. O., & Masten, A. S. (2006). Resilience processes in development: Fostering positive adaption in the context of adversity. In S. Goldstein & R. B. Brooks (Eds.), *Handbook of resilience in children* (pp. 17–37). New York, NY: Springer.

INDEX

American Psychological Association, 225
American Society on Aging, 217
Anderson, R., 143
Antigay discrimination, 143
Antigay views, 143
Arts domain (spirituality), 96
Assisted living, 148–150
Asthma, 60, 201
Azidothymidine (AZT), 83

Baby boom cohort
    as caregivers, 37
    historical context of, 79–80
    social context of, 30
    stigma faced by, 92–93
Barker, J. C., 182
Bartlam, B., 142
Bauer, G. R., 112n1
Beemyn, G., 196–199, 209, 210
Behaviors
    maladaptive, 60
    risk, 201
Being closeted, 34. *See also*
        Concealment
Bengtson, V. L., 73, 85, 93
Benjamin, Harry, 195
Bias, 16, 116, 155, 202, 210
Bill C-150 (Canada), 114
Birth cohort, 79
Bisexual individuals
    families' acceptance of, 178
    older, future research on, 44,
        183–184
    and sexual identity, 221
    social networks of, 182
Bisexual men
    in "40 and forward," 155
    health disparities among, 28, 60, 146
    prevalence of HIV among, 60, 146
    and singlehood, 59
Bisexual women, 28, 60, 146
Blando, J., 100, 118
Blank, T. O., 37
Blosnich, J. R., 156
Bono, Chaz, 209
Bossarte, R. M., 156
Boulder County Aging Services, 150
Brennan, M., 37–38
Burgess, D., 152

Calhoun, L. G., 61
California Health Interview Survey
        (CHIS), 27, 39
California state, x
Canadian health and social care, 111–132
    enhancing access to services, 129–131
    future research on, 131–132
    key issues in, 113–115
    and LGB aging, 115–122
    and life course perspective, 125–128
    limitations of research on, 123–125
    and transgender aging, 122–123
Canadian Nurse magazine, 113
Cancer, 28, 60, 142, 201
Cantor, M. H., 37–38
CAP (Caring and Aging with Pride),
        31–38
Cardiovascular disease, 28, 146
Care (psychosocial stage), 76
Caregiving
    community resources and
        government services for,
        150–151
    as family issue, 180–181
    by LGBT baby boomers, 37
    in LGBT community, xii, 37–38
    by LGBT elders, 65–66, 180–181
    limitations to, 100–102
Caring and Aging with Pride (CAP),
        31–38
CBPR (community-based participatory
        research), 221–222
Children. *See also* Adult children;
        Grandchildren
    coming out to, 179
    transgender individuals' relationships
        with, 203
CHIS (California Health Interview
        Survey), 27, 39
Chosen families. *See* Families of choice
Cisnormativity, 112n1, 113
Civil Marriage Act (Canada), 114
Cochran, S. E., 146
Cochran, S. S., 58
Cognitive ability (ADDRESSING
        framework), 12
Cohler, B. J., 183
Cohort effect
    in ADDRESSING framework, 7–11
    considered in research, 127

Cohorts
   age, 29–30
   baby boom, 30, 37, 79–80, 92–93
   birth, 79
   differences in, 184
   older adults, 172
   "oldest old," 159
   "old-old," 159
   "young-old," 159
Cohort theory, 79–81
Collaborative stance, importance of, 223
Coming out
   familiarity with process of, 186
   to grandchildren, 180
   as individualistic life experience, 15
   in later life, 173–174
   to own children, 179
   in psychosocial stages, 76
Coming-out stories, 86
Community-based participatory
      research (CBPR), 221–222
Community connectedness
   and caregiving, 66
   and community resources/
         government services, 155
Community groups, 221–222
Community resources and government
      services, 141–160
   accessing senior services, 144–145
   caregiving, 150–151
   and community connectedness, 155
   future research on, 158–159
   and health disparities, 145–147
   health insurance coverage, 153–154
   and hospitals, 151
   housing and assisted living, 148–150
   and immigration policy, 158
   income support programs, 156–157
   and life course perspective, 142–143
   mental health services, 152–153
   and Older Americans Act, 147–148
   and sexual health education, 151–152
   Veterans Affairs, 155–156
Competence (psychosocial stage), 75–76
Concealment, 34–35
   of gender identity, 199
   by LGBT elders, 219–220
   personal history of managing, 15
   by transgender individuals, 205
Congestive heart disease, 201
Congregate meal programs, 155

Connidis, I. A., 178, 184
Conron, K. J., 28
Convoy theory, 81–84
Cook-Daniels, L., 197, 199–204, 208
Coping skills, 85–86
Crawford, B., 143
Crenshaw, K., 127–128
Criminalization, of sexual orientation, 30
Crisis competence, 38, 85–86
Crisp, C., 225
Culture
   dominant discourse within, 16–17
   future research on, 124

Dannefer, D., 126–127
D'Augelli, A. R., 58, 66, 155
De Beauvoir, Simone, 84
Defense of Marriage Act, x, 39, 57
Dementia
   lifestyle interventions to prevent, 12
   and spirituality, 97–98
Demographic information, 158–159
Department of Health and Human
      Services (DHHS), ix, x, 26, 151
Department of Housing and Urban
      Development (HUD), 40, 149
Depression, 202
Depressive symptoms
   among LGBT individuals, 60
   and social support networks, 155
Detailed care plan, 103
De Vries, B., 65–67
DHHS. See Department of Health and
      Human Services
Diabetes, 28, 60, 201
Dibble, S. L., 28, 143
Disabilities
   among LGBT elders, 27, 60
   among transgender individuals, 201
Disclosure. See Coming out
Discrimination
   antigay, 143
   due to sexual orientation/gender
         identity, 40
   in early life, negative health effects
         of, 200
   against LGBT elders in Canada,
         115–117
   against LGBT individuals, 33
   in minority stress model, 34
   and transgender individuals, 197–199

of LGBT individuals, 182
as social convoy members, 222
as social support networks, 37
support given by, 66–67
of transgender individuals, 203–204
Frost, D. M., 62
Fruhauf, C. A., 14, 120, 179, 180
Future planning, 64–65
for end-of-life decisions, 103
service providers trained for, 43

Gans, D., 73
Garland, Judy, 82–83
Gates, G. J., 100
Gay Grandfathers, 180
Gay men
in "40 and forward," 155
health disparities among, 28, 60, 146
HIV risk for, 60, 146
and singlehood, 59
social networks of, 182
socioeconomic status of, 14
Gay Men's Health Crisis (GMHC), 83
Gay-related immune deficiency (GRID),
9, 83
Gender
in ADDRESSING framework, 16
discrimination reported by, 34
and physical health, 32
Gender identity
in ADDRESSING framework, 16
concealment of, 199
criminalization of, 30
as demographic information,
158–159
disclosing to health providers,
146–147
discrimination due to, 40
effect on aging, 77–78
evolving throughout life, 210
friends and families coping with,
203–204
health disparities due to, 26–29
legal protection of, in Canada, 114
pathologization and criminalization
of, 30
and sexual orientation, 204–205
socioeconomic status affected by, 31
of transgender individuals, 211
Gender identity clinics, 194

Gender-neutral pronouns, 208n3
Gender roles, 63
Generational time (life course
perspective), 93–94
Genet, Jean, 84
Genital surgery, 207
George, L. K., 7, 126
Gerontological research, 159
Gerontological Society of America, 217
Giwa, S., 124
GMHC (Gay Men's Health Crisis), 83
Gordon, T., 225
Government services. See Community
resources and government services
Grandchildren
family issues with, 178–180
future research on relationships with,
184–185
LGBT elders relationships with, 120
Grant, J. M., 150
Greatest Generation, 30
Greene, B., 14
Greensmith, C., 124
GRID (gay-related immune deficiency),
83
Grief, disenfranchised, 176
Grossman, A. H., 37, 58, 66, 143, 155
Guidelines for Psychological Practice
With Lesbian, Gay, and Bisexual
Clients (APA), 225
Guilt (in psychosocial stages), 75

HAART (highly active anitretroviral
therapy), 83
Haber, D., 100
Haile, R., 61–62
Halkitis, P. N., 96, 101–102
Hate crimes, 40
Hays, P., 5–6
Health and well-being, 25–45
background characteristics affecting,
31–33
and education of service providers,
42–43
future research on, 43–45
and health disparities, 26–29
and life course perspective, 29–30
policies to enhance, 39–41
resources affecting, 36–39

Palliative care, 99–100
Parenting challenges, 178–179
Pathologization of sexual orientation, 30
Personal care aides, 150
Personalogical paradigm, 126
Phillips, J., 119
Physical ability (ADDRESSING
    framework), 8, 12
Physical health
    and access to services, 35
    and age, 32
    and chronic stress, 33–34
    disparities in, 27
    and gender, 32
    and isolation, 36
    and marriage, 32
    and socioeconomic status, 31–32
    and transgender individuals, 200–201
Pizer, J. C., 58
Planning
    end-of-life decisions, 104–106
    for the future. See Future planning
    health care, 121
    legal, 181, 196
    for long-term care, 175
Planning guides, 104–105
Plans
    detailed care, 103
    401(k), 157
    retirement, 157
Policies
    changes needed in, x
    to enhance health and well-being,
        39–41
    immigration, 158
    to improve transgender issues,
        212–214
Ponce, N. A., 58
Positive aging, 56
Positive marginality, 60–67
Preventive care, 12, 29
Previous opposite-sex marriages, 175
Price, E., 180–182
Project Visibility, 150
Psychosocial development stages, 75–77
Public bathroom use, 208
Purpose (psychosocial stage), 75
Putney, N. M., 73

Qualitative Research, 67, 221
Quam, J., 65

Race
    in ADDRESSING framework, 13
    discrimination due to, 104, 142–143
    future research on, 124, 183
    and health outcomes, 35
    and prevalence of HIV, 146
Racialized communities, 129n4
Rancourt, R., 113
Rankin, S., 196–199, 209, 210
Rawlings, D., 99
Relationship domain (spirituality), 96
Relationships
    in convoy theory, 81
    with family members, 171, 178
    health benefits of, 38
    same-sex vs. heterosexual
        couplehood, 174–175
    severed, as result of transgender
        transitions, 195
    as social support, 119–120
    strengthened by stigma, 62
    with transgender individuals,
        176–177, 203–204
Religion
    in ADDRESSING framework, 13
    in end-of-life planning, 105
    as social support, 37
    and spirituality, 94–95
    transgender individuals'
        participation in, 211
Religion domain (spirituality), 96
Religiosity, 94–95
Reporting traumatic incidents, 57
Residential care, 121–122
Resilience, 217–225
    among LGBT elders and their
        families, 218
    due to family issues, 177–178
    in face of AIDS epidemic, 15
    future research on, 44, 219–222
    increased interest in, 56, 218
    practices to enhance, 222–224
    theories to study, 222
    of transgender individuals, 210–211,
        213–214
Resources, influence of, 36–39. See
        also Community resources and
        government services
Retirement plans, 157
Riggle, E. D. B., 62

Social Security, x, 31, 156–157, 174, 196, 207
Social support networks
   created by activism, 64
   future research on, 44–45
   and health and well-being, 36–37
   in palliative care, 99
   and positive marginality, 62
   preferences about, in Canada, 119
   and successful aging, 155, 182
   of transgender individuals, 211
Societal roles, freedom from, 62
Socioeconomic status
   in ADDRESSING framework, 14
   affected by sexual orientation/gender
      identity, 31
   future research on, 123–124
   and health, 31–32
   of lesbians, 14, 174
   in same-sex vs. heterosexual
      relationships, 174–175
SOFFAs. See Significant others,
      families, friends, and allies
Spirituality, 91–99
   and accessing care, 95–97
   in ADDRESSING framework, 13
   and dementia, 97–98
   in end-of-life planning, 105
   and life course perspective, 93–94
   and religiosity, 94–95
   as social support, 37
   spiritual reminiscence as, 98–99
Spiritual reminiscence, 98–99
Spyer, Thea, x
Stigma, 55–68
   enacted, 57
   faced by transgender individuals, 202
   felt, 57–58
   as individualistic life experience, 15
   internalized, 58–59
   and minority stress model, 59–60
   and positive marginality, 60–67
Stonewall riots, 7–8, 82–83, 101, 114
Strengths-based approach, 223
Stress
   and access to services, 142
   accumulation of, 55–56
   and dementia, 12
   future research on, 44
   health problems due to, 33–34

Strong, S., 62
Subject orientation, 85
Substance use
   among transgender individuals, 201
   in LGBT individuals, 35–36
Successful aging model, 84–86
Suicidal ideation, 202
Survivor guilt, 175

Talamantes, M., 104
Tan, P. P., 95–96
Tasker, F., 120
Tedeschi, R. G., 61
Terndrup, A. I., 63–64
Time, in life course perspective, 93–94
Tobacco use, 201
Toronto Long Term Care Homes and
      Services, 131
Training-related competencies, xi, 42
Tran, A., 152
Transgender individuals, 193–214
   access to services, 202–203
   adult children of, 179
   and age, 38
   alcohol and substance use among, 36
   concealment by, 34–35, 173
   and congruence of self, 63
   de-transition considered by, 174
   discrimination and health among, 33
   employment and income disparities
      for, 199–200
   family and friend relationships of,
      203–204
   future research on older, 44, 183–184
   health and social care in Canada for,
      122–123
   health care discrimination against, 200
   health disparities among, 27, 60, 146
   and health risk behaviors, 201
   and hormone use, 29
   as invisible, 194–196
   legal protection of, in Canada, 114
   and life course perspective, 208–210
   mental health of, 202
   nonconsensual outing of, 205–207
   physical health problems of, 200–201
   policies to improve issues for,
      212–214
   public bathroom use by, 208
   relationships with, 176–177

ABOUT THE EDITORS

Nancy A. Orel, PhD, LPC, received her doctorate in counselor education from the University of Toledo in 1999. In 2000, she joined the faculty of Bowling Green State University, where she is a tenured professor in the Department of Human Services. Dr. Orel currently serves as associate dean of the Gerontology Program (College of Health and Human Services), and graduate coordinator for the Master of Science in Interdisciplinary Gerontology. Dr. Orel's research and publications have focused on intergenerational relationships within diverse family structures and the needs and concerns of vulnerable populations of older adults (e.g., lesbian, gay, bisexual, and transgender elders; older adults living with HIV/AIDS).

Christine A. Fruhauf, PhD, received her doctorate in human development from Virginia Polytechnic Institute and State University in 2003. The same year, she joined the faculty of Colorado State University, where she is a tenured associate professor in the Department of Human Development and Family Studies (HDFS). She serves as director of the HDFS Extension and Coordinator of the Gerontology Interdisciplinary Minor. Dr. Fruhauf is currently treasurer elect to the Association for Gerontology in Higher Education and serves on the editorial board of the *Journal of GLBT Family Studies* and the *Journal of Intergenerational Relationships*. Her research interests include grandparent–grandchildren relationships, young adult caregivers, and gerontological education and instruction.

PROPERTY OF
SENECA COLLEGE
LIBRARIES
KING CAMPUS